Science Education Leadership

BEST PRACTICES FOR THE NEW CENTURY

Science Education Leadership

BEST PRACTICES FOR THE NEW CENTURY

Edited by Jack Rhoton

NSTApress

National Science Teachers Association

National Science Teachers Association

Claire Reinburg, Director
Jennifer Horak, Managing Editor
Andrew Cocke, Senior Editor
Judy Cusick, Senior Editor
Wendy Rubin, Associate Editor
Amy America, Book Acquisitions Coordinator

ART AND DESIGN
Will Thomas Jr., Director
Tracey Shipley, cover and interior design

PRINTING AND PRODUCTION
Catherine Lorrain, Director
Jack Parker, Electronic Prepress Technician

NATIONAL SCIENCE TEACHERS ASSOCIATION
Francis Q. Eberle, PhD, Executive Director
David Beacom, Publisher

Library of Congress Cataloging-in-Publication Data
Science education leadership: best practices for the new century / Jack Rhoton,
Editor.
    p. cm.
  Includes index.
  ISBN 978-1-936137-00-8
  1. Science—Study and teaching—United States. 2. Leadership. I. Rhoton, Jack.
  Q183.3.A1S3544 2010
  507.1'073—dc22
                                2009047474
eISBN 978-1-936137-83-1

CONTENTS

Section One:

The Science Education Challenge: Redefining Science Education Leadership for the 21st Century

Chapter 1

Looking Forward Into the 21st Century: Implications for the Science Leader

Chapter 2

New Models of Leadership and Collaboration to Improve Science Education: The Role of Business

Chapter 3

A New Challenge for Education Leaders: Developing 21st-Century Workforce Skills

Section Three:

School and District Science Leadership: Rationale, Strategy, and Impact

Chapter 9
Technology Leadership for the 21st Century

Chapter 10
The Role of Leadership in Fostering Inquiry-Based Learning and Teaching

Chapter 11
Bending the Professional Teaching Continuum: How Teacher Renewal Supports Teacher Retention

Chapter 12
No Boundaries: The Role of Mobility in Recruiting New Teachers and Developing New Leaders

Section Four:

School Improvement Processes and Practices: Professional Learning for Building Instructional Capacity

Chapter 13
Professional Learning Communities: School Collaboration to Implement Science Education Reform

Section Five:

Leadership That Engages the Public in the Understanding of Science

Foreword

Brenda Wojnowski
NSELA President 2009–10

The United States is at a critical juncture as many states, districts, and schools struggle to develop strategies and methodologies to prepare our students for life in this still relatively new century. We are well aware of the significant changes we, as educators, must make in our ways of thinking and doing in educating our populace, from preK education through career inservice. The need is critical; the structures and thought patterns which must be developed and implemented within our education system is the crux of the struggle. According to Tom Friedman, "the school, the state, the country that empowers, nurtures, enables imagination among its students and citizens, that's who's going to be the winner" (Pink 2008).

The Partnership for the 21st Century (2008) identifies the forward-thinking learning and innovation skills that are critical to students as (1) creativity and innovation skills, (2) critical thinking and problem-solving skills, and (3) communication and collaboration skills. To attain these skills, our students must be able to interact both with their immediate neighbors and with other students and potential workplace partners around the globe. We must develop mindsets that allow our students to understand and be sensitive to the intricacies of cultures that are very different from our own. At the same time, we must help our students to develop the science/technology/engineering/ mathematics strengths that will allow the United States to prosper and thrive in the modern world.

The chapters within this volume address many of the issues that currently occupy education leaders who are working to address the skill sets needed for 21st-century success in a global community and marketplace. *Science Education Leadership* will aid leaders in guiding the teaching and learning occurring within our classrooms as well as the thoughts and policies being formulated within our state and federal departments of education. The work of 21st-century education is imperative—the timing of the guidance and planning is crucial.

The National Science Education Leadership Association is pleased to be a part of the infrastructure that stands in support of quality publications that will be used to improve education and inspire the future of young people throughout the United States and the world.

References

Partnership for the 21st Century. 2008. *21st century skills, education, and competitiveness: A resource and policy guide.* Tucson, AZ: Partnership for 21st Century Skills.

Pink, D. 2008. Tom Friedman on education in the "flat world." *The School Administrator* 2 (65): 12–19.

Preface

Jack Rhoton

At no other time in the history of science education has the need for leadership been more important to ensure that all students in our nation's schools get the training they need to succeed. It has almost become a cliché to recognize that we live in the Information Age, an age that has mushroomed into the globalized knowledge economy. There is no doubt, however, that there is extensive support for the notion that science is vital for our economic competitiveness and for a science-literate public that can share in discussions—and make intelligent decisions regarding—science issues. In order to prepare students for success, we must instill in them the ability to constantly adapt through lifelong learning. Clearly we operate within a very complex educational system, and this will require strong science education leadership from a wide of array of individuals, businesses, organizations, and institutions.

Just as change is a permanent attribute of our time, leadership in science education needs to be continuously exercised with the ultimate goal of improving student learning. We all know that leadership takes on many forms, but a common theme in leadership is that leaders have vision. Leaders are able to develop a consensus around an idea, goals, and a course of action. They are able to mobilize people's commitment to improve. They make it possible for others to do good work. However, different leaders take on different roles and may have different ways of clarifying a vision. For example, some science leaders may craft futuristic models of science education or examine the impact of brain research on the teaching and learning of science. Some leaders may be able to impact science education through policy initiatives, others through their writing, and still others by defending the integrity of science. Science teachers can also be leaders in their individual classrooms and schools.

The community of science education is made up of systems and subsystems, all of which consist of individuals and groups with different agendas and goals for improving science education. Science teachers, science educators, administrators, curriculum directors, university personnel, scientists, business and industry, Congress, and members of the current administration all have unique roles to play in advancing the support of science education. Science education leaders must know their constituents and be able to enlist people in a vision. Leaders must understand their needs, speak their language, and fashion a unity of purpose that enables constituents to share in a vision. These visions are played out in different ways. Not all in the science education community can or should be engaged in research, crafting curricular materials, developing technology programs, or providing professional development. We all have distinct talents, roles, and responsibilities. If we take action, we can turn our vision for a better tomorrow into initiatives that become actions that will make a difference for our students. Leadership is the conduit that can assemble the various components of science education reform efforts in ways that improve instruction and learning at all levels.

It is my belief that the central goal of science education should be to allow every student to achieve high levels of scientific literacy. Achieving this type of literacy for all students requires science education leadership from all constituent groups. Furthermore, all groups must communicate and work together toward clearly identified, mutually agreed upon objectives. Leadership must forge connections between the important components of the science education system, including national, state, and local science programs, as well as individual classroom practices such as teaching, curriculum design, and assessment. Collaboration will be required of science education leaders as they work in an increasingly complex educational environment.

With these challenges in mind, this book addresses issues and outlines the practical approaches needed to lay the foundation upon which science education leaders—at all levels—can work together to develop a more science literate society. This book shares the research, ideas, insights, and experiences of individuals representing a wide array of constituent groups, ranging from science teachers to science supervisors to university personnel to those who work for agencies representing science education. The authors discuss how to contribute to the success of science education and how to develop a culture that allows and encourages science education leaders to continually improve science programs.

The 18 chapters in *Science Education Leadership* are organized into five major sections. This organization places each chapter within a general theme. The intent is not to provide an exhaustive coverage of each section, but rather to present a stimulating collection of essays on relevant issues. Those major themes are:

The Science Education Challenge: Redefining Science Education Leadership for the 21st Century. Whether in the classroom, the curriculum office, or the boardroom, the science education leader has a desire to inspire others and pioneer changes that build stronger science education programs. Leaders are willing to relinquish familiar and commonly held practices and embrace change. We introduce this theme in "Looking Forward Into the 21st Century: Implications for the Science Leader." Next, we consider the leadership exhibited by business leaders and how they are investing resources and energy to target systemic reform initiatives in science education. This is followed by a look at the challenges that science leaders face as they develop ways to imbue upcoming generations with 21st-century workforce skills. The section concludes with a look at the many faces of leadership found in a complex educational environment.

The Role of School and District Science Leadership for Building Instructional Capacity. Strong science education leaders are needed to build and organize an infrastructure that supports deep learning for both teachers and students. Instructional leadership consists of actions that promote improved student learning not only in one's own classroom, or one's own school, but throughout an extended community. Therefore, science education leaders not only view instructional quality as a top priority,

they also encourage others around them to share this priority. Successful science programs involve many participants—among them teachers, principals, and science supervisors. This theme develops over four chapters that examine the impact of instructional leadership on instructional quality and student outcomes. See in particular, "Content Coverage and the Role of an Instructional Leader."

School and District Science Leadership: Rationale, Strategy, and Impact. Science education leaders can create a robust digital age educational community that supports the use of advanced technologies in the teaching and learning of science. This section begins by addressing the critical role of transformational leadership in the science education community for effective and appropriate infusion of educational technology as a fundamental component of K–12 education. This topic is followed by examples of leaders who foster inquiry-based learning and teaching in a variety of settings, including classrooms, local communities, schools and districts, college science classrooms, teacher preparation programs, and professional experiences. Other chapters in this section address teacher preparation, induction, and ongoing professional development as well as the role of graduate mobility in recruiting new teachers and developing new leaders.

School Improvement Processes and Practices: Professional Learning for Building Instructional Capacity. The role that professional learning communities have in improving and coordinating our efforts to establish higher expectations for students, improve instructional practices, and increase student achievement outcomes through a shared curriculum-focused vision is of inestimable value. This theme emerges most fully in "Professional Learning Communities: School Collaboration to Implement Science Education Reform." Other topics in this section include leading through collaboration, assessing assessment to inform science leadership, and professional development.

Leadership That Engages the Public in the Understanding of Science. This country places a high value on science and science teaching, and this content area is well established in the American school curriculum. Our nation invests a significant amount of resources in science education at all levels. We value science, because our society believes it is important for preparing our students for the 21st-century workforce, preparing future scientists, and providing nonscientists with the science knowledge necessary to make informed decisions about issues affecting their everyday lives. However, the results of efforts to engage the general public in science have been mixed. For this reason, an argument is made that education and science education leaders should be prepared to communicate with the public, media, and decision makers to facilitate a better exchange of information between science professionals and society as a whole. These themes are highlighted in two chapters in this section: "Leadership for Public Understanding of Science" and "Science Communication and Public Engagement With Science."

In addition to the themes described above, the need to address local, state, and national science standards is prominent throughout the book.

Previous publications in this NSELA/NSTA series are *Issues in Science Education, Professional Development Planning and Design, Professional Development Leadership and the Diverse Learner, Science Teacher Retention: Mentoring and Renewal,* and *Science Teaching in the 21st Century.*

Science Education Leadership: Best Practices for the New Century captures the best thinking and best practices for science education leaders. Science educators can use it to vitalize their work. The book is directed at science teachers, science department chairs, principals, science supervisors, curriculum directors, superintendents, university personnel, policy makers, and any other individual who has a stake in science education. The final determinant of success in our effort to improve science education will be the degree to which we achieve high levels of scientific literacy for all citizens. The exercise of science education leadership is of the utmost importance if we are to achieve this goal.

Acknowledgments

Jack Rhoton

I wish to express my sincere appreciation to the individuals who made this publication possible. In particular I would like to thank the authors. In all cases, they addressed the theme, submitted manuscripts in a timely fashion and responded to reviewer recommendations. No volume is any better than the manuscripts that are contributed to it; we appreciate the time and effort of those whose work lies within the cover of this book.

I would also like to thank and acknowledge the support, help, and encouragement of my colleagues in the National Science Education Leadership Association (NSELA): Brenda Wojnowski, president; Linda Adkins, past president, for their suggestions and guidance in the early stages of the project, and executive director Susan Sprague in the later stages of the project. The support and advice offered by Pat Shane, NSTA President, is very much appreciated. I also thank and acknowledge some long-time professional colleagues: LaMoine Motz, Gerry Madrazo, Nicola Micozzi,

Acknowledgments

Ken Roy, Emma Walton, and Fred Johnson, for the impact they have had on science education leadership at the K–12 level.

We are deeply appreciative of all the support and assistance provided through the outstanding staff at NSTA Press including David Beacom, Claire Reinburg, and Andy Cocke. And last but not least, I express my deepest appreciation to my graduate assistant, Amy Selman, who did a yeomen's job revising manuscripts and keeping track of hundreds of important details.

About the Editor

Jack Rhoton has devoted his entire career to teaching, writing and advocating for the support and advancement of science education at all levels, K–16. He began his career as a high school science teacher and subsequently served as a K–12 science supervisor for fourteen years. He joined East Tennessee State University as professor of science education in 1987 where he is currently serving as executive director of the ETSU Center of Excellence in Mathematics and Science Education. He has served as president of the National Science Education Leadership Association (NSELA), Tennessee Academy of Science (TAS), and the Tennessee Science Teachers Association (TSTA). Among his many publications are several NSTA edited books, including *Teaching Science in the 21st Century*. Rhoton earned a bachelors of science in biology from East Tennessee State University, masters in biology from Old Dominion University, masters in science education from the University of Virginia and a doctorate in science education from the University of Tennessee. He has received many honors, including the National Science Teachers Association Distinguished Service Award.

Section One

The Science Education Challenge: Redefining Science Education Leadership for the 21st Century

Chapter 1

Looking Forward Into the 21st Century
Implications for the Science Leader

Jeanne Century

It is easy to welcome change when the changes we imagine are those that will support and reinforce the goals we already care about. We can embrace change when we believe it is calling for different behaviors and actions on the part of those who have stood between us and our goals. We are excited to consider shifts in structures and policies that have inhibited our ability to act. We think to ourselves, "Finally! Perhaps now we can make some progress."

On the heels of the turning century, we in the United States have a new presidential administration, coupled with an explosion of technology and globalization. With this we see that, indeed, some of the political, regulatory, and technological structures that have made high-quality teaching and learning difficult may be opening to make room for new ideas. All of this is good news, but along with this opportunity, we must consider that the changes that need to happen for the 21st century aren't going to stem from the shifting environment. They need to come from us.

Finding the will and capacity to change is a long-standing concern in education in general, with science education no exception. In the 1990s, national efforts to bring about change through systemic reforms grew from the premise that by changing all of the elements of the system in coordination with one another so that all efforts would be aligned, we could change the system and move it toward our shared goals. These efforts met with only limited success. Not only were there limitations in terms of funds and time, but also a flaw in the logic. Reformers invested in systems in which they could not pause to reflect or adapt; nor did these systems have the capacity to change.

While we recognize the need to change the system in which we operate, the changes need to come from changes in *ourselves*. As science education leaders today, we see that the contexts and conditions that can support changes are here. However, this does not mean that we can breathe a sigh of relief that we stand in an environment supportive of our long-standing goals in science education. Rather, just as the contexts and conditions have changed, so must we shift *our goals* so that we can achieve a fit between the two that will move us forward.

Specifically, we have viewed ourselves as operating exclusively in the field of science education and science teaching. But this is a time when the borders we have used to define ourselves must be permeable on some boundaries and disappear entirely on others. This isn't easy; it can be uncomfortable to think about changing the ways we do our work, and that discomfort can cause us to be critical or dismissive of new ways of thinking and protective of our points of view. However, in the end, if we fail to adjust our point of view, we may preserve our positions but fail to make any progress toward our goals.

Some might say this is a time to *shift* our thinking, but shifts can be small and do not necessarily require crossing or opening boundaries. Instead, this is a time to *open* our thinking, broaden our perspectives, and expand our focus beyond the well-understood goals for science education that we have held tightly over the years, and start asking questions about what those goals should be. This is the time to look at the standing questions we have been asking in our field but consider the answers from a different point of view. This is a time to embrace the changes around us—even when it means giving up some of the investments we have in how to do things—for the greater end of furthering our collective, ultimate goal of healthy, participatory students engaged in their world. Let us begin by considering some of our familiar questions.

What Are Some of Our Most Pressing Needs in STEM Education?

This first question is a simple one on the face of it. We read it and begin to consider some of the common challenges for science education, such as the importance of developing quality assessments, the need for science to have a higher priority in the instructional day, the necessity of having sufficient materials, and the need to emphasize science in preservice teacher education programs. However, we need to acknowledge that the question is not asking about *science* education; it is asking what the literature says about our needs in *STEM* education.

Science education and STEM education are often used interchangeably, but we know that many of the supports and barriers that affect each branch of STEM education—science, mathematics, technology, and engineering—are different. Leaders in each of these disciplines function in fields that have progressed differently, have different priorities and resources, and, perhaps most importantly, have different perceptions about their prioritization in the school day. As a result, they have differing needs not met easily with one strategy, though we refer to them with a single convenient term.

Because STEM groups disciplines that have been treated very differently, we engage in muddied conversations that do not further all four fields (S, T, E, and M) equally. Rather, we find that discussions of STEM are often really discussions about S (science) and M (mathematics), and even more frequently, they are discussions about one *or* the other. One could make a case that we need to address the disciplines separately so we can clearly identify how to support each in their particular context. However, rather than treat the disciplines separately, we need to recognize that there is no well-developed answer to the question, "What are some of our most pressing needs in STEM education?" because we, as members of these four fields, do not have a uniform understanding of the term "STEM."

We need to realize that STEM is more than the compilation of its component parts of science, technology, engineering, and mathematics. This is not a new idea, but these are new times, and the idea that STEM is more than just an acronymic home for "science" has not been embraced by science educators. Rather than ask, "What are the implications of the research for STEM?" the real question should be, "What are the implications of STEM for research?"

As science educators in search of our place in STEM education, we face a professional identity crisis. Even as we recognize the relationships between science and the other disciplines of STEM, we take up residence squarely in the field of science education and use the boundaries around our field to define ourselves. We recognize that we reside in a discipline that does differ from the other three but at the same time, we observe that the distances between each are getting increasingly smaller. We face the dilemma of how we retain our goals for strong science education while recognizing and acknowledging that we are part of a 21st-century community of STEM educators?

Let us begin with one of the major challenges we face as science educators—assessments. The creation and implementation of high-quality assessments—both affordable and efficient—have been long-standing challenges in science education and now, more than ever, they have high visibility and increased importance. When we discuss what we want to assess, however, our conversations take us beyond the facts and procedures of science to other important outcomes. We value students who are problem solvers, who know how to think critically about their world and environment, who can support conclusions with reasoned evidence, who can apply their knowledge to new and novel situations, and who can communicate with and transfer that knowledge to others. These important outcomes are not only elements of science education, but of STEM education as well.

The call for shared or common standards is another increasingly visible issue. We have both the standards developed by the National Academy of Sciences and the AAAS benchmarks, but these documents are not at the forefront of more general and public conversations about standards. The reasons for creating high-quality, common standards in science (and other subjects) are plain. But, as one moves from the commitment to ensuring that all students are held to high standards to the implementation of that idea, additional challenges arise. Science is a rich discipline comprised of many parts. Earth science, life science, physical science, and space science all have components with increasing levels of specificity. At a time when we are trying to provide a coherent learning experience for students, how do we give sufficient attention to the disciplines and their divisions while bringing *less* fragmentation to education, not more? Again, rather than ask ourselves "What are the implications of the standards for STEM?" we should be asking, "What are the implications of a STEM perspective for standards?"

The need for high-quality mathematics and science teachers has also been a long-standing issue. We hear calls for strategies to bring qualified teachers with degrees in their disciplines into these difficult-to-fill positions using incentives and targeted programs. There is no doubt that a teacher who knows the subject is better equipped (though far from fully equipped) to be a good teacher. But does our commitment to developing well-trained teachers make it difficult to bring meaningful coherency to STEM? Our students know, as do we, that in the real world, STEM operates as STEM, not as separate disciplines. Thus, as we prepare our teachers, we should think about the implications of STEM for teacher preparation and inservice development. We need not give up on the importance of teacher disciplinary content knowledge, but we may need to be more open to changing the organizational and institutional structures and processes that currently isolate rather than unite the disciplines, so the student learning experience in the school is more coherent and consistent with the real world.

We must focus not only on the commonalities between S, T, E, and M and the implications of STEM as a whole, but also on what it means for schools to address these disciplines as a reflection of the ways they interact outside of school. The walls between the classroom and the real world are becoming increasingly thin, and we can resist their disappearance or we can benefit from embracing it to help us look to the future. As we think about needs, we must consider more than the reasons for those needs from the past. Instead, we must look at the circumstances we are in now and anticipate what will happen in the future.

What Are the Short-Term and Long-Term Challenges For the STEM Community?

As we look ahead, it is clear that the STEM community will need to be more than an association that comes about by way of an acronym. Instead, we need to become a STEM *community*—an institution that embraces a collective identity.

With this in mind, it is easier to speculate about the long-term challenges, because the development of such a community calls for changes in our behavior that are more palatable when at least partially postponed. It can be much more comfortable for us to think about how things could be sometime in the future, far away from the immediate steps we need to take tomorrow. Right now, however, even as leaders of S, T, E, and M recognize their shared goals for instruction and teacher-student interactions, they maintain their focus (particularly leaders of M and S) on the needs of their own disciplines. We are left wondering then, how do we adjust our mindset?

Practically speaking, we need to consider how our immediate decisions on pressing issues such as standards, assessments, and instruction will impact the long-term prospects of moving toward a STEM community. For example, as we participate in conversations about national standards, we should ask ourselves how the process of creating those standards, their organizing principles, and the ways the disciplines are represented might have an impact on the STEM community in the years to come. It is difficult to make progress toward a STEM perspective when we work in isolation of one another to create standards for isolated disciplines. While integrated standards may not be the answer (or even a possibility), if the standards we use today are going to provide the guidance that moves us toward the instruction we need for the future, there needs to be a means by which disciplinary relationships and connections are drawn.

There is also the question of how movement toward those standards should be measured. STEM is not necessarily well-suited to conventional instructional materials and pencil-and-paper tests. It needs to be applied and assessed in practical, problem-solving settings. This requires movement in our thinking about standards, as well as a change in the curriculum and assessments that would support those standards. STEM calls for students who know how to transfer and apply their knowledge. This suggests, then, that when students have experiences outside of the traditional school setting, those experiences could be legitimate measures of their learning. As leaders looking forward, we need to imagine scenarios where the curriculum includes learning inside and outside of school walls and assesses that learning by looking at its application in the real world, which is ultimately where our students will need to use their knowledge.

When we talk about needs for students, we seem to still do so with an anticipation that the 21st century is still around the corner. But, of course, it is here now. For years we have been trying to accomplish what are sometimes referred to as 21st-century goals; we have long wanted students who could think critically, collaborate, and solve problems. But in action, we have given these goals only secondary attention, and until now, we have been able to do so without dire consequences. Although we are working harder to accomplish our 21st-century goals, if we focus *only* on those goals, we will find ourselves in trouble again in the future. We do need to work toward these goals, but as we do, we also need to develop a process of continuous improvement that will help us learn, identify new goals that come from anticipation of the 22nd century, and move us toward accomplishing those goals as well.

What Type of Leadership, at All Levels, Is Needed to Address These Issues?

We have a formidable task ahead of us. To accomplish it, leaders need to have all of the essential skills, and more. There is no question that leaders need to be passionate about the importance of STEM education for all kids, and they need to be able to communicate, facilitate, and manage, in ways that engage others. These are the usual qualities of leaders we identify in STEM education. But looking forward, we need leaders with additional leadership qualities, such as a willingness to give up familiar common practices, an openness to moving into the unknown, and an ability to embrace change.

These qualities must arise from a change in perspective; one that decreases the emphasis on specific programs or reforms as the "answer," and increases the emphasis on building *our capacity* to reach those goals through learning and continuous improvement. In other words, leaders need to place what we want to accomplish in the foreground and the particular programs that they believe will get us there in the background. Too much personal investment in a particular reform or program can cloud our ability to look at it objectively and consider whether it is helping us reach our goals, identify the parts that do and do not work, and make the adaptations necessary to move us forward. If we invest too much in the *reform* and not enough in our *capability and will* to reflect on and change it as necessary, we may unintentionally jeopardize our abilities to accomplish our goals.

The notion of divesting from our change strategies seems a little counterintuitive. Certainly, leaders should be thoughtful and committed to improvement through concrete strategies. However, leaders need to recognize those strategies for what they are and what they are not. We pursue interventions because we believe that they will help us bring about the changes we need to make in education. Whether through instructional materials programs, teacher training programs, or school redesign approaches, if we choose wisely, we will identify programs that research tell us have the potential to meet our needs. We trust these interventions because they have been tested in the conditions and contexts in which we function. However, this very fact is also why we should not be too invested in the programs themselves. This statement warrants explanation. First, consider the fact that programs with proven effectiveness had to have been tested in a time frame constrained by the resources of the study. Most often this is a short time frame, from one to five years. Thus, we don't know what the impact of those same programs might have been if they had been tested over a longer period, say 10 or 15 years. Second, consider that the conditions and contexts in which the program works now is certain to change in the future. Thus, our intervention will need to change as well.

No reform is a silver bullet that is going to solve our problems, even if it is implemented well. Research tells us that programs always adapt when enacted in different settings. Thus, the promise of improvement comes not from the reform itself, but from leaders who can focus on enacting them while always tracking both *if* they are working (the extent to which they are being fully implemented and are working as anticipated) and *how* they are working (the extent to which they are adapting to current contexts and conditions).

In addition to carefully implementing reforms, 21st-century leaders need to be able to facilitate trust and build collaboration. There is no doubt that it is important to execute a strong intervention, but even the best intervention can be of no value if its implementation does not address the factors that influence its ability to work and last. The literature tells us that leaders need to attend to internal environmental factors like social climate and the role of networks and they need to attend to external factors such as political climate. But leaders also need to monitor the human elements of the process, including ensuring collaboration at all levels, building trust, providing appropriate incentives, and demonstrating that the new direction is a good fit with current needs. We have known about these elements for some time but have treated them like extras of implementation—activities and behaviors that are nice to have but not necessary. In fact, these are the very actions that will make a difference. These actions will determine whether a teacher enacts a practice when the classroom door is shut—because she believes in it and trusts that it will work—even if it is difficult at the outset.

Finally, 21st-century leaders need to model the very behaviors we are working to develop in students in the new century. Reform leaders have to do more than identify, implement, and spread reforms; they need to enact new practices, develop innovations, and be creative. Classroom teachers must facilitate change in our students by solving problems and thinking critically; programs are only their tools. School, district, and state leaders must themselves become catalysts for changing behavior, not only the conduits through which change models make their way to schools. Lastly, researchers need to step away from a publication dissemination model to one that engages others in the generation, enactment, and use of their findings. Programs may come and go, but individuals working collaboratively in the system have the capacity to make the programs work, and that collective capacity is the key to long-term improvement.

Do We Have Some Effective Programs or Models Already in Place?

With the understanding that leaders should be less invested in the programs themselves, it is still important to seek out the programs and models we know are effective. However, as we do so, we need to broaden our question to ask, "*In what ways* and *for whom* are programs or models effective?" In order to bring about improvement, leaders seek strategies that can be broadly implemented, with the expectation that the strategies will be replicated as close to the original as possible. But that premise—that the path to improvement is the replication of tested effective programs—is itself not research-based. Research tells us quite the opposite, in fact. It shows that practices are not replicated when they spread; rather, they are always adapted. When we think about it objectively, that process is sensible. Contexts and conditions always vary from place to place. We would not expect that a practice that works in one setting should transfer directly to another. Instead, it *translates.*

There is no question that we need good, well-tested examples. But we need to give up the oversimplified expectation that we can take these models and "scale them up" exactly as they were when they were developed and tested. Certainly, reforms based on broad principles are, by their nature, applicable in different places. Likewise, their broadness leaves them open to many different interpretations and enactments. More specific interventions, such as instructional materials programs, leave less room for interpretation but still have room for variation and adaptation.

Schools everywhere are different, and teachers in those schools are different. So, rather than strive to implement models with as much fidelity as possible, we must find ways to systematically and rigorously capture the variations in the enactment of the model. In this way, we as a field can learn from the use of the model in multiple disciplines. Rather than overlook variability, we need to embrace it, systematically, so that we can understand how effective models and their comprising elements do (and do not) work in particular contexts and conditions. Thus, if our goal is to develop lasting improvements that can be implemented on a larger scale, the answer lies in the processes we use to implement the new practices and not in the intervention itself. As we move from a *product-focused* approach to a *process-focused* approach, here are three considerations that must be accounted for:

- First, we need to consider the separation between the research and practitioner community. In the typical scenario, researchers do their research, draw their conclusions, and then publish their results with the expectation that they will be applied. However, we know that this is a very ineffective way to generate knowledge. Some researchers talk about needing to "translate" research for teachers, but this assumes that research takes place outside of the teachers' understanding and engagement. Rather than thinking about translating research, we need to engage leaders (including teachers) as collaborators in research, involved in identifying the research questions and helping to shed light on the purposes and applications of the research. We should shift our perspective from one of bridging the two communities, to one that strives to meld these separate communities into one, single community.

- Second, we need to ensure that we have some shared understandings about our language. Why, for example, has there been such confusion about whether inquiry is an appropriate strategy for science education? Are we really in such disagreement about what good instruction is? The problem is less from disagreements about what good instruction is and more from a lack of shared understanding about what we mean by *inquiry*. Two leaders may discuss the merits of inquiry, yet have quite different understandings of what inquiry is and never know that they are talking about two different things. Our failure to find shared language reaches far beyond this particular topic. To grow a collaborative learning community, we have to find a way to identify common concepts and the language to discuss them. Then, we can begin to learn.

- Third, we need to orient ourselves to long-term change, not short-term fixes. As we work to do the best we can for students in school now, we should recognize that some of the required steps may not appear to have immediate returns but will serve these students and their children in the future. We see growing discussion about sustainable development for the environment that focuses on replenishing or replacing resources, and this is how we need to start thinking about sustainable reform in education. We cannot focus solely on replacing the resources that we had available to us. Instead we need to take steps to ensure that the students of the future have what they will need, which may very well be different from what students need today. As we think about effective reforms, we need not only reforms that are effective now, but ones that will establish a foundation for what could be effective in the future.

Do We Need a National Vision for STEM Education?

There has never been a time when the need for a national vision for STEM education was more critical. The leaders of our country must demonstrate their commitment to STEM education as a priority, and that commitment must be consistent and completely clear. We need to have a nation that embraces STEM in our daily lives and recognizes it for what it is—a way of understanding and interacting with our world and the people in it. We need a vision for STEM education that moves citizens away from the perception that STEM is something that is foreign and "not what I do." We need our leaders to communicate that the goals we have been working toward in STEM education for the last 50 years and more are possible to achieve.

But much more importantly, we need leaders who will recognize and communicate that, even as we work toward the goals first articulated long ago, we should reframe how we think about those goals. Much of the vision that has been driving science education in this country is over half a century old and while some, if not most, of those goals are still worthy of our attention, they place us in a fixed mindset that prevents us from thinking about the next 50 years. As we address the challenges we have today, we can create an environment in which every student has an equal opportunity to learn the beauty and wonder of the natural and manufactured worlds and to become a critical, thoughtful problem solver and a clear, engaging, collaborative communicator. At the same time, we need to use our own imaginations and think about where we need to be in another 50 years and begin to work toward that now.

Imagine where we could be today if those charged with bringing improvement to science education 50 years ago had thought about "sustainable education." At that time, the nation was fixed on creating scientists, and educational leaders did so by creating instructional materials programs that increased the visibility and placement of science in the curriculum. These actions were an important step toward meeting our needs at the time, but those needs have changed over the last 50 years. Investments in instructional materials (or any single strategy) may fail to consider the needs for improvement that the future might bring. Thus, a step toward sustainable education might be understood as one that focuses on investing in our capacities to continuously improve and adjust according to our changing needs and the changing world.

That is why we need to think about STEM. The disciplines need to come closer together, not become more separate. We need to think about how to engage students in activities for learning that reflect the skills and behaviors we know they will need, as well as those we speculate they are likely to need in the future. We know this now, and yet we struggle with the overwhelming pull of focusing on our immediate problems. Leaders today must carefully balance their focus by giving attention to immediate needs while stepping outside of the boundaries of the disciplines and considering ways to change practices and behaviors that have been in place for decades. Change is uncomfortable. But it is that discomfort that tells use we are on the right track; that we are doing something different. Indeed, the biggest challenge is not changing the education system; it is changing ourselves. The rest will follow.

Chapter 2

New Models of Leadership and Collaboration to Improve Science Education

The Role of Business

Chris Roe and Natalie Nielsen

In the first months of his administration, President Obama set ambitious goals for improving science education in the United States. He pledged to elevate the status of science in his administration and enhance America's competitiveness by cultivating the next generation of top scientists and engineers from among the ranks of U.S. students (Obama 2009). These commitments are evident in his fiscal year 2010 federal budget as well as the American Recovery and Reinvestment Act, which includes a number of provisions to encourage states to improve their math and science curricula, standards, and assessments.

Meeting these goals will require systemic changes to increase students' interest and achievement in science. A number of these changes will require more effective collaboration among K–12 education, higher education, and business stakeholders. For example, partnerships that leverage the particular strengths of these sectors can greatly enhance efforts to

- align K–12 teaching and learning with the skills and knowledge required for success in higher education and the workforce;

- strengthen the connection between science education and science careers; and
- recruit, prepare, and support teachers who have the requisite content knowledge and pedagogical expertise to improve science achievement.

Given their interest in developing a highly qualified workforce, it is not surprising that business leaders in the United States have a long history of supporting education. However, they have also been quite vocal in their demand for education reform. Indeed, the business community spearheaded the drive for state-based reforms in the wake of *A Nation at Risk* (National Commission on Excellence in Education 1983). They also helped to propel the standards movement in the 1990s and the reauthorization of the Elementary and Secondary Education Act—more commonly knows as the No Child Left Behind Act—in 2002. More recently, a number of prominent business leaders and organizations have undertaken a coordinated national effort to improve education related to key workforce issues in science, technology, engineering, and mathematics (STEM). This involvement has been prompted by growing concerns over the inability of the United States to keep pace with the demand for highly skilled workers and teachers in these critical fields, particularly among underrepresented minorities and women (BHEF 2005, 2007; TAP 2005, 2008).

Historically, business involvement in education has most often focused on school-business partnerships—in which businesses become directly involved in supporting a local school or set of schools—and "checkbook philanthropy," the practice of donating small amounts of money for specific requests without long-term or active involvement by business. Today's increasingly complex challenges call for more systemic approaches that use new technologies and business models that have emerged during the past decade. These models offer business leaders opportunities to change the nature of their involvement in education and strengthen the nation's scientific talent pool.

This chapter provides a brief overview of traditional business involvement in education improvement and then explores new models of involvement by business leaders to improve student outcomes in science education. The new efforts we examine encourage innovation and blend best practices from business and industry in order to bring diverse stakeholders together with a common goal. While some of these efforts are too new to have yielded measurable and lasting effects on science education policy, practice, or achievement, their early success and far-reaching potential makes them worthy of closer examination by all stakeholders interested in improving science education outcomes.

Business Leadership in Education Reform and Improvement Efforts

Corporate support for education has grown steadily over the past decade—both in terms of overall dollars and in-kind support—becoming tied with health and social services as the largest single area of investment by corporate philanthropy (CECP 2009). Although the business community's support for education is varied among a number of disciplines and types of programs, the majority of America's largest corporations support the priority of ensuring that all students in the United States graduate from high school prepared to succeed in college and the workplace (IHEP 2008). To achieve this goal, students must have a rigorous and high-quality math and science curriculum (ACT 2007).

Despite this growing support and recognition of key educational challenges, the business community's record of driving real and lasting education improvement has been mixed. For example, Grissmer and Flanagan (1998) argued that business leadership was the most critical factor contributing to rapid achievement gains in North Carolina and Texas during the 1990s. In those states, business leaders were involved in developing strategic improvement plans, convening multiple stakeholder groups, and supporting legislative changes. According to Grissmer and Flanagan, "the business community in both states was the single most stable, persistent, and long-term influence for the reform agenda implemented" (1998, p. ii). However, others have argued that despite significant annual investments, business support for education reform has typically not been strategic or high-leverage in nature (National Alliance of Business 1987; BHEF 2005).

In order to address this, the National Alliance of Business developed a classification system to better understand business's role in education and encourage adoption of higher impact activities. This involvement, depicted in Figure 1 (p. 20), ranges from high-impact and high-commitment activities (e.g., policy changes and systemic improvement efforts) to lower commitment activities (e.g., support for classroom enrichment or special services) that yield a lower level of impact.

Figure 1. Types of Business Activities to Improve Education

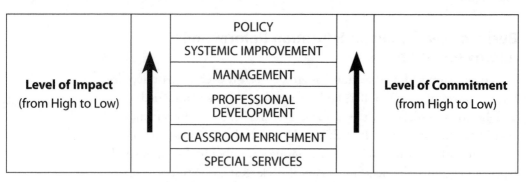

Level of Impact (from High to Low)		POLICY		Level of Commitment (from High to Low)
		SYSTEMIC IMPROVEMENT		
		MANAGEMENT		
		PROFESSIONAL DEVELOPMENT		
		CLASSROOM ENRICHMENT		
		SPECIAL SERVICES		

ADAPTED FROM BUSINESS-HIGHER EDUCATION FORUM (2005) AND NATIONAL ALLIANCE OF BUSINESS (1987)

It is interesting to note that although high-impact activities require a significant time commitment from individual business leaders, they do not necessarily require high levels of financial support. Indeed, in the examples of North Carolina and Texas, a critical role for business was to forge compromises among competing interests, an activity that did not require significant financial resources (Grissmer and Flanagan 1998).

Low-commitment activities such as professional development, classroom enrichment, and special services partnerships (which provide short-term support to address a specific problem or need) are attractive to business leaders because they respond to specific, localized needs and are often highly valued by those served. However, most low-commitment activities are also low-impact because they are normally not of the size or duration required to influence large numbers of students or to make fundamental and lasting changes to the overall system (BHEF 2005). Once the episodic support for these efforts disappears, the system is likely to revert back to old patterns.

Our focus in this chapter is on the approaches business leaders are taking to implement high-impact activities to improve science education in the United States. First, we describe two common ways that business leaders have encouraged policy and systemic improvement. We then explore new models of leadership and collaboration that have the potential to spur innovation and involve multiple stakeholders in science education improvement efforts.

Traditional Models of Business Involvement in High-Impact Partnerships

Among the various approaches that business has used to try to strengthen science education and related outcomes for students, we have selected two approaches that meet the definition of *high-impact*, meaning they focus on coordinated and continuing change of an entire education system: (1) advocating for policy changes and (2) aligning corporate resources and investments with education reform efforts.

Advocacy

Business leaders have played significant roles in advocating for improved science education policy and greater investments at the national and state levels. A number of reports from government and industry in the past decade sounded the alarm about the nation's diminishing leadership in scientific discovery and investment and pointed to lagging student interest and achievement in the STEM disciplines as foreshadowing a long-term decline in U.S. economic competitiveness (National Science Board 1999; National Commission on Mathematics and Science Teaching for the 21st Century 2000; BHEF 2005).

Concerned about this trend, the Tapping America's Potential (TAP) Coalition was formed in 2005 by 14 leading business associations. Together they issued a report that stressed the importance of STEM education as a central component of maintaining American economic competitiveness (TAP 2005). Citing lagging achievement and interest by American students in these disciplines and careers, this group called for doubling the number of students who obtained a degree in a STEM major by 2015. They also recommended a number of actions to be taken by various stakeholders, including the government and business. These actions included building public support for STEM disciplines; motivating U.S. students and adults to study and enter STEM careers, with a special effort geared to those in currently underrepresented groups; and upgrading K–12 math and science teaching to foster higher student achievement (TAP 2005).

Following soon thereafter, the release of the landmark report *Rising*

Above the Gathering Storm (Committee on Prospering in the Global Economy of the 21st Century 2007) helped galvanize support among business, scientific, and education coalitions to achieve broad bipartisan agreement among federal lawmakers regarding the urgent need for action. This advocacy campaign helped shape President Bush's 2006 American Competitiveness Initiative and passage by Congress of the America COMPETES Act in 2007—historic legislation that authorized major new federal investments in math and science education, teacher recruitment and training, and science and engineering research, among other areas.

The TAP Coalition and its individual members have been a positive force in influencing national opinion and support for science, technology, engineering, and math; nevertheless, they also acknowledge that much work remains. According to the TAP Coalition's 2008 report:

> Since the TAP report was issued three years ago, Congress and the administration appeared to get serious about addressing America's competitiveness challenge but have failed to provide matching federal money for STEM education and science and engineering research. The America COMPETES Act, signed into law last year, represents a substantial step forward toward the realization of the TAP innovation agenda. Follow-through by Congress and the administration on spending bills over the next several years will be necessary, however, before the vision of significantly enhanced U.S. innovation capacity embodied in the Act becomes reality (p. 12).

This important advocacy work seems to have been influential in shaping the policy environment in early 2009 that helped form President Obama's opinions about the importance of STEM education and guided his inclusion of a number of science education initiatives and programs as part of the American Recovery and Reinvestment Act and his FY2010 federal budget.

Aligning Business Investments With the Systemic Reform Agenda

A number of business leaders and their organizations have taken steps to move beyond checkbook philanthropy and school partnerships to align their own company's investments with systemic education reform initiatives, including those targeted at science education. In addition to aligning their grant-making activities, a number of corporations are beginning to also align other types of support around priority areas, including employee volunteerism, public relations, and even governmental affairs activities.

One such company is ExxonMobil, which employs almost 81,000 workers, including approximately 15,000 scientists and engineers. While they have invested in a wide array of education programs for over 30 years, concern about their continued ability to recruit a highly skilled workforce in science and math fields led them to identify STEM education as a priority for ongoing corporate investment.

ExxonMobil has chosen to focus its outreach and investments on programs that increase students' engagement with and performance in math and science courses and promote math and science careers. In addition, they have recently made substantial, long-term investments in two new programs that recruit, train, and provide ongoing professional development for math and science teachers—the National Math and Science Initiative and the Mickelson ExxonMobil Teacher Academy.

The National Math and Science Initiative (NMSI) was launched in 2007 with an initial contribution of $125 million from ExxonMobil to support scaling up two proven programs: Advanced Placement courses and UTeach, a program pioneered at the University of Texas–Austin that has a highly successful track record of teacher recruitment, training, and retention in math and science. The university's program focuses on recruiting math and science majors to enter the teaching profession and includes an integrated degree plan, financial assistance, and early teaching experiences for undergraduates. To date, NMSI has funded programs at 13 additional universities to replicate the UTeach model.

The Mickelson Academy was launched in 2005 and supports the professional development of nearly 600 teachers of grades three, four, and five each summer from school districts across the country. The academy partners with Math Solutions and the National Science Teachers Association. These two education groups design the curriculum, provide the instructors, and manage the daily activities of the academy.

ExxonMobil employees and their families also donate considerable time through company-sponsored volunteer activities in their local communities. In 2007, more than 15,000 employees logged some 686,000 hours of volunteer labor to support more than 5,400 charities around the globe. In addition, employees provided almost $33 million in donations through Exxon's employee giving, disaster relief, and matching gift programs (ExxonMobil 2007).

A number of other businesses both large and small have also aligned their investments and ongoing engagements around high-impact strategies that support science education, including Amgen, Boeing, Dow Chemical, General Electric, Merck, and Pfizer. In addition to examples of individual corporations, a number of nonprofit organizations representing business and industry, such as the Boston College Center for Corporate Citizenship, the Business-Higher Education Forum, the Committee Encouraging Corporate Philanthropy, and the U.S. Chamber of Commerce, conduct research, develop resources, host conferences and institutes, and provide technical assistance for business executives and philanthropic staff to increase the effectiveness of corporate engagement and investments in education reform and improvement. Together, these organizations provide a critical service in both encouraging and supporting more strategic and productive engagement by corporations with education.

New Models of Business Leadership to Support Sustained Improvement in Science Education Outcomes

The previous examples reflect a 20th-century model for business involvement in education. Although these types of activities continue to be important, during the past decade new types of high-impact approaches have become available as business leaders consider their involvement in education. Factors leading to these new approaches include the widespread advent and adoption of new business models, such as open innovation, and new technologies, such as social networking tools, simulation modeling, and data visualization. In the following section we discuss some examples of ways that business leaders are applying these new business approaches and technologies to improve science education.

The Emergence of Open Innovation

Fueled by new technologies and tools, individuals, organizations, and industries have begun to embrace the use of *open innovation*, a concept that involves open and flexible networks of participants who participate in the coidentification of complex problems and the cocreation of new solutions.

Henry Chesbrough (2003) is regarded as the first to coin the term. In 2006, he and his colleagues defined open innovation as:

> the use of purposive inflows and outflows of knowledge to accelerate internal innovation, and expand the markets for external use of innovation, respectively. [This paradigm] assumes that firms can and should use external ideas as well as internal ideas, and internal and external paths to market, as they look to advance their technology (p.1).

The Linux operating system, Mozilla Firefox, and Wikipedia are examples of the power of open innovation to harness the skills, expertise, and passion of large numbers and diverse types of individuals to cocreate new products that solve unique and complex problems.

The use of open innovation requires a fundamental shift in mindset among its participants, however. In the past, innovation was largely an activity done by individuals or organizations, usually in a closely guarded and proprietary fashion. Most discovery and innovation—whether in the realm of basic or applied scientific research or product development—often relied upon a secretive and isolated search for answers that frequently was focused on small-scale, incremental experiments.

In an open innovation environment, however, participants work in a fundamentally different manner, usually in unstructured and loosely coordinated environments and using real-time discovery, learning, and cocreation tools. Individuals in the information technology field were among the first to adopt this paradigm, but a large number of corporations in other domains, such as Procter & Gamble, also have begun to adopt open innovation processes to strengthen their business models by speeding innovation and product development.

Working in open innovation environments is becoming more commonplace among scientists as well. In the past, when results of scientific experiments were made public through journal articles, other researchers would then be able to test the results to verify or refute findings, and, perhaps, subsequently build upon them with further research and discovery. However, by adopting open innovation techniques, scientists and their benefactors—whether they be private corporations, the government, or the public—can make more rapid advances in discovery and innovation.

An example of open innovation is the Science Commons, established to speed the translation of scientific data into discovery. Its goal is to develop strategies and tools to allow for faster, more efficient Web-enabled scientific research, to craft policy guidelines and legal agreements to lower barriers to research, and to develop technology to make research, data, and materials easier to find and use. Likewise, the Human Genome Project involved large numbers of researchers who collaborated to map the human genome. By using open innovation, the project was able to complete the rough draft of the human genome a year ahead of schedule.

Although this process is becoming more widely used and accepted in industry and across a number of domains of scientific inquiry and discovery, including the social sciences, open innovation has yet to be embraced by the field of education. However, the potential applicability of open innovation processes is appealing given the complex nature of the educational improvement challenge and the persistent obstacles faced by education practitioners and policymakers in identifying best practices and scaling effective programs and policies.

Harnessing the Power of Open Innovation Networks to Strengthen Science Education

In terms of improving science education policy, practice, and outcomes, the real value of open innovation lies in the power of networks of individuals and organizations to pool their individual experiences and expertise to collectively address and solve complex challenges. Here we highlight two different efforts that use open innovation principles to improve STEM education. These examples illustrate some of the permutations of open innovation networks and the role of business leadership in addressing today's challenges.

Ohio STEM Learning Network

The Ohio STEM Learning Network (OSLN) was created in 2008 as a private-public partnership to advance high-quality STEM education for Ohio students. The goal of the OSLN is to build Ohio's capacity in STEM education by creating and sustaining new STEM schools, implementing new business models for STEM schools, and developing and sustaining a powerful network of schools, universities, businesses, and other community partners that more closely connect education and economic development in the state.

The partnership is managed by Battelle, a leading international research and development (R&D) organization that manages a number of Department of Energy national labs and conducts R&D in national security, energy technology, and health and life sciences.

The OSLN provides infrastructure and technical support for five STEM schools established by state legislation and supported by private and public investments totaling some $50 million. The network also leverages the expertise and capacities of Ohio's businesses, institutions of higher education, K–12 communities, and private foundations to support these "platform schools" and to drive innovative best practices throughout each region within the state and beyond. In its role, Battelle and its affiliates advise the state, connect all grantees to maximize impact, share research and data on STEM-education best practices, and connect the effort with other state and national efforts.

The first platform school in the network was Metro Early College High School, formed in 2006 by a partnership among Battelle, The Ohio State University (OSU), and the Education Council, which represents the 16 school districts in Franklin County. Battelle contributed $560,000 for the school's initial year of operation, helped to develop the school's curriculum, and established mentoring programs for students. OSU committed space on its campus worth $1.2 million for the school's building lease for three years, and assisted in the development of the school's curriculum through its colleges of Education, Mathematical, and Physical Sciences, and Biological Sciences. The university also hosts students at learning centers throughout its campus and conducts research on best educational practices, including mentoring and how to train scientists to be educators.

Metro Early College High School is a public, open enrollment school that enrolls students chosen by lottery from the 16 Franklin County school districts. It is the first STEM high school in Ohio, and it utilizes a mastery approach to learning. This model requires students to take accelerated classes in their first two years to demonstrate mastery of the core college preparatory curriculum. Upon demonstrating mastery of these subjects and a set of core competencies, students take classes at OSU and other centers of learning. In addition, they are required to engage in math- and science-focused apprenticeships that include problem solving, critical thinking, and innovation with organizations such as Battelle and other local companies with a STEM focus.

While it is still early, the results of Metro's approach appear to be promising. The first group of Metro sophomores scored impressively on the Ohio Graduation Tests when compared with their peers in Franklin County and statewide. For example, in 2008 Metro ranked 20th in passing rates among 610 school districts statewide. They achieved this result despite the fact that the school does not have any admission criteria. According to an interview with Education Council CEO Brad Mitchell, Metro's students come from diverse backgrounds and have a wide range of preparation. Specifically, about 25% of Metro school students had an A average in middle school, while the majority earned low B-minus to high C-minus grades, mirroring overall student averages in the Franklin County feeder school districts (Richards 2008).

STEM Research and Modeling Network

In 2008, the Business-Higher Education Forum (BHEF) launched the STEM Research and Modeling Network (SRMN), an open-innovation network established to better understand the U.S. STEM education system and increase the number of students who enter the STEM workforce or STEM teaching. The network includes members from K–12 and higher education, business and industry, government and nonprofit organizations, and philanthropy.

The SRMN partners came together, in part, to advance new methods of STEM education reform. Specifically, the SRMN was formed around the idea of using modeling and simulation tools to strengthen U.S. STEM education. The use of modeling and simulation—widely used in fields ranging from climate change to urban planning to business management—is a valuable tool when one cannot actually experiment on the system. Although they have historically been used rarely in education, modeling and simulation tools have the potential to

- offer an organized and comprehensive approach to understanding the complex, multilevel nature of the U.S. education system;
- provide a common platform for analysis, research, and dialogue among often disconnected education stakeholders including practitioners, policymakers, researchers, and funders; and
- identify gaps in the existing research base and inform the development of a more robust, coherent education research agenda.

Raytheon CEO William Swanson, co-chair of the Business-Higher Education Forum's STEM Initiative, helped conceive the idea for the project in 2006 as a means of exploring alternative policies for improving student outcomes in STEM. His vision was to harness the potential of systems dynamics modeling—a tool widely used by Raytheon and in engineering-based industries—to help solve the problem of too few STEM graduates. To this end, he deployed teams of Raytheon systems engineers over a period of 18 months to build an initial prototype model of the U.S. STEM education system.

This initial model included 227 independent variables for influencing the number of students who are capable and interested in pursuing careers in STEM disciplines. The model tracks the flow of students as they progress through the PreK–16 educational system from elementary school to middle school and then high school, and subsequently into college as STEM majors and either careers in STEM teaching or STEM industry. The model developers worked with Business-Higher Education Forum staff and other education experts to examine published causal research on STEM education and to develop and test the model's hypotheses, identify the variables that influence STEM persistence, and determine the relationships between those variables. This research forms the basis for the mathematical formulae that underpin the model and for the coefficients that determine the strength of various influences on STEM proficiency and interest.

At the K–12 level, the model demonstrates the influence of teachers on students' STEM proficiency and points to the positive effect of increasing the number of STEM-capable teachers on the overall number of students who pursue a degree in a STEM major. The postsecondary portion of the model highlights the importance of supports—such as social networks, mentoring or bridge programs—that influence student persistence in STEM majors.

Since the prototype model was completed in 2008, the SRMN has been improving the model before making a new version available for open-source use in mid-2009. The revised model will provide

- *researchers* with the ability to translate high-quality research into an applied tool;
- *policy makers* with a low-risk means of exploring the possible impacts—intended and unintended—of proposed legislation and other policy changes;

- *practitioners* with the ability to simulate the effects of scaling up specific programs and practices over the course of time; and
- *funders* with the potential to gauge effective and successful education investments.

By making the model available in open source, any individual will be able to download a free copy of the model for the purpose of experimentation or to suggest changes that will make the model more robust. In addition, individuals will be able to adapt the model to their own unique contexts if they wish.

The SRMN provides technical assistance to individuals, organizations, and policymakers in using the model, including training for model developers and users. It also advocates for the use of these kinds of techniques to inform policymaking and research. Finally, the network has begun to identify and develop other models and data visualization tools that can help practitioners and policy makers better understand the potential impacts of changes to education policy and practice.

As with any innovation, it will take time before the benefits of open innovation networks and modeling tools extend to students' science achievement. Nonetheless, these kinds of models and the networks that surround them have the potential to profoundly affect decision-making processes, which can result in noticeable changes to policies, funding strategies, research priorities, programs, and—eventually—practice.

Conclusion

Despite many well-intentioned and successful efforts, business investments in education have had too little overall cumulative effect on real and lasting science education reform that leads to improvement in student outcomes. Now is the ideal time, however, for the business community and its leaders to reexamine its approach to engaging with and investing in education, and in particular, science education. The widespread advent and adoption of new technologies, tools, and business models provides tantalizing opportunities for educators, business leaders, and other stakeholders to drive real and lasting improvements in science education that can result in significant gains in interest and achievement among all students.

It is too early to know if the new approaches described in this chapter will drive science education reform and whether they will be widely adopted or sustainable. However, it is clear that these examples reflect a shift from the historical approach, which asked, "How can business help education?" to the more contemporary, "How can business and education collaborate to address our common concerns?" By involving multiple stakeholders and adopting best practices from business and education, these efforts may help pave the way for more innovative and effective approaches to science education reform.

References

ACT. 2007. *Rigor at risk: Reaffirming quality in the high school core curriculum.* Iowa City, IA: ACT.

Business-Higher Education Forum (BHEF). 2005. *A commitment to America's future: Responding to the crisis in mathematics and science education.* Washington, DC: Business-Higher Education Forum.

Business-Higher Education Forum (BHEF). 2007. *An American imperative: Strengthening the recruitment, retention and renewal of our nation's mathematics and science teaching workforce.* Washington, DC: Business-Higher Education Forum.

Chesbrough, H. W. 2003. The era of open innovation. *MIT Sloan Management Review* 44 (3).

Chesbrough, H. W., W. Vanhaverbeke, and J. West, eds. 2006. *Open innovation: Researching a new paradigm.* New York: Oxford University Press.

Committee on Prospering in the Global Economy of the 21st Century. 2007. *Rising above the gathering storm: Energizing and employing America for a brighter economic future.* Washington, DC: National Academies Press.

Committee to Encourage Corporate Philanthropy (CECP). 2009. *Giving 2008.* New York: CECP.

ExxonMobil. 2007. *2007 corporate citizenship report.* Fairfax, VA: CECP.

Grissmer, D., and A. Flanagan. 1998. *Exploring rapid achievement gains in North Carolina and Texas.* Washington, DC: National Education Goals Panel.

Institute for Higher Education Policy (IHEP). 2008. *Corporate investments in college readiness.* Washington, DC: IHEP.

National Alliance of Business. 1987. *The fourth R: Workforce readiness.* Washington, DC: National Alliance of Business.

National Commission on Excellence in Education. 1983. *A nation at risk: The imperative for educational reform.* Washington, DC: U.S. Department of Education.

National Commission on Mathematics and Science Teaching for the 21st Century. 2000. *Before it's too late: A report to the nation from the National Commission on Mathematics and Science Teaching for the 21st Century.* Washington, DC: U.S. Department of Education.

National Science Board. 1999. *Preparing our children: Math and science in the national interest.* Arlington, VA: National Science Foundation.

Obama, B. 2009. Remarks of President Barack Obama to the National Academy of Sciences. Washington, DC: April 27.

Richards, J. S. 2008. Fledgling school fares well on state graduation exams: Metro High kids focus on science, math; scores top many across state. *Columbus Dispatch.* July 27.

Tapping America's Potential (TAP). 2005. *The education for innovation initiative.* Washington, DC: Business Roundtable.

Tapping America's Potential (TAP). 2008. *Gaining momentum, losing ground: Progress report 2008.* Washington, DC: Business Roundtable.

Chapter 3

A New Challenge for Science Education Leaders
Developing 21st-Century Workforce Skills

Rodger W. Bybee

The dawn of the 21st century shed light on a variety of new challenges for the United States in general and science education in particular. Popular books such a Thomas Friedman's *Hot, Flat, and Crowded: Why We Need A Green Revolution–And How It Can Renew America* (2008) and Fareed Zakaria's *The Post-American World* (2008) sent powerful signals that all was not well, and now is the time for change. While Thomas Friedman directs attention to the environmental crisis, economic instability, and population problems, the theme of Zakaria's book can be expressed as "the rise of the rest." That is, this era is less about the decline of America and more about the rates and directions of economic growth of other countries. Since these books were published, the global economy has experienced the worst decline since the Great Depression.

Few question the observation that the United States is losing its competitive edge in the global economy. Central to the global economy is scientific progress and technological innovation. The United States needs a workforce with higher levels of scientific and technological literacy in general and thus there is a need for talented individuals to enter scientific and engineering careers.

With these ideas in mind, I brought up the need for 21st-century skills and abilities as learning outcomes during a recent conversation with several science education leaders. The colleagues indicated that many were talking about 21st-century skills, but few were making concrete the abstract nature of this goal. Actually, they had much shorter and more dismissive statements. Probing their response, I found that they generally agreed with the goal, but they thought there was a need to describe specific skills and indicate how those skills might be implemented in school programs and classroom practices—without changing or diminishing the primary goal of learning science content. Of course, I told them this was possible. I did this without noting that the primary goal of science education was to prepare citizens for life and work, not exclusively for careers in science and engineering. They countered with a request for concrete, practical examples of the 21st-century skills and ideas for school science programs and classroom practices that would be appropriate responses. This chapter is my response to that request.

Business and Industry Signal the Problem

In September 2005, with support from the Office of Science Education at the National Institute of Health, Biological Sciences Curriculum Study (BSCS) compiled key recommendations from 20 major reports from business, industry, government agencies, and associated groups (see Table 1). The process synthesized recommendations for K–12 science and technology education. The panel directed attention to science and technology education, because the potential of these disciplines to contribute positively to the emerging goal of developing a 21st-century workforce had not been fully recognized. The resulting report was published in January 2007 under the title, *A Decade of Action: Sustaining Global Competitiveness* (BSCS 2007).

One finding of this effort was disturbing. Almost without exception, the various examined reports mentioned the critical role of science and technology in the economy, but they seldom addressed the topic of science and technology education specifically; literacy and mathematics were the leading disciplines. Most would agree that education has to account for increased reading and mathematics achievement, but science and technology education also must be seen as fundamental to achieving workforce competencies, especially when those competencies include critical thinking,

Table 1. Twenty Contemporary Reports Reviewed

Achieve, Inc. 2005. *Rising to the challenge: Are high school graduates prepared for college and work? A study of recent high school graduates, college instructors, and employers.* Washington, DC: Peter D. Hart Research Associates.

Achieve, Inc., and National Governors Association. 2005. *An action agenda for improving America's high schools.* Washington, DC: Achieve.

American Electronics Association (AeA). 2005. *Losing the competitive advantage? The challenge for science and technology in the United States.* Washington, DC: AeA.

American Electronics Association (AeA). Business-Higher Education Forum, Business Roundtable, Council on Competitiveness. Information Technology Association of America, Information Technology Industry Council, et al. 2005. *Tapping America's potential: The education for innovation initiative.* Washington, DC: Business Roundtable.

Barton, P. E. 2002. *Meeting the need for scientists, engineers, and an educated citizenry in a technological society.* Princeton, NJ: Educational Testing Service.

Business-Higher Education Forum (BHEF). 2003. *Building a nation of learners: The need for changes in teaching and learning to meet global challenges.* Washington, DC: BHEF.

————. 2005. *A commitment to America's future: Responding to the crisis in mathematics and science education.* Washington, DC: BHEF.

Coble, C., and M. Allen. 2005. *Keeping America competitive: Five strategies to improve mathematics and science education.* Denver, CO: Education Commission of the States.

Committee for Economic Development (CED). 2003. *Learning for the future: Changing the culture of math and science education to ensure a competitive workforce.* Washington, DC: CED.

Council of Chief State School Officers (CCSSO). 2006. *Mathematics and science education task force: Policy statement executive summary.* Washington, DC: CCSSO.

(continued on next page)

Table 1. Twenty Contemporary Reports Reviewed (continued)

Donohue, T. J. 2006. *The state of American business 2006.* Washington, DC: U.S. Chamber of Commerce.

National Academies. 2005. *Rising above the gathering storm: Energizing and employing America for a brighter economic future.* Washington, DC: National Academy Press.

National Association of System Heads (NSAH). 2006. *Turning the tide: Strategies for producing the mathematics and science teachers our schools need.* Washington, DC: NASH.

National Center on Education and the Economy (NCEE). 2006. *Tough choices or tough times: The report of the new commission on the skills of the American workforce.* San Francisco: Jossey-Bass.

National Education Summit on High Schools. 2005. America's high schools: The front line in the battle for our economic future. In The High Point workforce preparedness study, ed. Herman Group, 175–180. High Point, NC: City of High Point.

Partnership for 21st-Century Skills. 2003. *Learning for the 21st century: A report and mile guide for 21st-century skills.* Washington, DC: Partnership for 21st-Century Skills.

———. 2006. *Results that matter: 21st-century skills and high school reform.* Tucson, AZ: Partnership for 21st-Century Skills.

Roberts, G. 2002. *SET for success: The supply of people with science, technology, engineering and mathematics skills.* London, UK: Institute for Employment Studies.

Secretary's Commission on Achieving Necessary Skills. 1998. *Learning a living: A blueprint for high performance.* Washington, DC: U.S. Department of Labor.

Task Force on the Future of American Innovation. 2005. The knowledge economy: Is the United States losing its competitive edge? *www.futureofinnovation.org.*

solving semi-structured problems, and reasoning: much like the abilities of scientific inquiry and technological design. Still, there was a need to move from broad, policy-level recommendations to more concrete and practical statements of skills and abilities.

Clarifying Future Skill Demands

I begin this section with one example that both illustrates skill demands and underscores the need for an emphasis on what is generally referred to as inquiry-oriented science. Figure 1 illustrates changes in skill requirements in the U.S. job market from 1960 to the early years of the 21st century. Note that the steepest decline during recent decades took place in routine tasks (mental tasks that can now be completed by computers). In contrast, jobs requiring high levels of abstract tasks—nonroutine analytic problem-solving—have increased. This also includes interactions with others, such as with group problem solving and interpersonal communication. One other feature of this chart that should be noted is that manual tasks have also declined.

Figure 1. Trends in Job Tasks

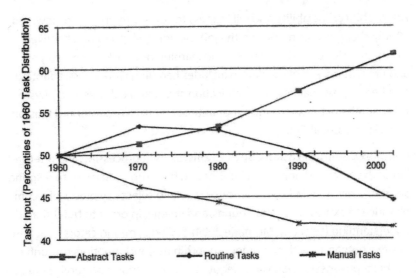

SOURCE: AUTOR, D. 2007. *TECHNOLOGICAL CHANGE AND JOB POLARIZATION: IMPLICATIONS FOR SKILL DEMAND AND WAGE INEQUALITY.* PRESENTATION AT THE NATIONAL ACADEMIES WORKSHOP ON RESEARCH EVIDENCE RELATED TO FUTURE SKILL DEMANDS.

What does this mean? If students in science classes only memorize and reproduce scientific knowledge, they are being prepared for jobs that are fewer in number and lower in skills and wages. In contrast, if students have experience solving problems, working in groups, and communicating conclusions using evidence, they are developing the knowledge, skills, and abilities to participate in this century's economy. Let's look more closely at details of 21st-century skills.

In 2007, the National Academies held two workshops that identified five broad skills that accommodated a range of jobs from low-skill, low-wage service to high-wage, high-skill professional work. Individuals develop these broad skills within contexts such as science and technology

---

Table 2. Examples of 21st-Century Skills

Research indicates that individuals learn and apply broad 21st-century skills within the context of specific bodies of knowledge (National Research Council 2008a, 2000; Levy and Murnane 2004). At work, development of these skills is intertwined with development of technical job content knowledge. Similarly, in science education, students may develop cognitive skills while engaged in study of specific science topics and concepts.

Adaptability: The ability and willingness to cope with uncertain, new, and rapidly changing conditions on the job, including responding effectively to emergencies or crisis situations and learning new tasks, technologies, and procedures. Adaptability also includes handling work stress; adapting to different personalities, communication styles, and cultures; and physical adaptability to various indoor or outdoor work environments (Houston 2007; Pulakos, et al. 2000).

Complex Communications/Social Skills: Skills in processing and interpreting both verbal and nonverbal information from others in order to respond appropriately. A skilled communicator is able to select key pieces of a complex idea to express in words, sounds, and images, in order to build shared understanding (Levy and Murnane 2004). Skilled communicators negotiate positive outcomes with customers, subordinates, and superiors through social perceptiveness, persuasion, negotiation, instruction, and service orientation (Peterson et al. 1999).

---

programs, a well as other settings (NRC 2008a, 2000; Levy and Murnane 2004). The skills identified, based on the National Academies workshops, are displayed in Table 2.

A review of Table 2 reveals a mixture of cognitive abilities, social skills, personal motivation, conceptual knowledge, and problem-solving competency. Although diverse, this knowledge—and many of these skills and abilities—can be developed in inquiry-oriented science classrooms. That said, it should be made clear that science programs cannot, and probably should not, assume complete responsibility for developing *all* 21st-century skills. Even so, inquiry-oriented science classrooms have the opportunity to make a substantial contribution.

Table 2. Examples of 21st-Century Skills (continued)

Nonroutine Problem Solving: A skilled problem solver uses expert thinking to examine a broad span of information, recognize patterns, and narrow the information to reach a diagnosis of the problem. Moving beyond diagnosis to a solution requires knowledge of how the information is linked conceptually and involves metacognition—the ability to reflect on whether a problem-solving strategy is working and to switch to another strategy if the current strategy isn't working (Levy and Murnane 2004). It includes having creativity to generate new and innovative solutions, integrating seemingly unrelated information; and entertaining possibilities others may miss (Houston 2007).

Self-management/Self-development: Self-management skills include the ability to work remotely, in virtual teams; to work autonomously; and to be self-motivating and self-monitoring. One aspect of self-management is the willingness and ability to acquire new information and skills related to work (Houston 2007).

Systems Thinking: The ability to understand how an entire system works, and how an action, change, or malfunction in one part of the system affects the rest of the system; adopting a "big picture" perspective on work (Houston 2007). It includes judgment and decision-making; systems analysis; and systems evaluation as well as abstract reasoning about how the different elements of a work process interact (Peterson et al. 1999).

Adapting 21st-Century Skills for Science Education Programs

This section provides an introductory description of the five skills (see Table 3, pp. 42-43, for specific examples) in the context of school science programs. Terms, strategies, and contexts that are used within the science education community will be used for descriptions of the skills and abilities. This discussion also presents connections to the *National Science Education Standards* (NRC 1996).

Adaptability

Science programs will provide learners with experiences that require coping with new approaches to investigations, analyzing less-than-clear data, using new tools and techniques to make observations, and collecting and analyzing data. Programs will include opportunities to work individually and in groups on science activities, investigations, laboratories, and field studies.

Specific examples from the National Science Education Standards (NSES) include

- Use appropriate tools and equipment to gather, analyze, and interpret data.
- Design and conduct a scientific investigation.

Complex Communication/Social Skills

Programs with varied learning experiences, including laboratories and investigations, will require students to process and interpret information and data from a variety of sources. Learners would have to select appropriate evidence and use it to communicate an explanation. Science programs would include group work that culminates with the use of evidence to formulate a conclusion or recommendation.

Specific examples from the NSES include

- Design and conduct scientific investigations (with a group).
- Communicate scientific procedures and explanations, as well as defend a scientific argument.
- Use technology and mathematics to improve investigations and communications.

Nonroutine Problem Solving

Science programs will require learners to apply knowledge to scientific questions and technological problems, identify the scientific components of a contemporary issue, and use reasoning to link evidence to an explanation. In the process of scientific investigations, learners will be required to reflect on the adequacy of an answer to a question or solution to a problem. Students may be required to think of another investigation or another way to gather data and connect those data with the extant body of scientific knowledge.

Specific examples from the NSES include
- Identify questions that can be answered through scientific investigations.
- Develop descriptions, explanations, predictions, and models using evidence.
- Think critically and logically to make the relationship between evidence and explanations.
- Recognize and analyze alternative explanations and predictions.

Self-Management/Self-Development

Programs will include opportunities for students to work on scientific investigations alone and as a group. These investigations would include full inquiries and may require learners to acquire new knowledge and develop new skills as they pursue answers to questions or solutions to problems.

Specific examples from the NSES include
- Design and conduct a scientific investigation.
- Use appropriate tools and techniques to gather, analyze, and interpret data.

Systems Thinking

School science programs would include the introduction and applications of systems thinking in the context of life, Earth, and physical science as well as multidisciplinary problems in personal and social perspectives. Learners would be required to realize the limits to investigations of systems, describe components, flow of resources, changes in systems and subsystems, and reasoning about interactions at the interface between systems.

Specific examples from the NSES include
- Identify questions that can be answered through scientific investigations.

- Design and conduct a scientific investigation.
- Think critically and logically to make the relationship between evidence and explanation.

Table 3 summarizes essential features of the skills and provides examples for school science programs.

Challenges for Curriculum, Instruction, and Assessment

Addressing the need to develop 21st-century workforce skills will require students to have experience with activities, investigations, and experiments. In a word, the curriculum needs to be *inquiry-oriented*. This orientation seems obvious, but it must be emphasized. Science education has an opportunity to make a substantial contribution to one of society's pressing problems. Science classrooms provide the setting for helping students learn most, if not all, of the workforce skills described in Table 2. In order to

Table 3. Adapting 21st-Century Skills for Science Education Programs and Practices	
Essential Features of 21st-Century Skills	**Examples of Contexts for School Science Programs**
Adaptability	
Cope with changing conditions Learn new techniques, procedures Adapt to different personalities and communication styles Adapt to different working environments	Work on different investigations and experiments Work on investigation or experiment Work cooperatively in groups Work on investigations in the laboratory and outdoors
Complex Communication Skills	
Process and interpret verbal/nonverbal information Select key pieces of complex ideas to communicate Build shared understanding Negotiate positive outcomes	Prepare oral and written reports communicating procedures, evidence, and explanations of investigations and experiments Use evidence gained in investigations as basis for scientific explanations Prepare a scientific argument Work with group members to prepare a report

Table 3. Adapting 21st-Century Skills for Science Education Programs and Practices (cont.)	
Nonroutine Problem Solving	
Uses expert thinking in problem solving Recognizes patterns Links information Integrates information Reflects on adequacy of solutions Maintains several possible solutions Proposes new strategies Generates innovative solutions	Recognizes the need to search for expert knowledge Recognizes patterns in data, evidence Connects evidence and information from an investigation with scientific knowledge from textbooks, the web, or other sources Understands constraints in proposed solutions Proposes several possible solutions and strategies to attain the solutions Proposes creative solutions
Self-Management/Self-Development	
Work remotely (individually) Work in virtual teams Self-motivated Self-monitoring Willingness and ability to acquire new information and skills	Work individually at home Work with a virtual group Completes a full/open investigation Reflects on adequacy of progress, solution, explanation Acquires new information and skills in the process of problem solving and working on investigation
Systems Thinking	
Understands an entire system Understands how changes in one part of system affects the system Adopts a "big picture" perspective Systems analysis Judgment and decision making Abstract reasoning about interactions among components of a system	Describes components of a system based on a system under investigation Predicts changes in an investigation Understands how small activity connects to big ideas Analyzes a system under investigation Makes decisions about best proposed solutions Demonstrates understanding about components and functions of a proposed system

accomplish this, science educators must provide opportunities for students to adapt to others' work styles and ideas, solve problems, manage their work, think in terms of systems, and communicate their results.

Learning outcomes aligned with inquiry and 21st-century skills can be attained using both full and partial inquiries. Central to these skills is group work and cognitive abilities such as reasoning. Although some may argue for full inquiries, and I agree that these should be part of a student's science experience, there is a place for partial inquiries. After all, the emphasis is on the learning outcomes, and these may be achieved with partial inquiry experiences. The important point is to give emphasis to the skills and abilities described earlier.

One challenge for curriculum, instruction, and assessment is implementing what I have called *integrated instructional sequences*. A National Research Council report, *America's Lab Report: Investigations in High School Science* (Singer, Hilton, and Schweingruber 2006) introduced the idea, saying, "Integrated instructional units connect laboratory experiences with other types of science learning activities, including lectures, reading, and discussion" (p. 4). I would argue that the BSCS 5E instructional model is an example of an integrated instructional unit. In a paper prepared for a National Research Council workshop exploring the intersection of science education and the development of 21st-century skills, I described the research supporting the 5E model and its links with 21st-century skills (Bybee 2009).

Using the BSCS 5E instructional model or another variation on the learning cycle provides connections among curriculum, instruction, and assessment and enhances students' opportunities to attain learning outcomes, including 21st-century skills.

Implications for Science Education Leaders

One of the consistent themes of educational leadership is that leaders have vision. Leaders with vision may, for example, have a long-term perspective, see large systemic issues, present future scenarios, or discern fundamental problems and present possible solutions, rather than spend time and energy assigning blame for the problems. Depending on their situations, leaders have diverse ways of clarifying a vision. Some may do so in speeches, others in articles, and still others in policies. One leader's vision may unify a group, organization, or community; another's vision may set priorities or resolve conflicts among constituencies. A leader's vision likely will have many sources and result from extensive review and careful thought. This is especially true in today's complex educational system.

It also is the case that a vision generally implies change. Seldom does one hear a leader announce that his or her vision is the status quo. Rather, visions clarify the need for and direction of change and the implications for improvement. Some educational changes in science education come from within the system. For example, state assessments have implications for adoption of curriculum materials and learning outcomes. From time to time, changes in society influence changes in science education. For example, a small satellite launched by the Soviet Union resulted in a space race and major reform of science education. The changes implied by the need for 21st-century workforce skills also have originated outside of the science education community.

Effective leadership includes a plan to complement the vision. I have heard from individuals with a great vision, but no plan. Not much happens without a plan. Conversely, I have seen individuals in leadership positions with limited visions and thorough plans. The result in these cases often was great management and maintenance of the status quo. So, the complement to a vision of developing 21st-century skills is a plan to implement the changes implied by the vision. Here are some concrete recommendations that science education leaders can use as they implement changes that will enhance 21st-century skills as learning outcomes.

- *Make sure all students meet the standards for scientific inquiry and technological design.* Beginning with the national standards and extending to state and local standards, abilities related to scientific inquiry are included as learning outcomes. Statements of the need to develop the abilities of scientific inquiry and technological design can be the connection between what many will perceive as the abstract vision of 21st-century skills and the concrete context of science teaching.

- *Build on the opportunities that already exist in school programs and teaching practices.* Understandably, many will see the call for development of 21st-century skills as a major change, one beyond their capabilities and interests. Centering the changes on opportunities that already exist in investigations, laboratories, and activities will soften the resistance to change. In many cases, science teachers already contribute to the development of these skills; the change is one of clarity and emphasis. In particular, some of the changes that may be new for science teachers include placing an emphasis on individual and interpersonal skills.

- *Emphasize cognitive abilities and skills as learning outcomes.* Bringing the development of cognitive abilities and interpersonal skills to the foreground in the science classroom may be new to science teachers. Providing teachers with statements they can use such as "What is the evidence for that explanation?" "What alternative explanations have you heard from your team?" and "What goals of the investigation include working together to gather evidence and form an explanation?" will help.

- *Use the idea of integrated instructional sequences.* Helping science teachers connect lessons will provide the time and opportunity needed for the emphasis on 21st-century skills. In addition, it will enhance the opportunities for other learning outcomes. Of course, I recommend using the BSCS 5E instructional model. But, the important idea is to use an integrated instructional sequence, not one particular model.

- *Include basic skills of literacy and mathematics as part of learning outcomes.* Because part of the student's work will include presentation of results, graphs, charts, diagrams and reports, the inclusion of basic literacy and mathematics should be considered part of a new emphasis on 21st-century skills.

As the leader moves from a vision and a plan to initiatives and actions within the educational system, paradoxes will appear. What do I mean by paradoxes? A paradox is a statement or situation that on the surface seems contradictory. Earlier I mentioned an often-heard paradox in education— equity for all students versus excellence for a few students. A paradox differs from a dilemma. A dilemma involves the selection of one alternative from two balanced alternatives. Dilemmas often defy satisfactory solutions; paradoxes may satisfactorily resolve themselves. For example, a leader must maintain continuity with past science programs and institute the changes implied by the inclusion of goals for skills for this century. Paradoxes may be perceived and expressed as tensions, contradictory directions, or conflicting issues. However, the elements seen as countervailing components of a paradox may not be as contradictory as they seem to be. Leaders in science education must master the paradoxes they confront. Let me describe several paradoxes faced by leaders.

One of the classic paradoxes of science education leadership is encouraging change in science programs and practices while supporting maintenance of past programs and practices. The resolution may center on maintaining stability in the major concepts of science while adopting a new inquiry-oriented science program and emphasizing additional learning outcomes of inquiry and 21st-century skills.

A second example of a paradox that leaders face involves being consistent and having a clear direction while being open and flexible. The resolution here may center on ultimate and proximate goals. The leader may have a consistent view of the ultimate goal he or she wants to attain; however, for now, the leader may have to accept changes that only partially represent the final goal. In between, the leader remains flexible and open to new ways of achieving the vision.

Along with the central importance of resolving the tensions of paradoxes, I would also add the importance of a leader's ability to recognize and address the political realities of educational work. The leader has to recognize that initiating changes means addressing the politics. All issues of improving science achievement are not solely educational. Indeed, it may be that *all* educational issues ultimately are political issues. The paradox embedded here can be stated as achieving educational goals while addressing political realities. I have found that "either/or" thinking often expresses the paradox, while "both/and" thinking provides insights into the resolutions.

Conclusion

Contemporary justification for a vision of improved science education resides in themes such as education and the economy, basic skills for the workforce, and thinking for a living. Such themes differ from earlier justifications such as the space race and a nation at risk. In many respects the economic rationale has emerged from the realization that the U.S. economy is part of a global economy and that the educational level of our citizenship influences the rate and direction of this country's economic progress.

Our discussion here, while this century is still young, presents the occasion to review the need for a workforce with 21st-century knowledge, abilities, and skills. What is common to the work of leaders? I proposed establishing a clear and consistent vision combined with a practical and workable plan. The vision and plan will get the leader moving in directions that may involve curriculum reform, instructional improvement, or alignment of assessments. One crucial point is that leaders must hone their ability to realize and resolve paradoxes as they execute their plans. Effective leadership requires initiating bold new practices while maintaining past traditions or fulfilling a national mandate such as developing new skills while incorporating a local agenda. One of the most disheartening paradoxes is the reality of achieving the established vision and enduring criticism rather than reward for attaining the goal.

Leadership in science education extends from science teachers to the Secretary of Education and the President of the United States. It does not reside with only a few people in key positions. Numerous systems and subsystems, each with individuals who have power, constituents, and goals, contribute to a better science education for students. Not every member of the science education community can or should be involved in constructing assessments, developing curriculum materials, presenting the arguments for scientific inquiry, defending the integrity of science, or providing professional development. But all of us do have our roles and responsibilities, and the extent to which we fulfill those responsibilities will ultimately make a difference for students as they live and work in the 21st century.

References

Autor, D. 2007. Technological change and job polarization: Implications for skill demand and wage inequality. Presentation at the National Academies Workshop on Research Evidence Related to Future Skill Demands.

Biological Sciences Curriculum Study (BSCS). 2007. *A decade of action: Sustaining global competitiveness. A synthesis of recommendations from business, industry, and government for a 21st-century workforce.* Colorado Springs, CO: BSCS.

Bybee, R. 2009. The BSCS 5E instructional model and 21st-century skills. Presentation for The National Academies, Washington, DC.

Friedman, T. 2008. *Hot, flat, and crowded: Why we need a green revolution—and how it can renew America.* New York: Farrar, Straus and Giroux.

Houston, J. 2007. Future skill demands, from a corporate consultant perspective. Presentation at the National Academies Workshop on Research Evidence Related to Future Skill Demands.

Levy, F., and R. Murnane. 2004. *The new division of labor: How computers are creating the next job market.* Princeton, NJ: Princeton University Press.

Millar, R., and J. Osborne. 1998. *Beyond 2000: Science education for the future.* London: King's College, School of Education.

National Research Council (NRC). 2000. *How people learn: Brain, mind, experience and school.* Washington, DC: National Academies Press.

———. 2007. *Taking science to school: Learning and teaching science in grades K–8.* Washington, DC: National Academies Press.

———. 2008a. *Research on future skill demands: A workshop summary.* Washington, DC: National Academies Press.

———. 2008b. *Ready, set, science: Putting research to work in K–8 science classrooms.* Washington, DC: National Academies Press.

Peterson, N., M. Mumford, W. Borman, P. Jeanneret, and E. Fleishman. 1999. *An occupational information system for the 21st century: The development of O*NET.* Washington, DC: American Psychological Association.

Pulakos, E. D., S. Arad, M. A. Donovan, and K. E. Plamondon. 2000. Adaptability in the workplace: Development of taxonomy of adaptive performance. *Journal of Applied Psychology* 81: 612–662.

Singer, R., M. Hilton, and H. Schweingruber, eds. 2006. *America's lab report: Investigations in high school science.* Washington, DC: National Academies Press.

Zakaria, F. 2008. *The post-American world.* New York: W.W. Norton.

Chapter 4

The Many Faces of Leadership in a Complex Environment

James E. McLean

Providing leadership in the school environment today is very difficult. A school leader is pushed by the school board, the superintendent, and the principal (if a departmental leader) from one direction and pulled by the faculty, parents, students, the community, and other constituency groups from additional directions. This chapter recommends a leadership approach that promotes focusing on important outcomes in the midst of many competing agendas. The core of this approach is the establishment of a consensus on outcomes and using those outcomes as the focus for all decisions that are made. Some may feel that this is an oversimplification of leadership, but let me point to one of the greatest social feats of the 20th century to illustrate. In a popular book by Juan Williams, *Eyes on the Prize* (1987), the civil rights struggle in the United States is described. Williams chronicles the issues, tactics, and sacrifices that arose during the process, and yet, despite these challenges, the leadership of the movement kept their eyes on the prize to achieve success. It would be difficult to argue that leadership in schools presents a more complex environment than the struggle for civil rights, and I do not wish to equate school leadership with this struggle, but the analogy does provide a convincing argument that decisions based on specific goals (keeping your eyes on the prize) can be very effective. Finally, the leadership approach recommended in this chapter can be used at any level. It is equally effective whether used by a superintendent, a principal, or a science teacher. In fact, it is most effective when used at all levels of an organization.

The outcomes approach should appeal to science educators because it has its roots in the scientific method. A simplified explanation of the scientific method is (1) encountering a problem; (2) hypothesizing a solution (outcome); (3) gathering data; and (4) analyzing the data to arrive at a solution. As you will see, a more detailed description of my recommended leadership approach will demonstrate that these steps are embedded in the leadership and change process described in this chapter. The approach also suggests that one must be willing to make mistakes, but it builds in the opportunity to make appropriate corrections. Indeed, failures along the way are only evidence used to improve the final product. Outcomes-oriented leadership is not my own creation. It has been suggested by many others, particularly in the corporate world. For example, *Fail-Safe Leadership* by Martin and Mutchler (2003) provides one road map for using this method. In fact, many authors that deal with change leadership focus on goal-oriented leadership explicitly or implicitly (e.g., Fullan 2001, 2006; Leithwood, Jantzi, and Steinbach 1999). More direct support in science teaching contexts can be found in Designing Coherent Science Education edited by Kali, Linn, and Roseman (2008). This book recommends that science curricula focus on criteria identified to unify instruction, which is an outcome the method discussed in this chapter should help achieve.

While it is my belief that an outcomes- or goal-oriented approach is the cornerstone of good leadership, I do not mean to suggest that leadership stops with identifying outcomes. Indeed, identification of the outcome goals is only the first step. Leadership also involves managing the process to turn the goals into reality. Most of this chapter deals with six components of a leadership process that addresses the full range of leadership and management functions needed to put this approach into practice. These six components can be summarized as follows:

- Develop shared vision, mission, and goals
- Build a learning community

an excellent opportunity to involve various constituency groups in the process, without having any one individual or group exert undue influence on the results.

Even during this process, it is important to keep your eyes on the prize! In most educational situations, this prize is improved student achievement. Obviously, providing leadership in science should result in improved science achievement. Does that mean improved scores on state science achievement tests? That depends on whether the state achievement tests measure what you want students to know and be able to do. In this age of accountability, these tests are far more important to teachers and school administrators than to students, because teachers and school administrators are the ones who are held accountable for students' performance on these tests. Thus, student performance on these assessments is almost certain to be one of the outcomes of interest.

Build a Learning Community

Some of the issues involved in the creation of a learning community are the belief in common values and goals, the ability to learn from each other, and the idea of learning as an ongoing process. In order to have a learning community, the participants must arrive at a common set of values and beliefs about what they want to accomplish. The common learning process can be accomplished in multiple ways. One of the more widespread approaches is to participate in a common book experience. That is, select a book appropriate to the mission of the organization, have everyone read the book, and participate in group discussions regarding the content of the book. This approach allows participants to agree or disagree with points without fear of incrimination, since the topics under discussion are more abstract concepts not yet part of the organizational customs.

A common characteristic of successful organizations is that members of that group often engage in ongoing staff development. The common book experience described in the previous paragraph is one such example of a staff development experience that helps members of the group learn new things, share their interpretations of the information, hear others' interpretations, and focus on possible improvements to the organization. For example, suppose the science teachers at a particular high school were interested in improving the science achievement of their students. They decide, as a group, to read a book about the results of the Trends International Mathematics and Science Study (NCEC 2008) and discuss how the findings of that study might be used in their school. By sharing this experience, they could learn about the characteristics of science and mathematics programs that are highly effective and generate ideas about how to modify their own practices to improve the achievement of their students.

Just as the ideas of others are essential in the establishment of an organization's goals, the input of others is also essential to the overall success of the organization. Involving others in the process is important to building and maintaining the learning community. But more than that, bringing in the ideas of all of the people involved often results in a better idea. Multiple perspectives help to identify solutions or goals that avoid unforeseen problems, especially if there is input from those with the most direct experience. In addition, input from multiple constituencies can provide buy-in to the final solution. However, this does require that participants are not only willing to share their own ideas, but are also willing to listen respectfully to the ideas of others.

Diversity is an asset to a learning community. Diverse perspectives lead to creative solutions. From psychology, this can be explained in terms of the theory of cognitive dissonance. Cognitive dissonance, a concept attributed to Festinger (1957), suggests that when individuals are presented with concepts in conflict with one another, it creates an uncomfortable feeling that can be resolved only by modifying one's belief or understanding. It stands to reason that the more diverse the members of a learning community are, the more diverse the ideas that are likely to emerge. This should ultimately result in new ideas as contradictions are resolved. It is my contention that the leadership of the United States during the last century in the development of major patents (the airplane, television, the nuclear bomb, computer, and video recorder, for example) was partially a result of the coming together of people from varied backgrounds who challenged each other's ideas (the melting pot concept). This was cognitive dissonance in action.

Often, putting into place a solution developed by one person is like the carnival game "Whac-A-Mole." In this game, a mole's head pops up in various locations on the board and the player must use a mallet to pound it back down each time it pops up. As soon as one head is pounded down in one place, one pops up in another. This is much like a solution developed by one individual. As soon as the problem is solved, another problem pops up as a consequence of implementing the first solution. Using the knowledge of everyone involved in the process to arrive at a solution can often avoid these problematic outcomes.

A final issue relating to building a learning community has to do with the hiring process. Some experts believe that hiring decisions are among the most important a leader can make (Electronic Recruiting News 2008). This same concern can be extended to promotion decisions. Hiring and promoting people who are willing to participate in learning communities suggest that the individuals possess some important characteristics. For example, having people who work well with others and respect each other's ideas is very important in a learning community. The cognitive dissonance concept supports the hiring of a diverse workforce. Again, diverse ideas promote creative decisions. It is much easier to not hire someone than it is to deal with the adverse consequences of hiring the wrong individual.

Use Data to Inform Decisions

Just as in research, data should inform decisions, not determine them. Predetermined consequences or absolute polices often lead to bad decisions that are made without thought of the consequences. Data-determined decisions are analogous to zero-tolerance policies. Consider a school with a zero-tolerance weapons policy. Most people would agree with such a policy, even if that policy required the immediate suspension of a student who violates it. These types of policies often provide a definition of what constitutes a weapon, and that might include items such as guns, knives and other sharp objects, and chains. Suppose a heretofore honors student arrived at school one day with a wallet connected to his pants with a small chain. If this policy was implemented exactly as written, this student would be suspended immediately and sent home. It makes much better sense to use data to inform decisions rather than determine them. Other criteria, such as fairness, potential impact on others, and impact on the organizational goals would be much more productive in the long run. Policies should be selected based on their potential impact on the ultimate goals of the organization.

Another aspect of this component is the appropriateness of data that are used for making decisions. The recommendation here is that all the data (or information) relevant to the decision be brought into consideration. First, the data has to be relevant to the decision. It is unfortunate that we often use data that are easily available, rather than data that are appropriate. For example, to measure science achievement, the most common assessments use multiple-choice items that measure achievement primarily at the knowledge level when we all know that the ability to understand and apply scientific thinking is far more important. However, measuring students' ability to use and apply science is much more expensive and time-consuming. Thus, student knowledge is what is most often measured. While this is an example of a validity issue, the data should also be reliable in the sense that the data are replicable. If we tried to measure the height of a plant using a ruler made of rubber that stretched and contracted, we would get a different value every time we conducted the measurement. That would be an unreliable measurement. In the same manner, it may not be appropriate to use an opinion poll conducted immediately following a tragic event, unless similar results are gathered from additional samples taken throughout the course of the year.

Think Beyond Your Own Ideas

Just making data-informed decisions is not sufficient. We must have decisions that are appropriate to the problem and are not restricted by past practice. How can we come up with potential solutions that address the problem, particularly if previously tried solutions have not worked? One method of promoting creative thinking has already been discussed. That is, creating learning communities with diverse participants. However, none of us is an expert in all areas or has had experience with all situations. Thus, it is essential to gain input from those with that experience.

One of my favorite methods of finding new and creative solutions is to use the Decision-Making Talent approach that was part of a project called Talents Unlimited (TU). TU was originally developed in Mobile, Alabama for young children in the early 1970s (Mobile County Public Schools 2008) and later expanded to secondary school students (Schlichter and Palmer 1993). This approach begins by brainstorming as many solutions as possible to a problem, regardless of feasibility or associated shortcomings. Once possible solutions have been generated, the advantages and disadvantages of each are determined. Using these results, the best solution is usually considered to be the one that maximizes the advantages while minimizing the disadvantages. Often, some of the possible solutions can be eliminated because they have critical disadvantages. Using this process is even more effective when people from all of the constituency groups are involved in the process. This is an excellent approach to use in groups and with learning communities.

Share the Rewards

At first, it would seem that sharing rewards is not part of an outcomes-oriented approach to leadership. However, it is the people in the organization who attain the goals and accomplish the mission of the organization. Thus, considering the well-being and feelings of the people in an organization is an essential element of good leadership. We usually think of money when we think of rewards. Unfortunately, providing financial rewards is usually not possible in an educational organization. However, there are many other ways of sharing rewards. Merely pointing it out when people do a good job is a simple and effective one. This can be even more effective if it can be tied into a description of the positive impact someone is having. Good deeds should be publicized both inside and outside the organization using both formal and informal methods. For example, internal and external newsletters are formal methods, but e-mails and individual notes can also be effective. Another way is to celebrate group successes with group events. The leader should keep in mind that the collective good deeds of the people in the organization are what make the leaders look good. Of course, it is advisable to share financial rewards when possible. This approach can be even more effective if the rewards can be tied to the achievement of organizational goals.

Set an Example

A leader who appears to be above it all and does not follow organizational policies will often end up without the respect or support of the members of the organization. Once respect is lost, loss of support follows, and the ability to lead suffers. First, it is advisable to follow your own policies. If there is a dress code, conform to the dress code. If the organization has specific working hours, be there on time and do not leave early. It is also a good idea for policies to make sense and be designed so that following these policies impacts positively on the attainment of the mission. A corollary to this is to get rid of rules that have no positive function. I refer to these as "stupid rules." Stupid rules merely take up resources that are required for enforcement and anger people who have to follow rules that have no positive function. It is also clear that one must be fair and consistent in enforcing institutional policies. This is often easier said than done. An organizational leader is often approached by individuals with many types of requests. I try not to look at every request as an individual one, but to consider it as part of a class of requests. That is, think of the request as one of all possible requests of this type. In this way, it can be addressed in terms of an appropriate policy. You will not be treating one person one way and another person with a similar request another way. However, that is not to say that treating people equally is treating them fairly. Equal is not always fair because different people have different needs, and sometimes different approaches are fairer for one person than another. Finally, as an outcomes-oriented leader, each request should be considered in terms of the contribution its approval will have on attaining the organizational goals.

Some Practical Advice

Building a learning community with outcomes-oriented goals is analogous to having everyone in a boat paddling in the same direction. When everyone in the organization is pulling in the same direction, the organization moves more rapidly in that direction. Being the leader of such an organization means that before you make any decision, you should ask how this will help achieve the organizational goals. Before approval, an outcomes-oriented leader should also ask how it can be documented that this decision has had the desired impact. This means that every decision can be evaluated and is directly related to the desired outcomes. That is, its impact can be monitored and assessed.

One of the most neglected areas of leadership relates to the personal needs of the leader. Ambitious leaders often neglect their own well-being both in terms of physical needs and emotional needs. Addressing physical needs suggests that we get appropriate sleep, exercise, nourishment, and medical care. Yet, this does not ensure that we are addressing our emotional needs. Ginsberg and Davies (2007) developed an entire book on meeting the emotional needs of leaders. Decision making is not without its emotional consequences, and ignoring these puts the leader at peril.

Ignoring emotional needs can, at the very least, lead to burnout and, if allowed to progress, it can eventually lead to serious physical problems. Ginsberg and Davies (2007) suggest concrete steps leaders can take to develop one's own emotional plan. They refer to this as the "Emotional Dirty-Dozen" (p. 91). In many ways, the dozen suggestions are like a 12-step program beginning with acceptance that "leadership involves emotional experiences" (p. 92). Caring for oneself and being emotionally sensitive to others are among the other 11 suggestions. The bottom line is that it is necessary to be aware of the emotional toll that can result from the isolation and pressure of leadership. I find that having my own support system and a good hobby to take my mind off work are excellent ways to maintain emotional stability.

Leadership in science education often draws uniquely qualified individuals who come from a science background. These individuals tend to be experienced applying logical thought and concepts such as the scientific method to achieve desired results. As was presented in this chapter, those skills go a long way in preparing one to be an effective leader. Working with others to solve problems and using data to support decision making is already part of their psyche. However, other aspects of leadership might be a challenge for these people. It is not always clear how precise scientific thinking can be applied to what is essentially a people-oriented function like leadership. Going from an often deterministic world to a more probabilistic world can be frustrating. In this case, taking care of the emotional side of leadership is even more important.

This brings us back to where we began. While the full implementation of the leadership approach recommended in this chapter has many facets, the foundation of that leadership style is to "keep your eye on the prize." That is, every decision should consider at its nucleus how it will support the overall mission and goals of the organization. This is a leadership style that should work well with science educators, because its core principles are borrowed from the science community.

References

Bensoussan, B. E., and C. S. Fleisher. 2008. *Analysis without paralysis: 10 tools to make better strategic decisions.* Upper Saddle River, NJ: Pearson Education.

Electronic Recruiting News. 2008. Hiring decisions miss the mark 50% of the time. *www.interbiznet.com/ern/archives/081007.html*

Festinger, L. 1957. *A theory of cognitive dissonance.* Stanford, CA: Stanford University Press.

Fullan, M. 2001. *Leading in a culture of change.* San Francisco, CA: John Wiley & Sons.

———. 2006. *Turnaround leadership.* San Francisco, CA: John Wiley & Sons.

Ginsberg, R., and T. G. Davies. 2007. *The human side of leadership: navigating emotions at work.* Westport, CT: Praeger.

Goodstein, L. D., T. M. Noland, and J. W. Pfeiffer. 1993. *Applied strategic planning: How to develop a plan that really works.* New York: McGraw-Hill.

Kali, Y., M. C. Linn, and J. E. Roseman. 2008. *Designing coherent science education: Implications for curriculum, instruction, and policy.* New York: Teachers College Press.

Leithwood, K., D. Jantzi, and R. Steinbach. 1999. *Changing leadership for changing times.* Maidenhead, Berkshire: Open University Press.

Martin, L. L., and D. G. Mutchler. 2003. *Fail-safe leadership, Straight talk about correcting the leadership challenges in your organization.* Orlando: Delta Press.

Mobile County Public Schools. 2008. Talents Unlimited. *www.mcpss.com/?DivisionID=2142&DepartmentID=2004*

National Center for Educational Statistics (NCEC). 2008. Highlights from TIMSS 2007: Mathematics and science achievement of U.S. fourth and eighth grade students in an international context. *http://nces.ed.gov/pubs2009/2009001.pdf*

Schlichter, C. L., and W. R. Palmer, eds. 1993. *Thinking smart: A primer of the talents unlimited model.* Mansfield Center, CT: Creative Learning Press.

Williams, J. 1987. *Eyes on the prize: America's civil rights years, 1954–1965.* New York, NY: Penguin Books.

Section Two

The Role of School and District Science Leadership for Building Instructional Capacity

Chapter 5

Content Coverage and the Role of Instructional Leadership

William H. Schmidt and Neelam Kher

The seminal nonpartisan report, *Rising Above the Gathering Storm: Energizing and Employing America for a Brighter Economic Future* (COSEPUP 2007), highlighted the urgency of investing in science and mathematics education in the United States. This investment was considered critical for the country to "compete, prosper, and be secure in the global community of the 21st century" (p. 11). In his best-selling book *The World Is Flat,* Thomas Friedman underscored the same concerns: "The truth is, we are in a crisis now... and this quiet crisis involves the steady erosion of America's scientific and engineering base, which has always been the source of American innovation and our rising standard of living" (2005, p. 25).

The Gathering Storm identified the need for improvement of K–12 mathematics and science education as the most pressing issue currently confronting policy makers. At the convocation marking two years since the dissemination of the report, there was general consensus that "the report continues both to inspire and to guide the actions of policy makers, business leaders, and educators" (COSEPUP 2009, p. 18).

There is growing concern about the performance of U.S. students on international assessments such as the Third International Mathematics and Science Study (TIMSS) and the Program for International Student Assessment (PISA). Student performance on cross-national comparisons declines as they progress from elementary to middle to high school. Comparison of the TIMSS results from 1995 to current international assessments shows that the relative position of U.S. elementary students in the area of science has declined. Trend results in science from the National Assessment of Educational Progress (NAEP) show essentially no change in student performance over the past 30 years (Gross et al. 2005). These poor student outcomes reinforce the view that America is losing its competitive edge.

While outlining the education reform agenda for the new administration in March of 2009, President Obama articulated similar concerns: "The relative decline of American education is untenable for our economy, it's unsustainable for our democracy, and it's unacceptable for our children—and we can't afford to let it continue" (Obama 2009).

The Role of Standards

The National Research Council (NRC) and the American Association for the Advancement of Science (AAAS) had leadership roles in the development of standards for science education. The standards-based framework included recommendations for student outcomes in science as well as guidelines for science teachers (AAAS 1993, 2001; NRC 1996, 2000).

Researchers point out that the connection between these and state standards may be nebulous at best (Marx and Harris 2006). Additionally, some teachers have argued that the standards articulated by AAAS and NRC are incompatible with state-mandated curricula and accountability systems such as No Child Left Behind (Southerland et al. 2007).

According to DeBoer, the states' "focus on testing has ... led individual states to create curriculum standards that are more detailed and highly specific" (2002, p. 413). Such standards, with the extensive listing of topics to be covered in the year, have served to "prohibit a robust, clear, intensive treatment of foundational ideas" (Southerland et al. 2007). Wandersee and Fisher (2000) reinforced the notion that a focus on myriad facts and details prevents students from obtaining a "big picture" of the science being studied. In the recent report, *State of the State Science Standards*, the authors (Gross et al. 2005) indicated that 19 states, which serve about 55% of U.S. children, have science standards that are considered exemplary. However, that leaves 45% of students served by state science standards that have received grades of C, D, or F.

Standards and Instructional Time

The development of state standards in science has largely been in preparation for the NCLB science mandate that went into effect in 2007–2008. The initial NCLB accountability policies focused on mathematics and language arts. As a result, this led to a reduction of the emphasis and time devoted to science instruction, especially in elementary grades (Saka 2007). In many schools, instructional time allocated to science was left completely to the discretion of teachers. At other schools, teachers, at their principals' behest, only focused on NCLB accountability subjects, especially in the last several months preceding testing (Lee and Luykx 2005).

The Need for Instructional Leadership

The widespread push for educational improvement has included calls for coherent, rigorous, and focused content coverage in science. These concerns have been driven by the following international data: U.S. science standards lack coherence, include too many topics at each grade level, repeat many topics grade after grade, and are not very demanding. Those same studies show that the educational experience occurring in classrooms mirrors this characterization of the standards (Schmidt et al. 1999; Schmidt, Wang, and McKnight 2005). This has led to a reexamination of the roles and responsibilities of state and district superintendents and principals with respect to issues of curriculum. According to Elmore, improvements in instructional quality and student outcomes "[are] possible with dramatic changes in the way public schools define and practice leadership" (2000, p.2).

Elmore (2000) and other researchers (Rowan 1990; Meyer and Rowan 1992) maintain that the institutional structure of public schooling in the United States can best be understood through the lens of the institutional theory of "loose-coupling." Such a lens is useful for understanding why "the most durable innovations occur in the structures that surround teaching and learning, and only weakly and idiosyncratically in the actual processes of teaching and learning" (Elmore 2000, p. 6).

Educational leaders such as district superintendents and principals typically do not consider instructional leadership—and, in particular, content coverage—central to their role as administrators. Empirical evidence suggests that school administrators are least involved with issues related to direct instruction and that only a very small proportion of educational administrators consistently demonstrate instructional leadership (Cuban 1988; Murphy 1990). Heck (1992), in his summary of the literature on instructional leadership, contends that much of the effort related to improvement of student outcomes has been prompted by effective schools research. The basic premise undergirding this research is that "improved student outcomes can be attained through strategic school organization and strong principal leadership" (p. 21).

International reports based on TIMSS data (Schmidt et al. 1999) provide evidence for the notion that leadership that focuses on the central mission of an educational institution and promotes policies and practices that support teachers and student learning is crucial for positive student learning outcomes. In TIMSS countries such as Czech Republic, Germany, Hong Kong, Norway, Spain, and Switzerland, principals (headmasters) spent more than half of their professional time on teaching and administrative tasks directly related to the school's central mission. These studies also indicated that, in the United States, principals in schools of seventh and eighth graders did not view their mission as directly related to educational functions. Much of the principals' time was spent on internal/external relations, and little time was allocated to teaching or internal administration. Additionally, U.S. educational systems have the characteristic of being independent and organize curriculum at the local district level. This has led to variability in access to school curricula, which in turn is related to student achievement (Schmidt et al. 1999). Given the "loosely-coupled" structure of the U.S. educational system, especially with regard to curriculum, and the general lack of instructional leadership, the purpose of this chapter is to examine the factors necessary to address these issues and achieve improved student performance and equality of opportunity.

Background

Findings from TIMSS and PROM/SE (Promoting Rigorous Outcomes in Mathematics and Science Education) underscore the importance of content in student learning in both mathematics and science. When content coverage is coherent, focused, and coupled with rigorous expectations, student learning is increased.

For example, classroom level analyses of U.S. TIMSS data revealed that when instructional decisions are typically left to local districts or individual classroom teachers, the amount of time teachers spent on topics was related to achievement. Even after adjusting for prior learning and SES, increased time spent on topics was related to higher achievement scores. Further, such a relationship was stronger when the increase in time was allocated to tasks that were a departure from dull and routine procedure (Schmidt et al. 2001). TIMSS studies further suggest that when policies and school organization emphasize the importance of curriculum and communicate clear expectations about the quality of the implemented curriculum, more students learn at higher levels of attainment (Schmidt, McKnight, and Raizen 1997; Stigler and Hiebert 1999).

The connection between teacher time spent on content and student learning was established in the 1970s and 1980s (Bloom 1971; Carroll 1989; Fisher and Berliner 1985; Wiley and Harnischfeger 1974). Increasing time spent on learning has also been linked to enhanced skill development and deeper conceptual understanding (Clark and Linn 2003; Smith 2002). These and other studies show a positive correlation between time spent on content and student learning outcomes (Huyvaert 1998; Rangel and Berliner 2007).

The Curriculum Structure of TIMSS' Top Achieving Countries

As part of the comprehensive 1995 TIMSS study, researchers reviewed the textbooks and national standards of nearly 50 countries and coded the documents. The framework developed was based on a cross-national consensus regarding science topic coverage in grades 1 through 8 in the participating TIMSS countries.

Content standards of the four highest achieving nations (Singapore, Japan, Korea, and Czech Republic) were used to develop a model of coherent content coverage in science. For the mathematics curriculum, subsequent analysis of the model by research mathematicians indicated that the model was consistent with the logic intrinsic to the discipline (Schmidt and Houang 2007).

A coherent curriculum introduces topics and develops the ideas in a logical sequence (Schmidt and Houang 2007). Individual topics are connected via a systematic conceptual framework both within and across grade levels. In such a curriculum, a teacher introduces a simple concept and develops the concept fully before moving to more complex concepts. Once the development of a topic is complete, it is excluded from the curriculum in order to free instructional time for the introduction of more complex topics. In a focused curriculum, a relatively small number of topics are selected for inclusion, especially in the early grades.

Figure 1 depicts the common topics that 75% or more of the top-achieving countries intended to cover in grades 1 through 8. The data suggest a logical progression in the coverage of topics from the simpler/basic to the more advanced. When examined by scientists with whom we have worked, this progression is recognized as coherent. For this reason, we view this model as an example of curricular coherence.

While the data presented in Figure 1 depicts the *intended* science curriculum of high-achieving TIMSS countries, it also provides an analytical framework for assessing the coherence of state- and district-level curricular intentions. The framework is also useful for assessing the pattern of topic coverage by teachers. In this study, the number of instructional days teachers spend on topics that appear in the high-achieving science curriculum was determined.

The Role of Instructional Leadership

Recognizing the centrality of content to student learning leads to the additional realization that classroom activities and their relation to content coverage are one of the most important resources a school or district has. School time is a limited resource (180 days in a year, 6 hours per day), and the ways in which this time is used should be of central concern to instructional leaders such as principals and superintendents. Given the salience of content coverage to student learning, we argue that instructional leadership in this domain should be one of the most important responsibilities

Figure 1. Science Topics Intended at Each Grade by a Majority of TIMSS 1995 Top Achieving Countries

Topics	Grade							
	1	2	3	4	5	6	7	8
Organs, Tissues	☐	☐	☐	☐	☐	☐	☐	☐
Physical Properties of Matter	☐	☐	☐	☐	☐	☐	☐	☐
Plants, Fungi	☐	☐	☐	☐	☐	☐	☐	☐
Animals	☐	☐	☐	☐	☐	☐	☐	☐
Classification of Matter	☐	☐	☐	☐	☐	☐	☐	☐
Rocks, Soil	☐	☐	☐	☐	☐	☐	☐	☐
Light	☐	☐	☐	☐		☐	☐	☐
Electricity	☐	☐	☐	☐	☐	☐	☐	☐
Life Cycles	☐	☐		☐	☐	☐	☐	☐
Physical Changes of Matter	☐	☐		☐	☐	☐	☐	☐
Heat & Temperature	☐	☐		☐	☐	☐	☐	☐
Bodies of Water	☐	☐	☐	☐	☐	☐	☐	☐
Interdependence of Life	☐	☐		☐	☐	☐	☐	☐
Habitats & Niches	☐	☐		☐	☐	☐	☐	☐
Biomes & Ecosystems	☐	☐		☐	☐	☐	☐	☐
Reproduction	☐	☐	☐	☐	☐	☐	☐	☐
Time, Space, Motion	☐	☐		☐	☐	☐	☐	☐
Types of Forces	☐	☐		☐	☐	☐	☐	☐
Weather & Climate	☐	☐		☐	☐	☐	☐	☐
Planets in the Solar System	☐	☐	☐	☐	☐	☐	☐	☐
Magnetism	☐	☐		☐		☐	☐	☐
Earth's Composition	☐	☐		☐		☐	☐	☐
Organism Energy Handling	☐	☐		☐		☐	☐	☐
Land, Water, Sea Resource Conservation	☐	☐	☐	☐	☐	☐	☐	☐
Earth in the Solar System	☐	☐		☐		☐	☐	☐
Atoms, Ions, Molecules	☐	☐		☐		☐	☐	☐
Chemical Properties of Matter	☐	☐		☐		☐	☐	☐
Chemical Changes of Matter	☐	☐	☐	☐	☐	☐	☐	☐
Physical Cycles	☐	☐		☐		☐	☐	☐
Land Forms	☐	☐		☐		☐	☐	☐
Material & Energy Resource Conservation	☐	☐		☐		☐	☐	☐
Explanations of Physical Changes	☐	☐	☐	☐	☐	☐	☐	☐
Pollution	☐	☐		☐		☐	☐	☐
Atmosphere	☐	☐		☐		☐	☐	☐
Sound & Vibration	☐	☐		☐		☐	☐	☐
Cells	☐	☐	☐	☐	☐	☐	☐	☐
Human Nutrition	☐	☐		☐		☐	☐	☐
Building & Breaking	☐	☐		☐		☐		☐
Energy Types, Sources, Conversions	☐	☐		☐		☐		☐
Dynamics of Motion	☐	☐	☐	☐	☐	☐	☐	☐
Organism Sensing & Responding	☐	☐	☐	☐	☐	☐	☐	☐

considered when defining good leadership at all three levels—state, district, and school—of the American educational system. We further argue that this must be the role of superintendents and principals. Elmore's (2000) discussion of distributed leadership emphasizes the role of instructional leaders at various levels as buffers against the encroachment of noninstructional issues. Thus, superintendents are called upon to provide a buffer against noninstructional issues so that principals and teachers can focus on the instructional core. Similarly, at the school level, principals in their roles as instructional leaders buffer teachers from noninstructional issues so that they are able to concentrate on issues of instruction and content coverage.

State-Level Instructional Leadership

Instructional leadership related to content coverage at the state level may be manifested through the development and adoption of rigorous and focused content standards—the intended curriculum. In their analysis of 50 state science standards, Schmidt, McKnight and Raizen (1997) found a lack of uniformity in both content and quality; some state standards were weak and incoherent while others displayed rigor and coherence. Variability in focus and coherence led to curriculum frameworks and textbooks that were often unfocused and ineffective in supporting student learning. A more recent study of state science content standards corroborates the earlier findings (Gross et al. 2005).

An analysis of the intended curriculum of high-achieving TIMSS countries revealed that the articulated standards identified topic sequences that were logical across grade levels and, when appropriate, elucidated the hierarchical organization of the disciplinary content (Schmidt, Houang, and McKnight 2005). Such standards were considered coherent. Schmidt and Houang (2007) found that measures of curriculum coherence in mathematics were related to student achievement across some 30 countries.

District-Level Instructional Leadership

Instructional leadership at the district level may be manifested through textbook adoptions, prescription of instructional objectives, and assessment tests to accompany objectives (Floden et al. 1988). If instructional leaders at the district level encounter state standards that lack rigor and coherence, they find themselves in the position of needing to make judgments about standards and goals that might be better (for example, international standards). However, if schools are viewed as "loosely coupled" organizations, then policies adopted at one level of the organization may not be reflected in decisions at other levels. For example, researchers have found considerable variability in the implementation of district policies at the classroom level (Meyer and Rowan 1977; Resnick and Resnick 1985). This would imply a need for instructional leadership at the district level that insures consistency across schools, especially with respect to content coverage.

School-Level Instructional Leadership

Ultimately, all educational reform efforts involve teaching and learning and, as a result, the role of the teacher is pivotal. Educational researchers (Floden et al. 1988) recognize that teachers, because of their direct involvement in the instructional process, play a central role in the implementation of instructional reform. Even teachers who are committed to and have embraced change and reform may not implement the reforms that are intended (Gess-Newsome et al. 2003). Craig (2006) believes that teachers do not simply implement the curriculum but help shape the curriculum.

Principals, by exercising their role as instructional leaders, can frame and articulate school goals, provide instructional supervision, and protect teachers' instructional time (Blase and Blase 1999). Instructional leadership behaviors are known to be related to teacher commitment and professional involvement (Blase and Blase 1999) and exert an influence on teachers' instructional practices (Spillane, Hallett, and Diamond 2003). Purkey and Smith (1983) point out that effective schools—schools in which teachers are able to devote time to the core curriculum in ways that enhance student learning—are characterized by school principals that act as instructional leaders and the presence of an agreement regarding the school's educational goals.

In the absence of such instructional leadership at any or all of these levels, teachers make the decisions regarding which topics to teach, which to add or delete, or whether to reorder topic coverage defined by the prescribed textbook. Most importantly, teachers' decision making focuses on two crucial aspects of instruction:

- How to use the 45–60 minute class period for content coverage and

- How to allocate the total available instructional time in one academic year to specific topics.

Content coverage, as it relates to the choices teachers make in allocating instructional time to various science topics, must become a major concern for instructional leaders, especially principals. The management of this resource is the most important task a principal can undertake in order to improve student learning. This is especially germane in the United States because of the absence of national standards that are uniformly adopted and powerfully enforced. The result is that the curriculum that is implemented displays considerable variability across classrooms within a school, across schools within the district, and across districts within the state. This variability contributes to poor performance internationally as well as inequality in opportunities to learn.

If the focus of instructional leadership is on the central mission of schools, then evidence regarding the extent to which school districts, schools, and classrooms differ in their allocation of time in covering content must be considered invaluable toward understanding achievement gaps as well as understanding the severity of the current situation. Consequently, it is also essential for understanding the importance of pushing for instructional leadership. In school districts, schools, and classrooms, when there is a high degree of coordination or alignment between the intended (standards) and implemented (teacher coverage) curriculum, then one would expect to see, at a given grade level, little or no variability in content coverage among districts within the same states, schools within the same district, or classrooms within the same schools. Presence of large variation in topic coverage is indicative of unequal opportunities to learn science. This variability in content coverage is likely to produce differences in student learning outcomes, thereby creating achievement gaps that can be especially evident when considered according to region or SES.

It is this variability that is presented in this chapter in order to reinforce our view that the management of content coverage, including associated time allocations, is among the most important tasks for educational leadership. We review 53 districts—21 in Michigan and 32 in Ohio—by grade level and then analyze coherence and consistency within the districts and within the individual schools.

Method

The analyses presented here are based on data collected as a part of the PROM/SE project. The goal of the PROM/SE project, a comprehensive Mathematics and Science Partnership (MSP), was to stimulate systemic curriculum reform using an evidence-based model to promote change. The curriculum-sensitive data collected for the project was used to provide individualized curriculum portraits of a school district's mathematics and science content coverage, both at the district and at the classroom level. These curriculum portraits were designed to enable district and school level leaders, teachers, and curriculum experts to develop informed plans for the improvement of student learning in the areas of mathematics and science. The data were also useful for informing the design and delivery of PROM/SE-supported professional development activities for the participating districts.

Instrumentation

Several of the instruments used in PROM/SE were initially designed and used for the TIMSS. The TIMSS Curriculum Frameworks were employed to measure the curriculum at different levels. As a result, comparisons could be made across each level in which curriculum was measured, i.e., state and district (Intended), and classroom (Implemented). All results could also be compared to international benchmarks developed as a part of TIMSS.

In the study reported here, the Teacher Content Goals Survey was used. In its present version, this survey consists of a web-administered[1], self-report measure[2] of the implemented curriculum. In addition to background information, teachers were asked to indicate the number of class periods they used to teach specific science topics (Appendix A). The exhaustive list of school topics used in the study was obtained from the TIMSS Curriculum Frameworks (SMSO 1992a, 1992b).

---

1. A paper-and-pencil version was also made available for those who had difficulty accessing the web.
2. Self-reports have limitations, but validation studies have found an acceptable level of agreement between self-reports of curriculum implementation and direct observation (Porter 1993).

Participants

Data from 1,699 elementary and 373 middle school teachers were obtained between spring 2004 and spring 2005. These teachers represented 277 elementary schools and 144 middle schools from 53 school districts in two midwestern states. Response rates ranged from 55% for some school districts to around 90% for other districts.

For each of the identified topics the teacher was asked to address the following close-ended question: To what extent did you teach each of the following topics in the science course indicated in #1 above during the 2003–2004 school year? Teachers indicated the extent of topic coverage on the following scale representing class periods: 0; <1 or 1; 2–5; 6-10; 11-15; >15.

Index of Content Coverage

Data on the number of periods during the year that each topic was covered was first converted into percentage of teaching time and then into number of instructional days (out of the standard 180). The 24 topics at the elementary level and 35 topics at the middle school level were aggregated for some analyses to broader categories such as biology, life science, Earth science, physics, and chemistry. They were also aggregated by grade level in order to characterize the degree to which content coverage associated with the model of coherence.

Teacher content coverage data were grouped by state and district. Time allocations were averaged across all teachers in the district to produce an average for each district by grade level. For district level analyses, an average of instructional days on specific aggregations of topic areas were calculated at each grade level for each school. Next, within each district we identified the schools (at each grade level) with the highest and lowest average number of instructional days spent on these topics. The difference between the two averages provided the range of average days of instruction within districts. Districts with only one school were not included in these analyses. A low value for the range was indicative of small differences between schools within a district, on average, in the reported instructional time for specific areas of science.

For school-level analyses, the variability in topic coverage between classrooms within a single school at each grade level was calculated by determining the classroom with the largest number of instructional days spent on these topics and the classroom with the smallest number. Once the range (difference) for each grade level within a school was determined, we summarized the entire distribution of ranges across all schools, with the exception of two extreme range values at each grade level. Schools with only one classroom per grade were also excluded from the analysis.

Results

In this section, data are first presented regarding variation in reported science content coverage *among districts* within each of the two states. Variation in reported content coverage is also described *among schools within participating districts* and *among classrooms within a school*. Variation among districts within a state is relevant to issues of instructional leadership at both the state and district level, while variation among schools within a district is particularly germane for the instructional leadership provided by district superintendents and principals. Variation in content coverage between classrooms within the same school is the concern of principals, because they are potential leaders of school-level instruction.

The results for each of the three levels focus on the group of topics covered at each grade level by the model of curricular coherence, as well as those that fall into the broad topic areas of Life, Earth, and Physical Science. Variation in content coverage is reported by grade level: grades 1–5 for the elementary school and grades 6–8 for the middle school. To maintain the flow of the narrative, the use of figures is mostly limited to depiction of content coverage related to topics defined by the coherence model.

Districts Within States

Topics Covered in the Coherence Model

Teacher reports of content coverage of topics consistent with the model of coherence are summarized in Figure 2, page 78, for each of the participating school districts in Michigan and Ohio. At the elementary level, the model of curriculum coherence does not intend for introduction of science topics until grade 3. At grade 3, only seven topics are the focus of study. School districts in Michigan and Ohio at the third-grade level have a difference of about 50 days between the lowest and highest average total number of instructional days for those seven topics. In the Michigan and Ohio districts, respectively, a maximum of about 70 and 55 days are devoted to these topics. Thus, even in these districts, many instructional days are used for other science topics. Coverage of too many topics leads to an implemented curriculum that is diffuse and lacking in focus. Across the elementary grades, the school districts in Michigan showed a wider range of average instructional days allocated to the topics defining the coherence model at that grade level than districts in Ohio.

At sixth grade, the range of average instructional days is similar for districts in both states. At eighth grade the spread is the greatest, not only out of the middle school grades but out of all grades. Ohio had some districts with no time devoted to the topics defining the coherence model, and one district with schools that devoted 100 days to the same topics. This amount of variation occurring at such a critical juncture seems particularly important, especially to the students in these districts, and raises many questions related to issues of equality.

Figure 2. Average Number of Days Elementary and Middle School Teachers in Selected Michigan and Ohio Districts Spent on Science Topics Covered by the Top Achieving Countries

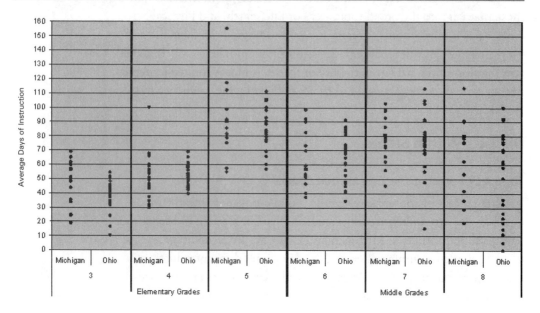

To illustrate the impact of such variability in average instructional days, we focused on data from a large urban school district (District E), along with data from four contiguous school districts (Districts A–D). District E is the largest school district and is located in a geographical area that houses many employers throughout the sectors of industry, government, and education. Although employment opportunities might be availed in District E, the population often makes the choice of residing in neighboring suburban areas (Districts A–D) and, consequently, providing children in the family with educational opportunities in these suburban districts. A non–geographically correct representation of the districts is depicted in Figure 3.

Figure 3. School Districts Neighboring an Urban District

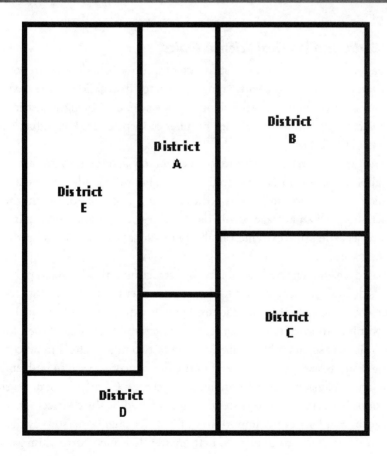

Across Districts A–E, in grades 3 and 4, the range of average instructional days varied by about 30 days. In grade 5, the range was considerably greater: District B devoted on average about 57 instructional days to topics in the model of coherence (approximately 32% of the instructional year) whereas District A spent 155 days (approximately 86% of the instructional year) on the same topics. Other similarly large differences existed between the districts. Given the close physical proximity and the integration of the suburban districts' population with that of the urban district in terms of employment, it seems incongruous that District A allocates almost three times more coverage to topics in line with the model of coherence than district B, especially since these five districts belong to the same county-based educational organization established to foster cooperation on matters such as curriculum.

Life, Earth, and Physical Science Topics

The data indicate that, in the first five grades, the school districts in both Michigan and Ohio had a wider range of average instructional days devoted to life science than to Earth science. In life science, Michigan districts had greater variation in the average number of instructional days than did districts in Ohio.

Michigan's districts continue to be extremely divergent in average time allocations for life science topics into the middle grades. Schools in one district spent no time at all on these topics, while schools in another district allocated an average of 109 days to the same topics. Districts in Ohio reflect the same extreme variability in allocation of time to Earth science topics.

Based on the reported variability in instructional time devoted to life, Earth, and physical science topics, it is apparent that school districts within the same state provide students with very different and unequal opportunities to learn science content. This variability is evident even for school districts separated by as little as one or two miles. The differences among districts within a state are of particular concern, because both states in this study have established standards for science. Clearly the state level intentions have not been consistently implemented by the districts. This once again emphasizes the importance of instructional leadership by the state and district superintendents. Left unattended, such curriculum gaps lead not only to inequalities in opportunity, but they most likely also result in achievement gaps.

Schools Within Districts

Topics Covered in the Coherence Model

When schools within the same district allocate different amounts of time to the topics in the coherence model, it is indicative of "loose-coupling" between district-level curriculum policies and school-level implementation of those policies. In the present study (see Figure 4, p. 82), in the elementary grades, there is at least one school district at each grade level whose schools demonstrate a consistency in instructional days allocated to topics in the coherence model, which means that the difference of the average instructional days is zero or close to zero. However, a majority of the districts have schools that, on average, differ in their allocation of time devoted to topics in the coherence model by at least two weeks. Furthermore, there are districts for which schools varied by about 100 instructional days within the same grade level. This is a difference of approximately 20 weeks of schooling. The outlier districts in Figure 4, including the one just described, are large urban districts where such differences are often related to SES. Differences of that magnitude make it difficult to imagine that these two schools are in the same district, or even the same state, yet such is the case.

At the middle school level, in the sixth and eighth grades, the largest difference between schools in the same district for average instructional days spent covering topics in the coherence model was 105 and 120 days, in Michigan and Ohio respectively. Thus, two middle schools within a single school district may be implementing very different science curricula, especially since there are only 180 days in a typical school year.

Life, Earth, and Physical Science Topics

The variability in topic coverage between schools within the same district mirrors the variability observed between districts within the same state. Schools in some districts do not differ in average instructional time allocated for life, physical, or Earth science topics. In these cases, the difference

Figure 4. Range of Average Instructional Days Elementary and Middle School Teachers Spent in Schools Within Districts on Science Topics in the Coherence Model

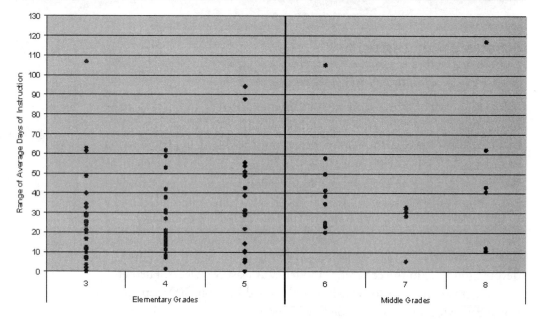

in the average instructional days might be three or fewer. Other districts have schools whose average days of instruction differ by 80 or more days. For the elementary grades, the greatest spread of differences in time allocation on science topics between schools in the same district occurs in grades one and three.

In middle school, variability in average time spent on topics is not only a function of the grade level, but also of the specific topics being covered (life, physical, or Earth science). At the seventh grade, districts seem to have the greatest spread of ranges in average instructional days. For example, in coverage of Earth science topics, two schools within a particular district were so varied in their time allocations that the difference in instructional days devoted to Earth science topics was almost 120 days. Thus, the seventh-grade classes at one school received 24 more weeks of instruction in Earth science than seventh-grade classes at another school in the *same* district.

Classrooms Within Schools

Topics Covered in the Coherence Model

The box plots for the range (difference between classrooms in the same school) of instructional days teachers spent on the topics in the coherence model are depicted in Figure 5. In the elementary grades, the median difference between two classrooms in the same school in the number of days allocated to these topics was between 17 and 21 days or between two and three weeks.

In middle school, the time teachers spent on science topics in the coherence model indicates that, in the lowest 5% of the distribution of schools, the classrooms did not differ in content coverage by more than five instructional days at grade 6, two days in grade 7, and less than two days in grade 8. However, the top 5% of the distribution revealed considerable differences between classrooms in the coverage of science topics. For the sixth through eighth grades, the largest differences in content cover-

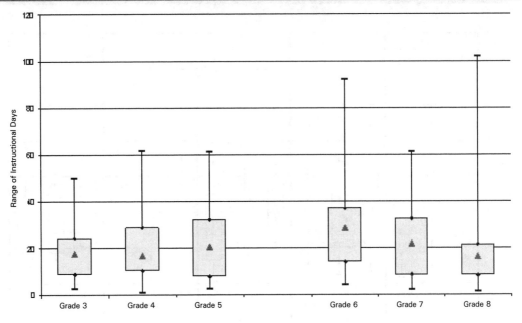

Figure 5. Box Plot of Range of Instructional Days Elementary and Middle School Teachers Spent on Science Topics Covered by TIMSS' Top Achieving Countries: Classrooms Within Schools

age between classrooms in the same school were 92, 61, and 102 days of instruction, respectively. Ignoring those schools with the most extreme differences, there is still substantial variation, and half of the schools at each of grades 6–8 had differences equal to or greater than three to six weeks, which is still a substantial variation that has important consequences for student learning in science.

Life, Earth, and Physical Science Topics

For the elementary grades, the median differences between two classrooms in the same school in instructional days spent on life, Earth, and physical science topics ranged from 17 to 21 days for life science topics, 15 to 24 days for Earth science topics, and 9 to 17 days for topics related to physical science. There seemed to be little consensus regarding instructional time for content coverage in life and Earth science topics between teachers, even those who teach at the same grade level in the same schools. These data are presented in Figure 6.

Figure 6. Box Plot of Range of Instructional Days Elementary Teachers Spent on Life, Earth, and Physical Science Topics: Classrooms Within Schools

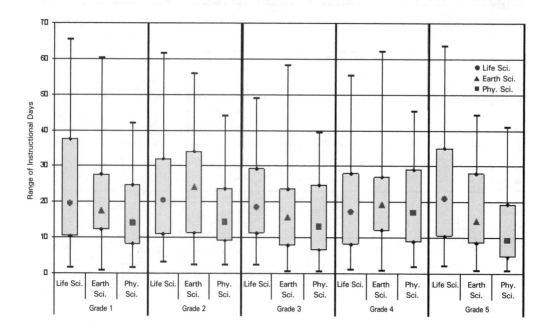

At the middle school level, the median differences between two classrooms in the same school are greatest for life science topics (Figure 7). In seventh and eighth grade, there is at least one school where classrooms differ by 94 and 152 days, respectively, in the coverage of these topics. This large difference suggests that students from different classrooms within the same school are experiencing distinctly different science curricula, even though the parents of these students expect their children to have the same opportunities to learn science. These extensive differences could adversely impact their readiness for the high school science curriculum.

Figure 7. Box Plot of Range of Instructional Days Middle School Teachers Spent on Life, Earth, and Physical Science Topics: Classrooms Within Schools

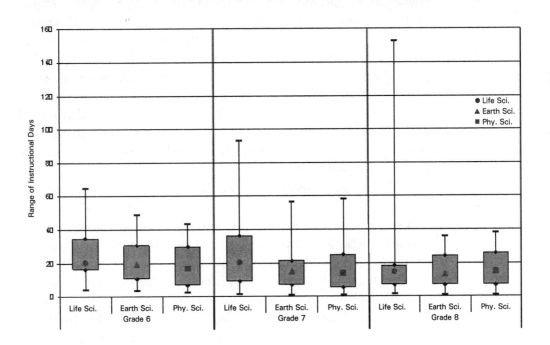

Chapter 5

Discussion and Implications

There is extensive variation in the amount of time allocated to science instruction at district, school, and classroom levels across elementary and middle grades in the 53 districts studied. This is true whether the definition of topics is given by the model of coherence, empirically derived from the science curriculum of the TIMSS high achieving countries, or by the traditional categories of life, Earth, and physical science. These findings suggest that instructional leadership from state superintendents, district superintendents, and principals is of enormous importance.

State standards for science do differ, which results in differences between the two states studied in terms of the content covered in life and Earth science and the grade level at which it is intended to be covered. Schmidt, McKnight, and Raizen (1997), in their analysis of 50 state science standards, reported a lack of uniformity in content and quality. However, when sharp differences *between* districts within the same state are observed (as is evident in the data presented), it may be indicative of either differences in interpretation and implementation of state standards at the district level or a disconnect between state and district curricular intentions. This becomes a leadership issue both for state leaders, because they should be concerned about district level variability, as well as district superintendents, because they should provide instructional leadership for the schools in their jurisdiction.

Wide variation in reported life, Earth, and physical science content is also evident among schools within the same school district. Districts may influence curriculum implementation in a variety of ways—textbook selection, articulation of instructional objectives, and assessments aligned with these objectives (Floden et al. 1988). Meyer and Rowan (1977) found considerable variability in the implementation of district policy at the classroom level. Our data corroborate these findings and reflect the view that schools are indeed "loosely coupled" organizations, so that district intentions and school-level implementation of the curriculum may reflect a wide variation. Instructional leadership of district superintendents and principals is particularly valuable in promoting coherent and consistent implementation of rigorous standards.

Loose-coupling is particularly challenging for students who are highly mobile and must move from one school to another during the span of their education. A recent report from the Wisconsin Center of Education

Research (WCER 2008) suggests that this type of mobility disproportionately affects low-income families. Thus, curricular variability across schools in the same district may have the greatest adverse impact on a subgroup that districts frequently view as "hardest to reach."

Additionally, we have evidence that variation in topic coverage occurs at the classroom level, which indicates that students within the same school at the same grade level are not experiencing the same science curriculum. As Craig (2006) points out, teachers do not simply implement a prescribed curriculum but shape it. This study indicates that the ways in which individual teachers shape the science curriculum is widely divergent between classrooms. Teachers may differ in their content coverage due to individual differences in their understanding of science content and district/state-level expectations. However, school-level policies (or lack thereof) may also be a contributing factor. Instructional leadership provided by principals, coupled with content-related professional development and policies such as common planning periods for teachers at the same grade level of instruction, may shrink the variation in content coverage across classrooms and offer students in different classrooms within the same school similar opportunities to learn.

In our analysis of teachers' reported content coverage of science topics in the TIMSS high-achieving curriculum, it is clear that there is considerable variation at state, district, and school levels. This variation seems to emerge in the early grades and persists (and widens) at the middle school level. The TIMSS high-achieving curriculum may be considered *one* example of a coherent curriculum. Research indicates that students' understanding of content is facilitated and enhanced when topics are presented in a logical sequence that provides students with the opportunity to connect disparate scientific ideas into coherent conceptual frameworks.

International assessments such as TIMSS and PISA have highlighted a decline in U.S. students' performance as they progress from elementary to higher grades. The variability in the implemented curriculum, both in terms of topics covered and the depth of topic coverage, may not only have an impact on students' opportunity to learn science topics in a focused and coherent way, but it may also place them at a comparative disadvantage in the global workplace.

Numerous studies have established the connection between instructional time spent on content and student achievement (Bloom 1971; Carroll 1989; Wiley and Harnischfeger 1974). These findings have also been substantiated in TIMSS studies (Schmidt et al. 2001), which show that more time spent on topics was related to higher achievement scores. The wide variability in instructional time devoted to science topics described in the present study creates inequality in opportunity to learn science. This variation and inequality has the consequence of reducing the mean performance of students, as well as increasing the variation in performance. The role of instructional leaders is critical in keeping the focus on the central mission of educational institutions, which should be to promote practices and policies that support positive student learning outcomes. Research clearly indicates that we cannot improve our national performance without a coherent and rigorous set of standards that are consistently implemented at the district, school, and classroom level. Variability in implementation results in a huge inequality of opportunity to learn science.

In order to "create a normative climate in which the improvement of instruction and performance is the central task," instructional leaders at the school and district level need to provide "direct oversight of classroom practice" (Elmore 2000, p. 28). Oversight related to coverage of specific content is critical to the success and realization of the vision of NCLB. The consequences that unequal opportunities to learn have on student learning and attainment are far too serious. With the call for large-scale improvement in the content and quality of instruction, it is imperative that we focus on "the way public schools define and practice leadership" (p. 2).

Strong leadership is needed at the state, district, and, especially, school levels. This leadership, unlike the way it has been traditionally defined, needs to center around curricular content. The leadership needs to define their central mission in terms of educational outcomes for students and promote the policies and practices that support consistent, coherent, focused, and rigorous implementation of curriculum in all classrooms so that *all* students have an opportunity to attain greater learning.

References

American Association for the Advancement of Science (AAAS). 1993. *Benchmarks for science literacy.* New York: Oxford University Press.

——. 2001. *Atlas of science literacy.* Washington, DC: AAAS and NSTA Press.

Blase, Jos., and J. Blase. 1999. Principals' instructional leadership and teacher development: Teachers' perspectives. *Educational Administration* 35: 349–378.

Bloom, B. 1971. *Handbook on formative and summative evaluation of student learning.* New York: McGraw-Hill.

Carroll, J. B. 1989. The Carroll model: A 25-year retrospective and prospective view. *Educational Researcher* 8: 26–31.

Clark, D., and M. C. Linn. 2003. Designing for knowledge integration: The impact of instructional time. *Journal of the Learning Sciences* 12 (4): 451–493.

Committee on Science, Engineering, and Public Policy (COSEPUP). 2007. *Rising above the gathering storm: Energizing and employing America for a brighter economic future.* Washington, DC: The National Academies Press.

———. 2009. *Rising above the gathering storm: Two years later.* Washington, DC: The National Academies Press.

Craig, C. J. 2006. Why is dissemination so difficult? The nature of teacher knowledge and the spread of curriculum reform. *American Educational Research Journal* 43 (2): 257–293.

Cuban, L. 1988. *The managerial imperative and the practice of leadership in schools.* Albany, NY: State University of New York Press.

DeBoer, G. 2002. Student-centered teaching in a standards-based world: Finding a sensible balance. *Science & Education* 11 (4): 405–417.

Elmore, R. F. 2000. *Building a new structure for school leadership.* Washington, DC: Albert Shanker Institute.

Fisher C. W., and D. C. Berliner, eds. 1985. *Perspectives on instructional time.* New York: Longman.

Floden, R. E., A. C. Porter, L. E. Alford, D. J. Freeman, S. Irwin, W. H. Schmidt, and J. R. Schwille. 1988. Instructional leadership at the district level: A closer look at autonomy and control. *Educational Administration Quarterly* 24 (2): 96–124.

Friedman, T. 2005. *The world is flat: A brief history of the twenty-first century.* New York: Farrar, Straus and Giroux.

Gess-Newsome, J., S. A. Southerland, A. Johnston, and S. Woodbury. 2003. Educational reform, personal practical theories, and dissatisfaction: The anatomy of change in college science teaching. *American Educational Research Journal* 40 (3): 731–767.

Gross, P. R., U. Goodenough, S. Haack, L. S. Lerner, M. Schwartz, and R. Schwartz. 2005. *The state of state science standards*. Washington, DC: Thomas B. Fordham Institute.

Heck, R. H. 1992. Principals' instructional leadership and school performance: Implications for policy development. *Educational Evaluation and Policy Analysis* 14 (1): 21–34.

Huyvaert, S. H. 1998. *Time is of the essence: Learning in schools*. Needham Heights, MA: Allyn & Bacon.

Lee, O., and A. Luykx. 2005. *Science education and student diversity*. New York: Cambridge University Press.

Marx, R. W., and C. J. Harris. 2006. No Child Left Behind and science education: Opportunities, challenges, and risks. *The Elementary School Journal* 106 (5): 467–477.

Meyer, J. W., and B. Rowan. 1977. The structure of educational organizations. In *Environments and Organizations*, eds. J. W. Meyer and W. R. Scott, 71–97. Beverly Hills, CA: Sage.

Meyer, J. W., and B. Rowan, eds. 1992. *Environments and Organizations*. Beverly Hills, CA: Sage.

Murphy, J. 1990. Principal instructional leadership. In *Advances in Educational Administration*, eds. L. L. Lotto, and P. W. Thurston, 163–200 Greenwich, CT: JAI Press.

National Academy of Science (NAS). 2005. *Rising above the gathering storm: Energizing and employing America for a brighter economic future*. Washington, DC: National Academies Press.

National Research Council. 1996. *National science education standards*. Washington, DC: National Academy Press.

———. 2000. *Inquiry and the national science education standards*. Washington, DC: National Academy Press.

Obama, B. H. 2009. Remarks to the Hispanic Chamber of Commerce, March, 10, 2009.

Porter, A. C. 1993. School delivery standards. *Educational Researcher* 22 (5): 24–30.

Purkey, S. C., and M. S. Smith. 1983. Effective schools: A review. *Elementary School Journal* 83: 427–452.

Rangel, E., and D. Berliner. 2007. Essential information for education policy: Time to learn. *Research Points: American Educational Research Association* 5 (2): 1–4.

Resnick, D. P., and L. B. Resnick. 1985. Standards, curriculum, and performance: A historical and comparative perspective. *Educational Researcher* 14 (4): 5–20.

Rowan, B. 1990. Commitment and control: Alternative strategies for the organizational design of schools. *Review of Research in Education* 16: 238–266.

Saka, Y. 2007. What happens to our reform-minded beginning science teachers? Unpublished doctoral dissertation. Tallahassee, FL: Florida State University.

Schmidt, W. H., and L. S. Cogan. 1996. Development of the TIMSS context questionnaires. In *Third International Mathematics and Science Study technical report*, eds. M. O. Martin, and D. L. Kelly, 1–22. Chestnut Hill, MA: Boston College.

Schmidt, W. H., and R. T. Houang. 2007. Lack of focus in the mathematics curriculum: Symptom or cause? In *Lessons learned: What international assessments tell us about math achievement*, ed. T. Loveless, 110–149. Washington, DC: Brookings Institute Press.

Schmidt, W. H., R. T. Houang, and C. C. McKnight. 2005. Value-added research: Right idea but wrong solution? In *Value-added models in education: Theory and applications*, ed. R. Lissitz, 40–81. Maple Grove, MN: JAM Press.

Schmidt, W. H., C. C. McKnight, L. S. Cogan, P. M. Jakwerth, and R. T. Houang. 1999. *Facing the consequences: Using TIMSS for a closer look at U.S. mathematics and science education.* Dordrecht, Netherlands: Kluwer Academic Publishers.

Schmidt, W. H., C. C. McKnight, R. T. Houang, H. C. Wang, D. E. Wiley, L. S. Cogan, and R. G. Wolfe. 2001. *Why schools matter: A cross-national comparison of curriculum and learning.* San Francisco, CA: Jossey Bass.

Schmidt, W. H., C. C. McKnight, and S. Raizen, eds. 1997. *A splintered vision: An investigation of U.S. science and mathematics education, Vol. 1.* Dordrecht, Netherlands: Kluwer Academic Publishers.

Schmidt, W. H., H. C. Wang, and C. C. McKnight. 2005. Curriculum coherence: An examination of U.S. mathematics and science content standards from an international perspective. *Journal of Curriculum Studies* 37 (5): 525–559.

Smith, B. 2002. Quantity Matters: Annual instructional time in an urban school system. *Educational Administration Quarterly* 36 (5): 652–682.

Chapter 5

Southerland, S. A., L. K. Smith, S. P. Sowell, and J. M. Kittleson. 2007. Resisting unlearning: Understanding science education's response to the United States' national accountability movement. *Review of Research in Education* 31: 45–77.

Spillane, J. P., T. Hallett, and J. B. Diamond. 2003. Forms of capital and the construction of leadership: Instructional leadership in urban elementary schools. *Sociology of Education* 76: 1–17.

Stigler, J., and J. Hiebert. 1999. *The teaching gap.* New York: Free Press.

Survey of Mathematics and Science Opportunities (SMSO). 1992a. *Mathematics curriculum framework* (research report series no. 38). East Lansing, MI: Michigan State University.

——.1992b. *Science curriculum framework* (research report series no. 37). East Lansing, MI: Michigan State University.

Wandersee, J. H., and K. M. Fisher. 2000. In *Mapping biology knowledge,* eds. K. M. Fisher, J. H. Wandersee, and D. Moody, 39–54. Dordrecht, Netherlands: Kluwer.

Wiley D. E., and E. Harnischfeger. 1974. Explosion of a myth: Quantity of schooling and exposure to instruction: Major educational vehicles. *Educational Researcher* 90 (2): 103–110.

Wisconsin Center for Education Research (WCER). 2008. Madison Metropolitan School District mathematics task force report: Review of mathematics curriculum and related issues. Madison, WI: University of Wisconsin–Madison.

	Class periods taught this year *(Check One Only)*					
EARTH SCIENCE	0	1 or <1	2 -5	6 - 10	11 - 15	>15
Earth Features: Earth's crust, mantle, and core; mountains, valleys, continents; oceans, lakes, rivers; atmosphere; types of rocks and soils	☐	☐	☐	☐	☐	☐
Weather: Weather maps; cloud formation; seasons of the year; types of precipitation; hurricanes and tornadoes	☐	☐	☐	☐	☐	☐
Earth Processes: Volcanoes and earthquakes; water and rock cycles	☐	☐	☐	☐	☐	☐
Historic Earth Processes: Fossil formation; fossil fuels; geologic timetable	☐	☐	☐	☐	☐	☐
Earth and the Universe: Planets, the Sun, and their effects on Earth; features of the solar system and universe; origin and history of the universe	☐	☐	☐	☐	☐	☐
LIFE SCIENCE						
Diversity of Living Things: Types and classification of plants, animals, and microorganisms	☐	☐	☐	☐	☐	☐
Human Health: Nutrition; types, causes, and prevention of disease	☐	☐	☐	☐	☐	☐
Human Biology: Structures and functions of organs and tissues; metabolism, respiration; reproduction, and inheritance	☐	☐	☐	☐	☐	☐
Structure and Function of Living Things: Types and features of cells; functions of organs and tissues (e.g., bird wings, plant leaves, earthworm circulatory system)	☐	☐	☐	☐	☐	☐
Life Processes and Systems: Respiration; digestion; reactions of living things to stimuli; photosynthesis	☐	☐	☐	☐	☐	☐
Life Cycles and Genetics: Life cycles of plants and animals; plant and animal reproduction; inheritance and variation; evolution and diversity	☐	☐	☐	☐	☐	☐
Interactions of Living Things: Ecosystems; habitats, niches; food webs, food chains; oxygen, carbon dioxide cycle	☐	☐	☐	☐	☐	☐
Animal Behavior: Migration; hibernation; social organization (e.g., elephant herds, beehives); communication	☐	☐	☐	☐	☐	☐

(continued on next page)

Appendix A. Elementary Science Areas Key (continued)

Class periods taught this year

(Check One Only)

PHYSICAL SCIENCES	0	1 or <1	2 -5	6 - 10	11 - 15	>15
Matter: Classification and structure of matter (elements, compounds, mixtures, atoms, molecules); physical and chemical properties (solids, liquids, gases; acids/bases)	☐	☐	☐	☐	☐	☐
Energy Types, Sources, and Conversions: Types of energy (mechanical, chemical); sources of energy (food, oil, wood); simple machines (levers, pulleys); work, efficiency	☐	☐	☐	☐	☐	☐
Energy Processes: Heat and temperature; sound, electricity, magnetism; light	☐	☐	☐	☐	☐	☐
Physical and Chemical Transformations: Changes in states (freezing, boiling, evaporation); chemical changes (burning, rusting, batteries, radioactivity)	☐	☐	☐	☐	☐	☐
Forces and Motion: Gravity and friction; speed; acceleration	☐	☐	☐	☐	☐	☐

ENVIRONMENTAL AND RESOURCE ISSUES

	0	1 or <1	2 -5	6 - 10	11 - 15	>15
Environmental and Resource Issues: Pollution; saving the rain forests; recycling garbage; effects of natural disasters; food supply and demand	☐	☐	☐	☐	☐	☐

NATURE OF SCIENCE AND SCIENTIFIC INQUIRY

	0	1 or <1	2 -5	6 - 10	11 - 15	>15
Science, Technology, and Society: Designing or making things (tools, bridges); use of technology in science (computers, microscopes); interactions among science, technology, and society	☐	☐	☐	☐	☐	☐
History of Science and Technology: Famous scientists; classic experiments; development of scientific ideas; scientific discoveries	☐	☐	☐	☐	☐	☐
Nature of Science: Methods scientists use (problem identification, observation; creating and testing hypotheses); basis and ways of making decisions	☐	☐	☐	☐	☐	☐
Scientific Measurement: How to use measurement tools; measurement procedures; making measurements	☐	☐	☐	☐	☐	☐
Data Analysis: Classifying, organizing, and representing data; having students interpret provided data; having students interpret gathered data; drawing conclusions from gathered data	☐	☐	☐	☐	☐	☐

Chapter 6
The Role of Teacher Leadership in Science Education

Julie Gess-Newsome and Barbara A. Austin

Leadership roles are not things that I seek out, but somehow I end up there. I think people see in me skills that I don't even see in myself. I keep getting thrust into the limelight and as people learn more about my abilities, they want to take advantage of them. I think it's important to stay open to those experiences and pursue them when they become available.
                              —Tammy, middle school teacher

Schools are complex places. As professional developers, much of our work is designed to help teachers deal with this complexity by refining their instructional practice. Professional development activities deepen content knowledge, support inquiry-based teaching, help teachers tap into student thinking, and assist in implementing curriculum materials and interpreting assessment systems. In short, professional development is focused on fostering science education reform. The outcome of this work is often increased excellence in teaching and improved student learning. In our work at Northern Arizona University (NAU), however, we have discovered a different and unanticipated outcome: the development of teachers as leaders. Many of the teachers in our inservice programs comment how, as a result of our programs, they have increased confidence in themselves as teachers and are willing to position themselves in leadership roles at the classroom, department, and district levels, as well as take on external leadership responsibilities in state and national science education professional societies that allow them to participate in policy development.

Methods

What does it mean to be a leader? Why do teachers elect to take on leadership roles? This chapter examines teachers as leaders and the ways that leadership impacts science education reform. Thirteen teachers were interviewed about their professional trajectory and the ways that they evolved into teacher leaders. The following questions were used to structure the interviews and organize the chapter:

- **Being a Leader:** What does it mean to be a leader? What does a leader do? How are you a leader? Why did you elect to take on leadership responsibilities?

- **Goals for Science Reform:** What does science education reform mean to you? What needs to happen for us to achieve your vision of science education reform?

- **Impact of Leadership:** In what ways do you, through your leadership, impact science education reform? What evidence do you have that your efforts have made an impact?

- **Cultivating Leadership:** What elements or experiences allowed you to become the leader that you are today? What sources of support do you draw upon to sustain yourself as a leader? What advice would you give to others that want to cultivate leadership in teachers?

This chapter is written through the voices of the teacher leaders. The teachers represent a variety of backgrounds, professional experiences, and leadership pathways. Teaching experience ranges from 5 to 36 years. Some were originally prepared as elementary teachers; others had bachelor's degrees in science and taught at the secondary level.

Some entered teaching following a career in science or after raising their children. Six of the informants are graduates of NAU's Master of Arts in Science Teaching program (MAST); others earned their academic credentials from other institutions. Today, seven of these individuals are fostering change while continuing as classroom teachers, four have taken on administrative responsibilities at school or district levels, and two are contributing to the preparation of preservice teachers at the university level. Within this group are presidents of state and national science education professional associations and nationally recognized teachers. Despite this diversity, common themes about leadership and science education reform emerged in our analysis of their interviews.

Being a Leader

None of the teachers interviewed set out to be a leader. Instead, leadership came about as a result of unexpected experiences and opportunities. As Dave said, "It creeps up on you and you find that you're in a leadership position." In fact, despite external recognition of leadership qualities, many of our participants were hesitant to label themselves as leaders. Gaylene noted, "I don't think of my everyday work as a leader in science reform. I am an advocate for science learning and for the science teacher." Through their conversations, we found consistent qualities that characterized these individuals. Foremost in this list is being open-minded, willing to pursue opportunities, and pursuing a commitment to lifelong learning. Vicki noted: "I'm on a leadership continuum. I have a long way to go, but that's part of the excitement. I keep learning." Kelli expressed a similar idea, "As a leader, I'm always getting training, going to professional development, always trying to learn and improve myself. I always want to be a better teacher."

Second, all teachers noted that leadership was not about personal gain, but advocacy for the student, honoring and supporting fellow teachers, and promoting public understanding of science.

Vicki: "As a leader, I need to be an advocate for what's best for children and science education. Leaders gather information and work side by side with others, facilitating and listening to teachers."

Laura: "I think a leader does whatever is necessary to facilitate others' improvement. I have found it fascinating that the higher you go in your profession, the more you become a servant for others. A good leader is a good servant."

Xan: "I've always wanted to make things better. Rather than complaining, I want to be part of the solution; a change catalyst. It's about changing the system, not about having people follow me."

Kelli: "I'm always looking at what is best for the student and trying to help other teachers teach in a way that is going to help benefit students the most."

These teacher leaders were quick to note that fostering change in others involves listening carefully, providing encouragement, and facilitating learning in a number of settings. This form of leadership is different from the management that occurs in other work settings.

Dave: "In industry, a leader manages people and directs employees toward a goal. In education, leadership looks different. You don't have the same power relationship. You don't manage peers. Instead, change comes with leading by example, gaining trust and respect, and building a reputation of excellence and innovation."

Gaylene: "In my role as a science supervisor, I have a lot of duties and responsibilities, but not much power. Our power is solely based on those who elect to follow us."

Laura: "Leadership in education is similar to being a good classroom teacher; you understand the subtleties of learning: When to nudge and when to push."

Janey: "Teacher leaders have to love shared collaboration. I mean true collaboration, not just imparting knowledge. They have to act as coaches and not just tell people what to do."

What allowed these individuals to move into leadership? Without exception, these teacher leaders developed confidence through learning a deep knowledge of science, an understanding of the research that supports the vision of science education reform, and having a "tool box" of professional development strategies that they experienced as learners and were then able to implement as mentors.

Janey: "Teacher leaders have to have deep content knowledge and pedagogical content knowledge. They need to have good questioning skills, be able to implement inquiry, and understand science as a process *and* a way of knowing."

Laura: "Going through the Math and Science Partnership program has made me so much more confident. I now see it as my responsibility to help others in my district."

Hank: "Prior to MAST, I taught as I had been taught. Now I know what the research says and why we should teach the way we teach. Now I have more confidence in what I do, I know *why* I do it, and can help others understand how to change their practice."

Vicki: "Leaders need a variety of tools that they gather from their own professional development experiences. When I work with a teacher, I can use my tool box and be selective about the strategies that I use based on their needs."

Kelli: "When I started the MAST program, I had absolutely no idea what it meant to be a good science teacher. But the classes really made me think about the changes needed in our school district. I wanted to part of the team to implement those changes."

Scott and Hank elaborated on the importance of professional development experiences that can be replicated with others. Recently, they were asked to team teach a course at Arizona State University–West for teachers about science and science teaching. In designing the course, they drew on their prior experiences. As Hank explained,

"The course is 20 percent pedagogy and 80 percent content. You have to know the content in order to do inquiry. We're using *Understanding by Design*, the 5E model, and levels of inquiry. We've drawn heavily from the program at NAU. Through using these materials with others, I am able to better understand what I learned in the program. We're making sure that the teachers have the foundations of reform and understand the history and philosophy behind it, the way it was done at NAU."

Similarly, Ava used a lesson taught in the MAST program as a tool in a school inservice. The activity involved collaboratively examining teacher-created assignments and student work in order to improve the assignment and investigate student learning. The activity was so successful that it was adopted districtwide.

Goals for Science Reform

When asked about the goals of science reform, two key ideas were mentioned: promoting the importance of science literacy and a robust understanding of science, and changing instructional practices to meet the needs of today's students. A number of teachers held sentiments similar to those expressed by Ava: "Quality science education is an investment in our future. We need to be able to compete in global markets, and students need to be skilled in making informed decisions." Xan agreed, saying, "We need to teach students to be critical thinkers and to have 21st-century skills. We need to be constantly aware that we're preparing students for careers and jobs that don't exist today."

Others noted the importance of allowing students to participate in the joy of science. Vicki recognized that when teaching in a gifted and talented classroom, that "science activities were able to grab and hold students' attention."

Gaylene: "We need to establish balance. We need an appropriate mix of content and detail with big ideas and conceptual understanding, as well as opportunities for students to appreciate and apply science to their lives. If we focus on too many standards and too much content, we'll limit real world applications and the magic of science. "

But the most consistent goal of science reform was to remove what Xan called the "silos" that we create within science and across other disciplines.

Dave: "We've separated our sciences into separate disciplines. We're pigeon-holing them into departments where in society they are integrated. We need to develop cross-curricular courses where all students can be successful."

Scott: "I want to help elementary teachers make the connection between science and reading and writing in such a way that they support each other and reinforce the importance of science and its interdependence with other parts of the curriculum. Teachers also need to make connections across the life, Earth, and physical sciences to help students recognize the application of science outside of the classroom and so that they can make informed decisions as citizens."

Another consistent theme was the importance of inquiry and the changing nature of students.

Dave: "Our instructional methods have to change. The chalk, talk, and regurgitation methods of the past don't work. We learn different today and use technology in new ways. Our classrooms need to reflect new thinking about teaching if we are to be successful and competitive."

Ava: "Teaching can't be designed to address only one way of thinking. Students need to engage in hands-on/minds-on activities. We need to make the curriculum more engaging, captivating, and relevant. We need them to buy into their own learning."

Scott: "Today's students interact through technology. Technology is how they think, and we need to adapt. We need to use technology to help them learn. Our students still have a spark for learning and are anxious to inquire. We need to help them think for themselves, show them that they can be successful and can learn from their mistakes."

In order to meet the goals of science literacy and inquiry-based teaching, two support structures were identified. The first was the need for systemic change, thinking about science reform across the P-20 continuum. Janey identified university-level science instruction as a critical locus of change, "In the university, students listen to lecture, take notes, and then take a big test. It's no wonder that teachers graduate and use this model for teaching science." While Janey looked at the impact of university instruction on teachers, Dave looked at the base of the continuum.

Dave: "If we want to create *real* change, we have to look further down from the high school to the middle and elementary schools. If we don't start to make changes at the elementary school level, we'll never be able to make changes at the university level. I'm hoping to be a conduit of science education reform across the continuum."

Scott and Hank are advocates for exactly such an approach. Calling themselves the "bookends," Scott purposefully moved to an elementary school that acts as a feeder to Hank's middle school. Positioned to teach fourth and seventh grades, Hank and Scott work to influence the science teaching in their own classrooms and schools while establishing a pipeline of exemplary science practice across some of the most important years in a student's development of science knowledge and attitudes. Through their efforts, they are trying to make sure that science is emphasized in the daily curriculum. The effectiveness of such an approach is reinforced by Gaylene. In her district, a team of teachers developed an inquiry-based freshman level science course. Multiple science topics were taught through the context of the Mars Student Imaging Project. Student reaction was extremely positive, and one student wrote an editorial for the school paper praising the course. As a result, changes in instructional practices were pushed up the educational continuum.

> **Gaylene:** "Teachers don't realize how often we're guilty of stringing together activities without a conceptual framework or indication of how students could apply the information. This project allowed us to build a curriculum within a context while infusing inquiry and research data. Now, the biology teachers are feeling pressure to change their instruction, because the students expect something different, something more."

In order to identify, characterize, and support this type of systemic change, Janey noted the need for formative assessment at all levels:

> **Janey:** "Science education reform rests on transformative assessment. Once teachers see success in their own students, they will change their beliefs. But reform can't take place without getting the building principals involved. They have to recognize a classroom that promotes, examines, and maintains student learning through evidence."

Impact of Leadership

Teacher leaders impact a wide continuum that includes students, teachers, districts, and even state policy. Teachers in the classroom see immediate impacts of their efforts to implement instructional change. As teachers reform the nature of their science teaching, students get excited and talk about it more at school and home. Laura said, "I had a student say, 'that was the coolest science class ever.' It gave me goose bumps, because I knew that we were on the right track." Many student outcomes are only evident long after the initial event. As programs develop good reputations, student enrollment increases. Students who experience effective elementary and middle school science instruction continue to enroll in science courses. As Tammy noted, "I prepare my middle school students for high school. Many times they will come back and tell me, 'I remember doing that in your class!' After the fact, they recognize that I had a reason for what I was doing."

All of our teacher leaders noted the impact of their leadership on other teachers. At the elementary level, many of our teachers acted as motivators for teaching science. By talking to teachers around them, assisting them in the design and implementation of lessons, and acting as a subtle reminder that science is important, science was taught more often.

Laura and Kelli talked about their experiences when their district recently adopted a new elementary science curriculum:

> **Laura:** "The enthusiasm is contagious as more teachers see that we have a research-based program that works with students. I had a teacher who was originally upset about having to teach science, but when she saw her students' excitement, she changed her attitude.'"
>
> **Kelli:** "Innovations need to spread teacher to teacher. It can't come from someone higher up in the school system. You create more buy-in from teachers when a fellow teacher is the one saying, 'this is what I do and it works!'"

Other teacher leaders provided professional development experiences, answered phone calls from teachers seeking advice, or acted as role models. Fostering change occurs through mentoring, patience, and skilled practice.

> **Janey:** "We bought release time for one of our teacher leaders. She was able to spend every afternoon in the classrooms of our grant participants. She helped with everything—classroom management, grouping strategies, and content and curriculum kit support. It worked so well that none of our new teachers left their schools."
>
> **Vicki:** "Working with teachers one-on-one in their classrooms is a powerful way to provide support. Rigor, relevance, and relationships are central to everything I do. If teachers respect me, they may follow my suggestions. Change happens one teacher at a time."

Our teacher leaders also recognized their role in positively impacting the next generation of teachers by acting as host teachers for student teachers or being an instructor in a university setting. Ava acknowledged, "By working with preservice teachers, I'm changing the future of science education." Barry agreed, "I'm developing the next generation of teachers. Along with that, I'm influencing the cooperating teachers with whom my student teachers are working, and I can apply great influence to the way they teach."

Several of the teachers were affecting change at district and state levels. Dave talked about the ways that some of his curricular initiatives influenced science teaching at a number of schools in his district.

> **Dave:** "I'm seeing outward growth in myself. People I've never worked with before want to involve me in writing grants to expand the programs I've developed. Originally, I was isolated in my classroom. Now

the doors have been blown open, and there are more opportunities than I anticipated."

Impacts exist at the policy level as well. Based on her reputation for creating a biotechnology school within a school, Xan was selected by the governor as the only active teacher to serve on a state level committee that examined educational issues in preschool through grade 20. The committee convinced the state legislature to increase statewide graduation requirements from two years of science to three.

> Xan: "Our superintendent of instruction was against the increase in graduation requirements, but I was able to convince the committee that when you increase expectations, students will meet them. They valued my participation and perspective about what is really happening in the classroom."

Obviously, our teacher leaders have made significant impacts at multiple points in the educational system.

Cultivating Leadership

Developing and growing as teacher leaders requires support from multiple sources. Many of our teachers noted the importance of support from families as they participated in growth opportunities. Attending weekend workshops, graduate programs at distant campuses, and professional conferences all necessitated time away from family.

While removed from daily instruction, district superintendents were an important source of support, especially for funding professional development and science support networks, such as district science coordinators. Kelli was able to implement professional learning communities (PLCs) at her school, because the district paid for her PLC facilitator training. She explains, "Science education reform in our building comes from the teachers utilizing PLCs by coming together and sharing what works in their classroom in a better and more effective way." Building principals also support science education reform and the development of teacher leaders. Principals establish the value of and commitment to (or lack of) science in the curriculum. Tammy stated, "If school administrators don't value science, even teachers that want to teach science at the elementary level won't do so." As Dave commented, "You have to have the support of the administration to take a chance on doing something new." For instance, Barry recalled the effect of a principals' support, "In my first job, we decided to revise the biology curriculum into eight quarter courses so students could choose the subjects they wanted to take." Ava noted that support through her principal allowed her to "have a voice in what goes on in the school."

Colleagues play a critical role in science teaching reform. Many of the teacher leaders recognize that change was difficult and not all teachers are capable of change. The idea of perseverance became a theme. Ava advised that as a change agent, she had to be careful "not to be quieted by archaic practices." Janey asserted that part of her role was to prepare the teachers she worked with for these nay-sayers: "The veteran teachers say, 'they tell you to do this but here's what I do.' We are aware of this and can address it with our teachers who are supportive of change." Hank concurs, "We're not going to be able to reach everybody. Instead, you work with those teachers who have the energy to change."

Colleagues support teacher leaders in a number of different ways. In some cases it's direct. Hank, Tammy, and Scott all commented about the importance of the network of colleagues that they established as part of the MAST program and noted how those relationships have created additional opportunities. As Hank explained, "Colleagues are our main support group. We are constantly seeking advice from each other and sharing new ideas." Others note the importance of colleagues in recognizing their leadership potential and acting as mentors. Xan described her experience: "Years ago my district specialist and science supervisor recognized something in me. They encouraged me to attend leadership institutes and put me on committees as a very young teacher. This grooming process has helped me be the person I am today." Finally, fellow teachers become a motivating force when they implement the changes advocated by the teacher leaders. As Ava recognized, "When I feel like I've made a difference, it encourages me to go on. "

> **Vicki:** "Even if one teacher gets excited about science teaching from something I've done, it motivates me. When I see their excitement, I know that what I'm doing is important and worthwhile. I'm providing a service to the profession."

Professional associations were described as a valuable source of collegial support. State level associations such as the Arizona Science Teachers Association and the Arizona Science Coordinators Association (ASCA) were credited with establishing networks of teachers with similar commitments. National associations such as the National Science Teachers Association and the National Science Education Leadership Association were appreciated for the knowledge disseminated through their publications and conferences, as well as offering an opportunity to expand leadership roles.

> **Barry:** "When issues arise, my colleagues in ASCA rally around and provide information, insight, and support. For example, when there was concern about district policies related to opting out of evolution instruction, we were able to quickly survey the policies in various districts. This quick move allowed us to deflect a few vocal people and focus on the really good things that we do."

Developing these communities of support at the local, district, and state level is an important impact of teacher leadership and helps educators to persist in their personal development as teachers and teacher leaders. As Barry explains, "To cultivate leadership in others, teachers have to have an opportunity to lead. You can be a teacher leader, but if you are in a department where everyone is a dinosaur, then it will be hard to go forward. We need to find places where like-minded teachers can get together for support."

Conclusions

Through the writing of this chapter, we have become convinced of two things. First, teacher leaders emerge from well-designed programs that have an intentional developmental trajectory, as opposed to a random set of courses, workshops, or experiences.

> **Hank:** "In order to produce teacher change, programs must educate teachers in the essential knowledge and tools that teachers' need. Through the MAST program, we were able to learn the research and experience firsthand the instructional practices advocated by science reforms. We were encouraged to construct a new set of thoughts, beliefs, and practices—a new philosophy in how and what to teach and the in-depth knowledge needed to sustain the change."

> **Scott:** "It was obvious that the MAST program purposefully spiraled ideas across the three summers. Things kept coming back around, which was important because I wouldn't have gotten it the first time. And it helped that the things that we learned during the summer were linked to assignments that we completed during the school year

in our classrooms. I still refer back to my papers from the program."
Second, there are many types of opportunities that contribute to the
confidence, skills, knowledge, and tools available to the teacher leader.
The MAST program was just one of many opportunities that these teachers pursued. Others participated in multiyear MSPs designed to develop
science content knowledge and pedagogy.

> **Laura:** "The three courses that I took in the MSP were the best I have
> ever taken in my whole entire life and were important in my learning
> to be a better science teacher. We were mentored, shown by example,
> and asked to do things the same way we are going to ask our students
> to do things. It really helped prepare me to be a leader for my district."

Others participated in research opportunities for teachers. Still others
were affected by serving on curriculum design or alignment committees,
were involved in the creation of district assessment tools, participated in
textbook selection, or were involved in the writing of grants to support
educational programs.

> **Kelli:** "Being a part of the districtwide leadership academy made me rec-
> ognize that many students are being poorly serviced in their classrooms.
> As a result, I now want to be an instructional coach so that I can help
> teachers become better. All students deserve an equal education."

All of our teachers talked about the importance of sharing what
they've learned and how, through the act of designing and teaching formal
and informal professional development sessions, they have deepened their
own knowledge of science education reforms and the materials, resources,
and activities that support the reform movement. Thus, no single set of
activities or single program was found to be the sole contributor to growth
of confidence and leadership skills. Perhaps, instead, growth should be
understood through the lens of those common characteristics that we saw
earlier in this chapter: a willingness to learn new things, a service commitment, a deep knowledge of science content and the goals of reform
that combine into a valid and robust educational philosophy, a passionate
advocacy for students and science, the willingness to persevere in the face
of obstacles, and the desire to share what they have learned. Programs and
policies that promote these characteristics through a variety of experiences
and opportunities will help develop teachers at all points along the continuum to teacher leadership and science education reform.

So what advice do our teacher leaders have for others who want to cultivate teacher leadership?

Laura: "Treat people with respect, honor their expertise, and value teachers. Give them the curriculum and support they need to teach science well. Help them learn from their mistakes and try again without fear. Recognize that they are in a learning curve and are out of their comfort zone."

Xan: "Draw on younger teachers and what they have to offer. Let them know that they're valuable and involve them in leadership. Be a mentor. Maintain a connected network. When I recognize leadership, I encourage teachers to participate in opportunities, such as copresenting at a conference. You need to offer opportunities for others to get involved."

Vicki: "Look for those rising stars and encourage them. Perhaps we should teach principals to identify and encourage leadership. Many rising stars have no idea how good they are. They assume that others are doing the same things that they are. They don't recognize that they are unique."

And what advice do they give to other teacher leaders?

Dave: "Become well versed in current research. Develop a thick skin. Be prepared to hear "no" many times, but have the perseverance to find the person who will say "yes." Stay grounded in the goal of the betterment of student learning in science."

Ava: "Don't take on too much. Be positive. Don't be afraid to change things. Be an outspoken advocate. Don't be afraid to challenge the norm. Draw on school resources."

Teacher leaders are not born, but are nurtured through associations with colleagues; administrators that support their development; well-designed professional development experiences; and participation in local, district, state, and national committees and organizations. These opportunities not only give them the knowledge they need to develop into teacher leaders, but also inspire them to share their vision of effective science teaching with others as a salient pathway in the pipeline to systemic science education reform.

References

When we started this project, our goal was to use the voices of teachers to depict the ways that professional development promotes teachers' self-identity as science education leaders and their understanding of science education reforms. As themes emerged during our analysis of the transcripts and we identified illustrative comments, we realized that the teachers' quotes accurately portray much of the current research about teacher leadership. We expect that many of the other chapters in this book will provide support from the research base and confirm the insights provided by our participants. We purposefully let their words internally substantiate and validate their views from the field.

Acknowledgments

We would like to thank the following teachers for sharing with us their thoughts and experiences in becoming teacher leaders:

Ava Bemer is in her sixth year of teaching sixth and seventh graders at Billy Lane Lauffer Middle School in the Sunnyside School Unified School District in Tucson, Arizona. She is a school science coordinator, the MESA (Math, Science, Engineering Achievement) club advisor, and a teacher trainer, and she has won multiple teaching awards.

Scott Currier is in his 14th year of teaching and currently teaches fourth grade in Deer Valley Unified School District. He is the chairman of the Friends of the Desert Outdoor Center at Lake Pleasant, Arizona, and is developing educational programs for the Sonoran Desert Center.

Janey Kaufmann is the district science coordinator at Scottsdale Unified School District in Arizona. Following 26 years in the classroom, she provides teacher mentoring as well as district level workshops. She is currently the president-elect of the National Science Education Leadership Association, NSELA.

Vicki Massey is a science specialist for Mesa Unified Public Schools. Following 24 years in the classroom, she coordinates district level professional development and serves in a leadership role for the Arizona Science Teachers Association, Arizona Association for Environmental Education, and the Arizona Science Coordinators Association.

Laura Mineer is a fifth-grade elementary school teacher that has taught in the Cottonwood/Oak Creek School District for the past 16 years. She serves as the district science coordinator for the K–8 schools, serves on the science curriculum committee, and has just finished science leadership training.

Tammy Naef has taught middle school science for 10 years and serves as the science curriculum specialist and curriculum mapping coordinator for Beaver Creek School District. Tammy has received multiple teaching awards and was named the 2005 Middle School Science Teacher of the Year by the Arizona Science Teachers Association (ASTA). She also served as the 2007–2008 president of ASTA.

Kelli Rhoda has taught middle and elementary science for seven years with Cottonwood/Oak Creek School District. In addition to teaching, she is a member of COCSD's Leadership Academy, Blueprint Committee, Curriculum Task Force and serves as a district Science Fair Coordinator. She is also PLC Facilitator for her Cottonwood Elementary School campus.

Barry Roth is the director of Teach Arizona, a Master's degree teacher certification program at The University of Arizona that emphasizes secondary science and mathematics. Prior to this position, Barry was the Science Curriculum Specialist for the Tucson Unified School District where he taught high school biology and chemistry for 30 years.

Hank Shoop has been teaching for 24 years in the Deer Valley School District. Currently Hank is the chair of the science department, teaches seventh-grade science, and serves on his school's data analysis team. Following numerous forms of recognition for this teaching, Hank has recently been nominated for the Presidential Award for Excellence in Mathematics and Science Teaching.

Xan Simonson is the biotechnology career and technical education specialist and team leader for Mesa Public Schools. Xan has received many honors including the 2000 Arizona Biology Teacher of the Year, 2007 Arizona Bioscience Educator of the Year, and was recognized as one of the top 20 Arizona Woman of 2020 by AZ *Woman* magazine.

Gaylene Swenson has been the secondary science curriculum specialist for Peoria Unified School District since 2004. Prior to this position, she taught high school science for five years. In her role, Gaylene conducts professional development activities and coordinates district curriculum and assessment development.

Dave Thompson is currently an assistant clinical professor/master teacher for the NAUTeach Program at NAU. He taught in the Flagstaff Unified School District for 21 years at the secondary level where he developed many new programs including CIT, a four-year science and technology magnet program. Dave has received numerous teaching awards including National Science Teacher of the Year.

Chapter 7
Getting Results From Science Teacher Leadership
The Critical Role of Principals

Carolyn Landel and Barbara Miller

Introduction

In this time of increased accountability, the principal's role as leader of school improvement is more important and more visible than ever before. School improvement is the process through which schools establish structures, processes, norms, and instructional practices to improve the academic performance of students over time. Successful and continuous school improvement requires leaders to have real knowledge and skills central to the goal of schools: *ensuring all students receive effective instruction in every subject every day*. School leadership is then fundamentally anchored in instruction.

The responsibility to improve instruction in every subject in every classroom for every student is an unreasonable expectation to have of even the most knowledgeable and skilled principal. This is, perhaps, most pronounced in science, because relatively few principals have strong science backgrounds. Effective science instruction relies on knowledge of science content, of how students learn science, of science-specific pedagogy

Chapter 7

to facilitate student learning, and of collaborative practices that allow knowledge to be generated and shared. No matter how effective a building principal is, the principal is just one person—one leader—with limits on his or her own individual knowledge and expertise. Principals must access and apply expertise beyond their own if they are to raise the performance levels of all students in science.

This chapter opens with a detailed look at the empirical and theoretical literature on models of teacher leadership as part of the solution to the demands of principalship. Researchers and practitioners alike have long observed that science teacher leaders, with their mastery of science content and instructional practices, credibility with colleagues, and proximity to students, offer valuable expertise central to school decision making and improvement efforts. There is growing evidence that teacher leaders and principals are indeed effective—and perhaps essential—allies in leading schoolwide improvements in teacher effectiveness and student learning. There is also evidence that suggests that all too often models of teacher leadership do not realize their potential and have only a limited impact on enhancing teaching and learning. According to Roland Barth, "The principal, it seems, has a disproportionate influence upon teacher leadership—for better or for worse" (2001, p. 447). In light of that significant influence, the chapter goes on to explore three core values central to the work of principals interested in getting positive results from teacher leadership and their implications for science teaching and learning in particular.

What Is Teacher Leadership?

The term teacher leadership is used broadly to describe the work of current or former classroom teachers working with other teachers or other educators in the school or district[1]. Teacher leadership is a strategy often invoked to support improvement in a specific subject matter, so a teacher leader is most often identified with a discipline. Mathematics teacher leader, literacy coach, and science specialist are titles that all fall within

---

1. The discussion of teacher leadership draws from a series of knowledge reviews prepared by the Mathematics and Science Partnership Knowledge Management and Dissemination Project, supported by the National Science Foundation under grant number EHR-0445398. These knowledge reviews include a discussion of what is known from empirical research and practice-based insights on a number of teacher leadership topics. www.mspkmd.net/index.php?page=03_2b.

the broader category of teacher leader. The work of teacher leaders is wide-ranging, and often includes observing and giving feedback to other teachers, coteaching, engaging in collaborative lesson planning, sharing materials, leading workshops, or doing demonstration lessons (Adey 1997; Gersten and Kelly 1992; Race, Ho, and Bower 2002). Other responsibilities that are less classroom-based, such as conducting parent outreach efforts, leading curriculum committees, and serving on building leadership teams, are also frequently assigned (Feldman and Tung 2002; Gillis et al. 1991; Ryan 1999; Vesilind and Jones 1998).

The amount and duration of support teacher leaders provide to other teachers is as varied as their job descriptions. In science, as in all other subject areas, there are teacher leaders who are released full- or part-time from classroom teaching to act as leaders in their school or district, as well as teachers who remain in their classroom and take on additional leadership responsibilities. Studies that observed teacher leaders who worked for limited periods (e.g., four half days a year, or biweekly in a six-week period) reported that this can be effective in impacting teacher practices (Adey 1997; Gersten and Kelly 1992). Similar results were noted in studies where teacher leaders worked with teachers over an entire year or more (Feldman and Tung 2002; Race, Ho, and Bower 2002). Though there is still much to be learned in order to understand which models work best in which contexts, tapping into the expertise of science teacher leaders clearly has the potential to benefit both teachers and students.

Why Science Teacher Leadership?

Improving student learning in science poses a host of challenges not always found in other disciplines, which argues even more strongly for capitalizing on teacher leadership to support improvements. At the elementary levels, few teachers have strong backgrounds in science content or pedagogy, which frequently leads to avoiding the science curriculum altogether. Moreover, mathematics, reading, and writing often consume the majority of instructional time in the early grades, making it almost acceptable to avoid teaching science. Effective models of elementary science teacher leadership can help principals and teachers alike ensure that science is not overlooked and that teachers have opportunities to develop their knowledge, skills, and confidence in science.

At the secondary level, principals often face difficult choices in hiring due to current shortages of certified science teachers. All too often, the qualifications of the available applicants fall short of content needs within the school, particularly in high-need schools. In these circumstances, the principal bears the responsibility of ensuring that new hires have access to professional development and support that will enable them to fill in critical knowledge gaps. Here again, a science teacher leader is a powerful ally to the principal in growing and sustaining an effective teaching staff.

The Impact of Teacher Leadership

Many examples in the professional literature advocate for teacher leaders as key figures in improving instruction (Fullan 1994; Lambert 2003; Lieberman and Miller 2004; Little 2003; Moller and Katzenmeyer 1996; Murphy 2005; Wasley 1991). Such advocacy is rooted in the belief that school leadership needs to be broad-based and include the specialized knowledge of teachers, alongside that of administrators. This collaborative approach and purposeful application of different knowledge sets is central to school success. There is mounting evidence that student achievement is tightly linked to the working habits of the adults in the school (Hord 1997; Louis, Marks, and Kruse 1996; Marks, Louis, and Printy 2000). Schools with strong professional learning communities—groups of teachers and administrators that take collective responsibility for student learning and work together toward a clear and commonly shared purpose—are effective in promoting student achievement (Du Four and Eaker 1998; Hord 1997). Teacher leadership is an important ingredient for supporting the collaborative work among teachers that is necessary to achieve that success.

The case for teacher leadership has been made by many, and their claims are beginning to gain greater support based on recent empirical studies that offer evidence of the efficacy and impact of teacher leadership[2]. These studies paint a compelling picture that suggests that teacher

---

2. The discussion of teacher leadership draws from a series of knowledge reviews prepared by the Mathematics and Science Partnership Knowledge Management and Dissemination Project, supported by the National Science Foundation under grant number EHR-0445398. These knowledge reviews include a discussion of what is known from empirical research and practice-based insights on a number of teacher leadership topics. *www.mspkmd.net/index.php?page=09_2b.*

leaders, particularly when engaged in practices focused on classroom instruction, make a difference in teacher practice and student outcomes.

In studies that report an impact of teacher leaders on teachers' classroom practice, the role of the teacher leader was primarily focused on providing instructional support to other teachers (Adey 1997; Feldman and Tung 2002; Gersten and Kelly 1992; Gillis et al. 1991; Race, Ho, and Bower 2002; Ryan 1999). The form of support that these leaders provided ranged from conducting and debriefing observations of classroom instruction, to demonstrating and debriefing effective lessons, to analyzing student work or discourse among groups of teachers. Many of these practices were situated in classrooms with teachers, but some took place outside the classroom. Here, teacher leaders engaged in practices that did not directly address classroom practice, but it has been suggested that they impact the school or classroom culture within which the teachers work. Commonly reported activities included promoting communication among teachers and with administrators, planning new school or district programs, or supporting school improvement plans (Feldman and Tung 2002; Gillis et al. 1991; Ryan 1999; Vesilind and Jones 1998).

The designs for these studies were not able to reveal which particular teacher leader practices had the greatest impact on instruction or student outcomes. However, one study (Coggins, Stoddard, and Cutler 2003) found that teacher leaders believed they were more effective when they were focused on instruction during debriefings of lessons or while analyzing student work than when fulfilling other responsibilities, such as finding resources for teachers or coordinating school reform efforts. Another study suggested that teacher leaders provide greater instructional leadership in teams of teachers when they are focused on specific subject areas (Keedy 1999). In these settings, teacher leaders draw upon their subject matter content knowledge, their experience in the classroom, and their facilitation skills. Teachers reported that teacher leaders who led subject-specific groups derived their credibility and influence from their subject area affiliation. In contrast, those who led interdisciplinary groups were more closely associated with administration or administrative authority.

Three studies pointed further to a positive relationship between teacher leadership and student learning in and attitudes about science or mathematics (Fancsali 2004; Johanson et al. 1996; Shanahan et al. 2005). In these studies, the teacher leaders were treated as classroom teachers, and the performance of their own students relative to comparison groups was measured. Students taught by teacher leaders performed higher than the comparison groups in all three studies. Other studies looked at teacher leadership as part of the school infrastructure in order to examine its impact on classroom organization and activities and outcomes for students (Hofman, Hofman, and Guldemond 2001; Ryan 1999). These studies reported that schools with active teacher leadership programs scored higher on measures of student opportunity to learn. Positive effects on student outcomes were also observed in schools where teacher leaders were actively engaged in decisions related to school policy.

Implications for Principals

Principal leadership is critical to supporting and sustaining teacher leaders in ways that will capitalize on their potential to enhance instructional practices and improve student learning throughout the building.[3] Many research studies, as well as observations from ongoing reform efforts, offer important cues for principals working to improve school effectiveness and student outcomes (Adey 1997; Fennell 1999; Ryan 1999; Silins, Mulford, and Zarins 1999; Silva, Gimbert, and Nolan 2000; Vesilind and Jones 1998). Though there are many ways a principal can incorporate teacher leadership into school improvement efforts, there are some core values and beliefs that are fundamental to success.

Imagine, for example, a principal, a team of teacher leaders, and a staff of teachers in a school you know. Do the observable actions and behaviors of the principal demonstrate that they regard teacher leaders as potential competitors or as collaborators? Is there evidence to support the claim that the principal views the teacher leader as an individual resource for periodic consultation or as a core contributor to the ongoing, long-term professional development plan for the school? Are there indicators that suggest that the principal places teacher leaders among teachers who work largely as isolated practitioners or do they function as collaborative professionals?

---

3. The discussion of teacher leadership draws from a series of knowledge reviews prepared by the Mathematics and Science Partnership Knowledge Management and Dissemination Project, supported by the National Science Foundation under grant number EHR-0445398. These knowledge reviews include a discussion of what is known from empirical research and practice-based insights on a number of teacher leadership topics. *www.mspkmd.net/index.php?page=11_2c.*

These questions provide a means of probing into some of the core values important for achieving results from teacher leadership in any discipline, including science. We explore each of these facets of principal leadership in an effort to better understand actions principals might take to embrace these values and maximize the impact of teacher leaders on science instruction and student learning.

Value and Access the Specialized Knowledge of Teacher Leaders

The ever-increasing expectation that principals ensure rapid and consistent improvement in student performance is daunting to new and experienced principals alike. The challenge of instructional improvement requires collaboration among key players who, together, offer a wide range of knowledge and experience. A principal's identity as a leader must shift away from that of the single, heroic, and often heavily burdened individual who typically acts alone, toward a model of leadership where the principal is a leader among other leaders. Science teacher leaders offer principals access to the specialized skills and knowledge of science content and pedagogy. When science teacher leaders and principals collaborate, it allows principals to use that knowledge to inform leadership decisions (Spillane and Camburn 2006; Wettersten 1994).

In many settings, principals' salaries, job security, and reputation depend on improvement of student test scores. It is understandable that a principal, responding to the pressures of accountability, might seek to control the situation by holding tight to the leadership reins. A principal might believe that admitting that she doesn't have the answers—or that someone else does—could diminish her status as a leader. Or, she might feel that relying on the expertise of others could render her less credible, or that identifying others as leaders could challenge her own authority and weaken her ability to lead. Teacher leaders, in this situation, would be perceived as competitors that could challenge the principal's status as a leader.

It is striking that those principals who actively seek out teacher leaders' input on instructional issues are the ones that have a positive impact on schoolwide instruction (Heller and Firestone 1995). By adopting a collaborative stance, a principal engages teacher leaders as colleagues to share leadership—and responsibility and accountability—for their common goal of instructional improvement. By acknowledging that she doesn't have to "know everything" and seeking out teacher leaders whose knowledge and experience complement her own, a principal embraces opportunities to learn from her support staff. Understanding that she doesn't have to be the lead on everything means that a principal supports models of shared decision making, distributes responsibilities among those best suited to fulfill them, and provides the time and resources needed to get the expected results. As one principal engaged in a large, regional science education reform effort noted, "The principalship is simply too big a job to do myself. I need the insights, expertise, and willingness of teacher leaders to effectively lead our school."[4]

Proactively Develop and Purposefully Engage Teacher Leaders

Effective principals actively engage teacher leaders as integral contributors to the larger plan for whole-school improvement. Principals often take advantage of discipline-focused, grant-supported programs through colleges and universities to provide both funding and experiences to develop science teacher leaders. A principal may encourage teachers to participate in these programs, applaud them personally and publicly for their commitment to personal and professional growth, and even appoint them as "science advocates" or "science leaders" for the building. Such an appointment often means that other teachers are informed of the teacher leader's newly developed expertise in science teaching and learning and encouraged to use them as a resource as needed.

Unfortunately, teacher leaders are severely limited in their ability to impact science instruction when engaged through this "as needed" approach. This approach does not authentically integrate the expertise of science teacher leaders and the activities they could support into the school professional development plan or improvement process. Without clearly defined pathways by which to use expertise to support instruction, they are

---

4. The principal quotes on teacher leadership in this chapter were taken from focus groups or interviews conducted by the North Cascades and Olympic Science Partnership, supported by the National Science Foundation under grant number DUE-0315060. Principals were selected on the basis of their demonstrated success at increasing student performance in science as measured by the state science assessment.

teacher leader in title only, not in action or results. In these circumstances, teacher leadership is viewed as purely happenstance, or worse, irrelevant. When a teacher leader from such a school leaves for a position elsewhere or retires, the loss may be acknowledged, but is rarely replaced. Another teacher leader may be named to "take her place," but the replacement will likely have different skills and experiences which may or may not meet the needs of other teachers in the building. These conditions perpetuate a cycle of idiosyncratic teacher leadership where benefits to other teachers are minimal and improvements in student learning outcomes are negligible.

A more systematic and purposeful approach engages principals and teacher leaders in selecting and participating in professional development programs based on real and verifiable needs in the building relative to student and teacher knowledge and skills. Principals support the development of teacher leadership by providing professional development opportunities for teachers to develop as leaders, inviting them to participate in school decision making, and creating an active community among teachers in the school. Teacher leaders develop into stronger leaders by working with principals who are actively involved in teaching and learning and supportive of opportunities for teacher leaders to participate in administrative decisions (Fennel 1999; Ryan 1999; Silins, Mulford, and Zarins 1999).

Effective principals then go on to create a school infrastructure that ensures a teacher leader's work doesn't depend on chance. Instead, they create defined and allocated ways for teacher leaders to work with other teachers. This is accomplished through development of a strategic and comprehensive plan that defines the content and focus of professional development experiences needed to develop teacher leaders, as well as a means to capitalize on that expertise once it is developed. In the words of a principal who had experienced consistent annual growth in science achievement scores, "Professional development has to be tied to a clear vision and focus for the building. Each teacher leader will have their own personal goals, but they must fall within the building focus." Another principal who had achieved similar results added, "Once you identify their passion and expertise, you have to create an opportunity to put that to work in a way that supports the building so that everyone can benefit. That's when real change occurs."

To accomplish these goals, a principal appoints science teacher leaders based on their individual expertise, but goes on to integrate them into a larger effort to improve the quality of science instruction in the school as a whole. He is aware of the knowledge and skills the teacher leader has to offer and understands how it can be used to benefit other teachers of science. The principal understands that science teacher leaders require professional experiences to explicitly address their leadership role, and recognizes that not all teachers require those same experiences. He makes a programmatic decision to promote instructional improvement by creating opportunities for teacher leaders to regularly work with other teachers as part of the school improvement effort. When a teacher leader in science leaves, the principal assesses the expertise that is lost, makes programmatic adjustments to fill that loss, and ensures that the leadership gap within the discipline is filled so that the improvement efforts can continue.

Create a Culture and Work Environment Conducive to Teacher Leadership

The principal is key in creating a work environment that allows teachers to flourish as collaborative professionals. The typical school includes a collection of classrooms, each led by a teacher for a given grade level or subject area. Most often, students enter and leave the classroom as they move among classes while the teacher remains in her classroom readying herself for the next set of lessons or the next group of students. While regular staff or department meetings address matters of school business, the daily routine of a practicing teacher during contract hours rarely includes interactions with colleagues to learn new teaching strategies, examine practice, or reflect on student learning. All too often, each teacher is left to operate as an isolated practitioner and to develop and implement his/her own approach to instruction.

The working premise for teacher leadership is to have teachers working with other teachers to improve instructional effectiveness and increase student learning. But even with sufficient preparation, resources, and support, placing a teacher leader into a school where staff has limited experiences and skills in collaborative practice will be largely ineffective. A science teacher leader can certainly help to promote collaboration among peer teachers but cannot single-handedly create or promote a school culture that values teachers working with other teachers, nor set an expectation for them to do so as part of their regularly assigned responsibilities.

Although a principal can simply decree, "Thou shalt work productively with one another," this strategy rarely succeeds. The reality is that the principal needs to act strategically to build a school culture that makes science classrooms open to observation by other teachers and administrators; challenges assumptions about appropriate science content, effective instruction, relevant laboratory experiences and phenomenon based on evidence from student discourse and written work; and expects positive results for each and every student without exception. As one principal who had worked tirelessly for five years to cultivate a community of teacher leaders stated, "Building a collaborative culture is something you have to train yourself to do. You read about it, you talk about it, and you practice it. In the end, you live it. Only then can you get others to live it too. Teacher leadership will only be successful when the principal is ready and able to live in that collaborative culture."

Several studies provide evidence of a higher incidence of effective teacher leadership in schools where principals' practices include building consensus among school faculty, participative decision making, making the school an active learning community for teachers, and offering support to individual teachers (Fennell 1999; Silins, Mulford, and Zarins 1999). In these settings, principals recognize and encourage the good work done by teacher leaders and create time for teachers and teacher leaders to work together to discuss instruction. In so doing, they create a school culture and work environment receptive to the work of teacher leaders and create mechanisms by which that work can occur.

Principals that abide by these principles create a collaborative culture by publicly supporting existing efforts of collegial work, particularly those efforts that have moved beyond talking about teaching and have genuinely taken on the hard work of deprivatizing practice and improving instruction. Together, the principal and the teacher leader establish common expectations for what it means for teachers to work as collaborative professionals. The principal acknowledges the situations where teachers are working collaboratively on issues related to science content and pedagogy as a model worthy of emulation in other disciplines. The principal allocates resources to support teachers working in collaboration, rather than isolation, and in turn looks for measureable results in exchange for continued investment. The principal might give priority to professional development experiences requested by a group of science teachers over those sought by

Chapter 7

an individual teacher, but the group must prove that the investment has led to improvements in their classroom practice and student experiences.

Influence "For the Better"

Returning to the words of Roland Barth, the three values of principal leadership explored earlier point to ways in which principal influence can be used "for the better" when linked to teacher leadership. Many schools and districts have invested time and money to develop teacher leaders to support school improvement. The ability of even the most knowledgeable teacher leader to have a positive impact on instruction and learning is inextricably linked to choices made by the building principal. These choices are perhaps most profound in the context of science because of the growing influence and impact of science on all facets of daily life. Science literacy is no longer a luxury for a few, but rather a necessity for all.

Though there is clearly a need for more research to inform which practices in which settings are most effective at supporting science instruction, both theoretical and empirical studies suggest that the expertise, knowledge, and commitment of science teacher leaders adds value to schools. This happens when the principal regards teacher leaders as collaborators who share in leadership responsibilities. To accomplish this, the principal engages teacher leaders as integral contributors to a long-term program of school improvement and, places them among teachers who operate as collaborative professionals ready to learn and improve. Those choices are rooted in core values and beliefs that must be continuously examined through thoughtful self-reflection and careful observation by critical friends in the spirit of self improvement and school improvement. A principal whose actions are rooted in these values will maximize the impact of teacher leaders on progress toward their shared goal of improved instruction and academic success for every student.

References

Adey, P. S. 1997. Factors influencing uptake of a large scale curriculum innovation. Paper presented at the annual meeting of the American Educational Research Association, Chicago, IL.

Barth, R. 2001. Teacher leader. *Phi Delta Kappan* 82 (6): 443–449.

Coggins, C. T., P. Stoddard, and E. Cutler. 2003. Improving instructional capacity through field-based reform coaches. Paper presented at the annual meeting of the American Educational Research Association, Chicago, IL.

DuFour, R., and R. Eaker. 1998. *Professional learning communities at work: Best practices for enhancing student achievement.* Bloomington, IN: National Educational Service.

Fancsali, C. 2004. *Teacher leaders for mathematics success (TL=MS). Final evaluation report.* New York, NY: Academy for Educational Development.

Feldman, J., and R. Tung. 2002. The role of external facilitators in whole school reform: Teachers' perceptions of how coaches influence school change. Paper presented at the annual meeting of the American Educational Research Association, New Orleans, LA.

Fennell, H. 1999. Encouraging teacher leadership. Paper presented at the annual meeting of the American Educational Research Association, Montreal, Canada.

Fullan, M. 1994. Teacher leadership: A failure to conceptualize. In *Teachers as leaders: perspectives on the professional development of teachers*, ed. D. R. Walling, 241–253. Bloomington, IN: Phi Delta Kappa Educational Foundation.

Gersten, R., and B. Kelly. 1992. Coaching secondary special education teachers in implementation of an innovative videodisc mathematics curriculum. *Remedial and Special Education* 13 (4): 40–51.

Gillis, L., L. Glegg, J. Larkin, and M. Ojo. 1991. *The summative evaluation of the Science Quality Education Project (SQEP).* Toronto: Ontario Educational Communications Authority. (ERIC Document Reproduction no. ED 328 453)

Heller, M. F., and W. A. Firestone. 1995. Who's in charge here? Sources of leadership for change in eight schools. *The Elementary School Journal* 96 (1): 65–86.

Hofman, R. H., W. H. A. Hofman, and H. Guldemond. 2001. The effectiveness of cohesive schools. *International Journal of Leadership in Education* 4 (2): 115–135.

Hord, S. M. 1997. *Professional learning communities: Communities of continuous inquiry and improvement.* Austin, TX: Southwest Educational Development laboratory.

Johanson, G., R. Martin, C. Gips, B. Beach, and S. Green. 1996. The evalu-

Chapter 7

ation of the lead teacher project. Paper presented at the annual meeting of the American Educational Research Association, New York.

Keedy, J. L. 1999. Examining teacher instructional leadership within the small group dynamics of collegial groups. *Teaching and Teacher Education* 15 (7): 785–799.

Lambert, L. 2003. Shifting conceptions of leadership: Towards a redefinition of leadership for the twenty-first century. In *Handbook of educational leadership and management*, eds. B. Davies and J. West-Burnham, 5–15. London: Pearson Education.

Lieberman, A., and L. Miller. 2004. *Teacher leadership.* San Francisco: Jossey-Bass.

Little, J. W. 1995. Contested ground: The basis of teacher leadership in two restructuring high schools. *The Elementary School Journal* 96 (1): 47–63.

———. 2003. Constructions of teacher leadership in three periods of policy and reform activism. *School Leadership and Management* 23 (4) 401–419.

Louis, K. S., H. M. Marks, and S. Kruse. 1996. Teachers' professional community in restructuring schools. *American Educational Research Journal* 33 (4): 757–798.

Marks, H. M., K. S. Louis, and S. M. Printy. 2000. The capacity for organizational learning: Implications for pedagogical quality and student achievement. In *Understanding schools as intelligent systems*, ed. K. Leithwood, 239–265. Stamford, CT: Jai Press.

Moller, G., and M. Katzenmeyer. 1996. The promise of teacher leadership. In *Every teacher as a leader: Realizing the potential of teacher leadership*, eds. G. Moller and M. Katzenmeyer, 1–17. San Francisco: Jossey-Bass.

Murphy, J. 2005. *Connecting teacher leadership and school improvement.* Thousand Oaks, CA: Corwin Press.

Race, K. E. H., E. Ho, and L. Bower. 2002. Documenting in-classroom support and coaching activities of a professional development program directed toward school-wide change: An integral part of an organization's evaluation efforts. Paper presented at the annual meeting of the American Educational Research Association, New Orleans, LA.

Ryan, S. A. 1999. Principals and teachers leading together. Paper presented at the annual meeting of the American Educational Research Association, Montreal, Canada.

Shanahan, T., K. Hyde, V. Mann, C. and Manrique. 2005. Integrating curriculum guides, quarterly benchmark assessments, and professional development to improve student learning in mathematics. Unpublished manuscript.

Silins, H., B. Mulford, and S. Zarins. 1999. Leadership for organisational learning and student outcomes. The Lolso Project: The first report of an Australian three year study of international significance. Paper presented at the annual meeting of the American Educational Research Association, Montreal, Canada.

Silva, D. Y., B. Gimbert, and J. Nolan. 2000. Sliding the doors: Locking and unlocking possibilities for teacher leadership. *Teachers College Record* 102 (4): 779–803.

Spillane, J. P., and E. Camburn. 2006. The practice of leading and managing schools: Taking a distributed perspective to the school principal's work day. Unpublished manuscript.

Vesilind, E. M., and M. G. Jones. 1998. Gardens or graveyards: Science education reform and school culture. *Journal of Research in Science Teaching* 35 (7): 757–775.

Wasley, P. 1991. *Teachers who lead: The rhetoric of reform and the realities of practice.* New York: Teachers College Press.

Wettersten, J. A. 1994. Low profile, high impact: Four case studies of high school department chairs whose transactions "transform" teachers and administrators. Paper presented at the annual meeting of the American Educational Research Association, New Orleans, LA.

Chapter 8

Developing and Sustaining Leadership in Science Education

Norman G. Lederman and Judith S. Lederman

Teaching is a difficult profession with too few external rewards. Teachers often work in isolation and typically do not get either financial or societal credit for the important work they do. Although professional development programs are prominent in most school districts, the quality of these programs is often suspect (Loucks-Horsley et al. 2003). For this reason and many others, it can be argued that the most important guiding force leading to a teacher's continued improvement is having a good role model, such as a colleague who is an experienced leader. Indeed, many university graduate programs have realized the value of instructional leadership.

Throughout the United States, as well as many locations internationally, teachers are required to pursue a master's degree or the equivalent, in order to maintain their teaching certificate and/or advance to a higher level on the pay scale. Quite often, degree programs designed for inservice teachers are called "leadership" programs, with the assumption that graduate coursework of any kind will help the teacher become an instructional leader in his/her school or school district. However, the ways in which the teacher is expected to develop leadership skills and use those skills is often unclear. These programs usually do not contain courses specifically designed to help teachers develop the skills and abilities necessary to become instructional leaders (Cochran-Smith and Zeichner 2005). This chapter will provide a detailed description of a master's degree program that specifically targets the skills and abilities necessary to become an instructional leader at the secondary level (grades 6–12). This cohort program has existed for five years and has engaged 119 teachers. Additionally, this chapter will describe methods used to ensure continued effectiveness following completion of the program.

What Is an Instructional Leader?

The term *instructional leader* can be defined in various ways, but most would agree that an instructional leader uses specific knowledge, abilities, and behaviors to provide the guidance to fellow faculty that improves the quality of instruction and student learning in a school or school district (Reeves 2006). In addition, an instructional leader is an individual who facilitates the dissemination of good practices to a broader audience in an effort to benefit the science education community beyond a specific locality. These are nice words, but what is it that an instructional leader needs to know and be able to do? The particular knowledge and skills related to leadership focused on within the program are:

- Curriculum development
- Action research
- Assessment and evaluation
- Subject matter knowledge, including inquiry and nature of science
- Advanced instructional strategies
- Supervision, mentoring, and peer coaching
- Expertise in connecting school curriculum to community resources and agencies
- Leadership skills
- Grant writing
- Contributions to the professional community

This chapter will examine the research-based leadership program at Illinois Institute of Technology. In addition to the specifics of program content, evidence for the success of the program and mechanisms designed to sustain leadership will be presented. The foci are discussed in the same sequence that they are presented within the program. The program takes 13 months to complete, beginning with an initial summer, followed by two academic year semesters, and then completed during a second summer.

Curriculum Development

Curriculum Development is one of the first two courses that the cohort completes during the initial summer. The focus of this course is on the nature and structure of secondary (6–12) science curriculum. The course begins with a historical study of science curriculum. The objective is to study the relationship between the science curriculum and the various factors that influence that curriculum. These factors include the social/historical climate, federal/national interests, state interests, local/community interests, parental interests, incumbent interests, and current theories on teaching and learning (DeBoer 1991). The teachers are asked to analyze formerly used curricula within their historical context and then apply the insight they have gained to currently used curricula in their schools and districts. Finally, teachers are asked to use the information they learned to develop their own curriculum focus and structure. The goal is to help teachers develop a more in-depth understanding of the nature of curriculum and its purposes so that they can address curriculum issues in their districts and schools with a more informed perspective. This background enables these teachers to provide leadership with regard to local curriculum initiatives. All too often, teachers feel that the science curriculum operates in a vacuum and does not extend beyond the content they teach. This is especially true with respect to the currently accepted theories of teaching and learning.

Action Research

The second course taken during the initial summer is Action Research. The subject matter covered in this course is further developed over the subsequent two semesters. During the summer, teachers learn to read both quantitative and qualitative research analytically and critique the methods and findings. They are then asked to apply the information they have learned from these critical discussions to develop a research study of high relevance to their current teaching situation. Teachers are given the option of working alone or in teams, depending on the availability of other teachers with similar concerns or interests. The goal is to have teachers develop the skills necessary to collect systematic data to answer teaching/learning questions relevant to their current situation. A basic assumption of the program is that leadership skills include those skills necessary to make data-driven decisions about the local concerns of teachers and administrators. Action research has long been advocated as an effective approach to teacher professional development (Sagor 2005; Spiegel, Collins, and Lappert 1995).

The program at IIT also assumes that the use of locally developed research investigation is an important skill of an instructional leader. The project planned during the summer is implemented during the fall and spring semesters, and the final report is due at the end of the spring semester. Consistent with the development of leadership skills, all teachers are expected to provide a copy of their results to their school administrator and present those results during a faculty meeting.

Assessment and Evaluation

As the teachers are carrying out their research projects during the fall semester, they are also enrolled in a course focusing on assessment and evaluation. Although the course primarily focuses on the development of valid and reliable assessments of student knowledge, it also covers the analysis of data as it pertains to making instructional decisions. The stress on data analysis is also useful in helping teachers analyze the data they are collecting as part of their action research projects.

As mentioned, the primary focus of this course is on the development and use of multiple assessment items to evaluate student understanding of subject matter, as well as affective outcomes. Stress is placed on authentic assessment items as well as alternative methods for assessing in-depth student knowledge. Teachers quickly become aware that certain assessment items are more amenable to certain learning outcomes as opposed to others. Teachers are asked to apply their new knowledge to the development

- Use data to inform decisions
- Think beyond your own ideas
- Share the rewards
- Set an example

Keeping one's eyes on the prize (outcomes) is the basis of the recommended leadership approach. However, these six components provide a more detailed process for implementing this leadership model. Except for the first component, they are not listed in order of priority. In fact, it is often possible to work on many of these components simultaneously. That is, several components frequently overlap and often enhance each other. Each of these components will be described and discussed.

Develop Shared Vision, Mission, and Goals

In order to be a goal-oriented leader, a prerequisite is the establishment of goals. Any visionary leader could develop a set of goals. However, doing that in isolation often results in goals that have very little support from those who must actually implement them. In fact, goals that come only from the vision of the leader often make it quite lonely at the top. A better approach is to involve others in the process of creating the goals. The alternative requires the leader to sell the goals to both those to whom the leader reports and to those who report to the leader. A collaborative process can result in more feasible goals and a broader commitment to implementation.

One effective practice to build consensus is for the leader to bring a vision to the table and work with the various constituency groups to refine that vision and create the organizational mission and strategic goals. It is not the purpose of this chapter to present a strategic planning process, as there are many excellent books on this topic (such as *Applied Strategic Planning*, by Goodstein, Noland, and Pfeiffer 1993). Approaching the planning process in this way provides an excellent opportunity to involve others in the activity and build a common commitment to accomplishing the goals that result. A widespread approach to strategic planning begins by examining the strengths, weaknesses, opportunities, and threats to the organization (often referred to as a SWOT analysis, discussed in *Analysis Without Paralysis*, by Bensoussan and Fleisher 2008). This approach also provides of an assessment that can be used with their own students. After the assessments are used, the teachers bring the data back to class to determine if the assessments were fair and valid. Item analysis procedures are used, and the teachers are asked to revise any flaws that were identified. Finally, the last part of the course is concerned with the assignment of grades within norm-referenced and criterion-referenced grading schemes. There is an emerging emphasis in schools on data-driven decision making. In terms of helping teachers develop into instructional leaders, this course helps to develop in-depth knowledge of assessment and ways to use assessments to evaluate student progress and program quality.

Subject Matter Knowledge, Including Inquiry and Nature of Science

The leadership program requires participants to complete three graduate courses in their content areas. Instructional leaders, or all teachers for that matter, benefit from continued study of their subject. Additionally, the program includes a specialized course dedicated to understanding scientific inquiry and the nature of science. Both of these areas have been heavily emphasized in recent reforms, but little change has been noted in science instruction. Quite simply, there is very little quality professional development related to nature of science. Teachers often complain that they need more practical experience addressing the nature of science through classroom instruction. To a lesser degree, the same is true when it comes to facilitating students' understanding about scientific inquiry. The current reforms emphasize both theoretical knowledge about and active participation in inquiry. This course, which counts as a subject matter course, helps develop teachers' understanding and facilitates development of pedagogical skills related to inquiry and nature of science. The research clearly indicates that most teachers do not possess an adequate understanding of inquiry and nature of science and lack the skills and knowledge necessary to effectively teach either concept (Lederman 2007). Within this course, teachers are given numerous opportunities to create and revise instructional materials that better address the nature of science and scientific inquiry.

Scientific inquiry and nature of science are two instructional outcomes considered to be critical for the development of scientific literacy. Hence, they are consistently stressed in both national and state level reform documents (AAAS 1993; NRC 1996). Instructional leaders need to be well-versed in the teaching of key areas addressed by current reforms. It is hoped that graduates of the leadership cohort program will provide staff development about nature of science and scientific inquiry to their colleagues.

Advanced Instructional Strategies

Advanced Instructional Strategies is one of two courses (the other being the final semester of the action research course) that cohort members attend during the spring semester. In this course, teachers develop and practice lessons that stress critical thinking and higher-level thinking. This course builds on the inquiry and nature of science course completed the previous semester by providing opportunities to actually practice teaching nature of science and scientific inquiry. Additionally, this course facilitates teachers' abilities to plan and implement lessons following instructional models such as concept attainment, inquiry, general inductive, and group interaction. Each of these instructional models places a strong emphasis on critical thinking and problem-solving skills (Eggen and Kauchak 2006). These models provide an excellent instructional platform in which to integrate nature of science and scientific inquiry. Teachers practice lessons in peer teaching/microteaching activities and receive feedback regarding their performance. The teachers are then required to re-teach the lesson with their actual students. The lessons are taped and brought back to the course for a group discussion.

Supervision, Mentoring, and Peer Coaching

One activity that an instructional leader performs is providing assistance to colleagues on instructional matters. In particular, teachers often have concerns about their own teaching, skills they are trying to improve, or new instructional approaches that they are trying to integrate. For this reason, the program has a course specifically dedicated to supervision and mentoring skills. This course is offered during the spring semester. The course focuses on a clinical supervision model (Acheson and Gall 2003) and gives the teachers experience with pre- and postobservation conferencing as well as objective data collection and data analysis in science classrooms. Teachers are given an opportunity to practice each of these skills during class meetings. Simulated conferences during which teachers' peers have an opportunity to discuss approaches to supervision/mentoring help further develop these skills. Teachers are then expected to arrange a supervision/mentoring experience with at least two colleagues from their district. The results of these experiences are discussed with other class members. The overall approach is to facilitate gradual development of the skills and knowledge needed to successfully serve as a teacher leader.

Expertise in Connecting School Curriculum to Community Resources and Agencies

Current reform documents strongly stress the importance of connecting schools with community resources (NRC 1996). The science curriculum can be greatly enhanced through the use of informal science venues (e.g., museums and zoos) because these venues can provide learning opportunities not available in schools. This course is a combination internship and university-based course. During the second summer of the leadership program, teachers are placed in various informal venues around the city (zoos, botanical gardens, museums). They spend eight hours per week at the venue and two hours per week in class. The teachers are exposed to a variety of experiences during their internship—docent, program designer, curriculum designer, and data collector for research projects, for example—and, depending on the needs of the venue, they assist the education unit in any ways that are appropriate. Consequently, these internships do not provide identical experiences for all teachers. The major project of the course is the completion of an instructional unit that intimately integrates the internship site into existing school curriculum. The goal is to facilitate the ability to productively integrate informal education venues into school curriculum to enhance students' science learning. The intent is also to impact teachers so that they will continue to use informal education sites after graduation from the leadership program. In terms of leadership, it is important for instructional leaders to be well-versed in various educational opportunities outside of the formal school setting that can be used to enhance learning. It is also hoped that these teachers will conduct workshops with their colleagues in their home schools and districts about using informal science venues to enhance science curricula.

Leadership Skills

The leadership skills integrated throughout the program are emphasized in a capstone course taken during the second summer. This course draws heavily on the work of Gabriel (2005), Reeves (2006), and Loucks-Horsley et al. (2003). During this course, teachers are expected to apply the skills and knowledge that they have gained throughout the year to develop a plan for instructional change intended to be enacted in their schools and districts the following year. This plan includes detailed descriptions of curriculum change and professional development sessions. One of the requirements for admission to the cohort program is a letter of support from the teacher's school administrator. Consequently, the expectation that the teacher will be submitting plans for school change is established prior to starting the program.

Grant Writing and Contributions to the Professional Community

The third course during the second summer of the program is a professional development practicum that focuses primarily on development of a professional portfolio. This portfolio contains many of the assignments completed in other program courses, and also includes detailed information about personal professional development projects, proposals for presentation at professional meetings, and a manuscript from the action research project that will be submitted to a professional journal. The professional development plan is the teacher's plan of activities that will ensure his or her continued professional growth for the next five years. Proposals for presentations at professional meetings typically include, but are not limited to, proposals for the National Science Teachers Association (NSTA), Association of Science Teacher Educators (ASTE), and the National Association for Research in Science Teaching (NARST). These activities are the future leader's opportunity to share knowledge with others in the field, which is something all leaders do. Some of the presentations are practitioner-oriented while others are oriented toward research. The manuscripts prepared for publication are submitted to a wide variety of professional journals.

The specific content requirements for the full professional portfolio are as follows:

- Title page

- Personal autobiography
  (includes certification area, current teaching responsibilities, personal history as a science teacher, and an explanation of ways the teacher has developed as a result of the program)
- Essays on domains of knowledge
  - subject matter knowledge
  - pedagogical knowledge
  - knowledge of learners
  - knowledge of curriculum
  - knowledge of schools
  - pedagogical content knowledge
  (essays should describe ways that the teacher has changed in each area and include specific examples from classes and current teaching experiences)
- Clinical supervision assignments (revised)
- Videotapes of two lessons and lesson plans
- Lesson plans (revised) illustrating each of the models from advanced strategies and reflections on the lessons taught
- Book reviews (revised) from the Inquiry/Problem Solving course
- Sample assessment "instrument" that illustrates knowledge of contemporary assessment/evaluation
- Informal practicum project
- Action research paper (revised)
- Professional development plan
- Completed/submitted grant
- Completed manuscript for publication
- Submitted proposal (or proposal prepared for submission) to a professional meeting

Evidence of Program Success

As mentioned previously, the described leadership cohort program is just completing its fifth year and has engaged 119 secondary level science teachers. Since the fifth year is not yet completed, 97 teachers have completed the entire program. Following development and implementation of this program, five outcomes were used as indicators of success in order to document that the program achieved its stated goal.

Department Leadership

Since completing the program, 32 of our teachers have assumed the role of science department chair in their school. Five teachers were already department chairs when they entered the program and continue to serve in that capacity. A quick analysis indicates that approximately one third of the teachers in the leadership program have achieved a leadership role in their schools. Given the various factors that influence who is appointed as department chair in a school, we feel that this can be considered evidence of program effectiveness.

District- and Schoolwide Professional Development

All teachers are required to present the results of their action research projects to their school faculty. It is also hoped that graduates of the program will provide professional development in their schools or districts with respect to curriculum, instructional innovation, and supervision. A total of 97 teachers (82%) have delivered professional development workshops in their school or district. The topics have included

- ways to teach nature of science,
- inquiry as subject matter,
- data-based decision making,
- reform-based curriculum,
- the value of Test-Prep for ACT scores,
- authentic assessment, and
- improving instruction through clinical supervision, in addition to other topics.

Eighty-two percent is an impressive number of professional development workshops, and furthermore, at least 15 of our teachers have presented additional workshops beyond the initial workshop.

Funded Grants

Of the 97 teachers who completed the leadership program, 24 (25%) have been successful in securing funding for instructional projects. Given that the typical success rate on the types of grants applied for is about 20%, the teachers in this program have been relatively successful. It is important to note that all teachers are required to submit grants as part of the leadership course at the end of the program. Grants were obtained through gardening organizations, energy companies, the state of Illinois, and various other businesses. Projects involved developing gardens on school grounds, installing solar panels, and curriculum revision initiatives. The teachers in the fifth iteration of the leadership program have not yet written grants.

Professional Meetings

All teachers are required to write at least one proposal for submission to a professional meeting. Forty-eight (49%) of the teachers have successfully presented at professional meetings. Some of these presentations involved more than one teacher. With two exceptions, all papers were presented at regional and national conferences of NSTA or Illinois/Chicago-based professional meetings for teachers. The two exceptions were research papers presented at the NARST and NCTM.

Journal Articles

All teachers were required to prepare manuscripts for publication in professional journals. At this time of writing, none of the teachers have published papers in national journals, but several are still waiting to hear from *The Science Teacher, Science Scope,* and *School Science and Mathematics.* Although we cannot claim much success in this arena, we are highly encouraged by the teachers' success in presenting at professional meetings. Given this consideration, we feel that the teachers simply need more practice and direction in terms of getting manuscripts published in peer-reviewed journals, and we will continue to focus on improving this aspect of the program.

Mentoring of Preservice Teachers

One of the original reasons for beginning the leadership cohort program was to develop a cadre of teachers who could provide exemplary sites for the supervision of student teachers. Indeed, applicants to the program were told that one of the "perks" of the program would be that they would be given priority as sites for student teachers. A total of 72 (74%) program graduates have successfully supervised a student teacher. This has greatly enhanced the IIT preservice program, and it has also allowed leadership graduates to continue their service as instructional leaders. In addition to providing leadership within their schools and districts, they are providing leadership to future science teachers.

Conclusion

This master's degree cohort program shows that leadership in teachers can be developed and sustained. Through carefully crafted programs, teachers can improve their skills and knowledge in curriculum, instruction, supervision, assessment, and other areas to an extent that enables them to benefit others. Universities can help sustain this leadership by continually providing opportunities for working with future teachers, involvement in the planning of university courses, and participation in collaborative research. Teacher educators and teachers have the same primary goals: improving the quality of teaching and learning of science. Because working collaboratively is much more successful than working independently, fostering the development of teacher leaders is expected to positively affect the quality of instruction provided by teachers acting in leadership roles as well as the colleagues that they influence.

References

Acheson, K. A., and M. D. Gall. 2003. *Clinical supervision and teacher development.* Hoboken, NJ: John Wiley & Sons.

American Association for the Advancement of Science (AAAS). 1993. *Benchmarks for science literacy.* New York: AAAS.

Cochran-Smith, M., and K. M. Zeichner. 2005. *Studying teacher education.* Mahwah, NJ: Lawrence Erlbaum Associates.

DeBoer, G. 1991. *A history of ideas in science education.* New York: Teachers College Press.

Eggen, P. D., and D. P. Kauchak. 2006. *Strategies and models for teachers.* Boston, MA: Pearson Education.

Gabriel, J. G. 2005. *How to thrive as a teacher leader.* Alexandria, VA: Association for Supervison and Curriculum Development.

Lederman, N. G. 2007. Nature of science: Past, present, and future. In

Handbook of Research on Science Education, eds. S. K. Abell and N. G. Lederman, 831–880. Mahwah, NJ: Lawrence Erlbaum Associates.

Loucks-Horsley, S., N. Love, K. E. Stiles, S. Mundry, and P. W. Hewson. 2003. *Designing professional development for teachers of science and mathematics*. Thousand Oaks, CA: Corwin Press.

National Research Council (NRC). 1996. *National science education standards*. Washington, DC: National Academy Press.

Reeves, D. B. 2006. *The learning leader*. Alexandria, VA: Association for Supervision and Curriculum Development.

Sagor, R. 2005. *The action research guidebook*. Thousand Oaks, CA: Corwin Press.

Spiegel, S. A., A. Collins, and J. Lappert. 1995. *Action research: Perspectives from teachers' classrooms*. Tallahassee, FL: Southeastern Regional Vision in Learning.

Section Three

School and District Science Leadership: Rationale, Strategy, and Impact

Chapter 9

Technology Leadership for the 21st Century

Karen E. Irving

Literacy in the 21st century comprises more than simply reading and writing. In 2002, a study at the University of California, Berkeley School of Information Management and Systems, estimated that 5 exabytes (10^{18} bytes) of new information were stored that year on paper, film, and optical and magnetic media (Lyman and Varian 2003). This represents about 800 MB of new information per human and would require about 30 feet of books per person. To grasp the size of this new content, it helps to consider that 500,000 new libraries the size of the Library of Congress print collections would be needed to hold this information on paper. Between 1999 and 2002, new information, 92% of which is stored on hard disks and other electronic devices, grew about 30% per year. As of 2003, around the world, about 600 million people had access to the internet, about 30% of them in North America (Lyman and Varian 2003). To be an informed citizen in our contemporary information age, digital skills are needed by students, teachers, library/media specialists, administrators, and parents (Brooks-Young 2006).

Despite the perceived slow pace of educational technology integration in modern schools, information and communication technologies (ICT) are a driving force for change in education (Gurr 2004). In U.S. public school instructional spaces, 93% reported having had internet access in 2003 compared to 3% in 1994. In those public schools with internet access in 2003, 95% used a broadband connection. The student-to-computer ratio in 2003 was 4.4 to 1, a decrease from the 12.1 to 1 ratio reported in 1998 (Parsad and Jones 2005). As brick-and-mortar schools struggle to integrate and take advantage of their digital resources, virtual schools continue to evolve. In the 2007–2008 school year, virtual schools attracted more than a million students, which was a 47% increase from 2005–2006 (Davis 2009). Adapting and responding to the shifting educational landscape requires knowledgeable and capable leadership. This chapter addresses (a) how transformational leadership in the educational community is crucial for effective and appropriate infusion of educational technology as a fundamental part of K–12 education; (b) how educational leaders can create a robust digital age educational community that supports the use of advanced technologies in teaching and learning; and (c) how effective infrastructure may be provided for educational technology in K–12 schools.

Transformative Leadership

While hierarchical relationships are usually clear in the corporate world, views of educational leadership differ from traditional, leader-centered, top-down positional roles to include a variety of descriptions that account for how leadership adapts to site-based needs (Gurr 2004; Ladyshewsky et al. 2008). Transformative educational leaders adjust not only to situational conditions in schools, but also to the rapid and continuous changes in educational technology. Modern electronic technologies differ from earlier technologies like books, chalkboards, mimeograph machines, and film strips by the apparent anti-humanistic culture of the computer and its conflict with the person-centered work of school (e.g., Turkle 1984). Teachers are often poorly trained in the use of modern technologies, and they struggle to figure out how or why to integrate electronic technologies in their instructional practice. Most of the factors that researchers cite for the failure of teachers to use educational technologies (lack of training, lack of materials, unrealistic goals, insufficient hardware/software) can be overcome. However, if school leaders do not believe in the importance and possibility of the innovation, then even the best conceived plans will lead to failure. Informed, transformational leadership that believes solutions are possible is critical to the success of educational technology integration in 21st-century schools (Kearsley and Lynch 1992).

From the variety of established theories on leadership, the cultural view best fits the ecology of technology in the school (e.g., Schein 1985). The cultural view of leadership is an evolutionary perspective in which the dynamic creation of culture and the shaping of that culture by its leaders are two sides of the same coin. A successful leader is able to view the culture that created the leader from an outside perspective, to identify the limitations of the culture in light of difficulties, and to initiate any needed adaptive changes. Building a school culture where educational technology innovation and integration are both accepted and expected requires engaging in shared values and beliefs. Participants at all levels, from teacher to state superintendent, must believe in what they are doing, be involved in the change process, and have a voice in the process. Otherwise, the well-documented obstacles of innovation diffusion will doom the initiative to failure (Rogers 2003). Different leadership skills and responsibilities fall to different levels of school administration, as illustrated in Table 1. Despite distinctions in responsibilities for individuals at different levels of governance, a commitment to a set of beliefs and values as well as emotional, political and financial support must occur at all levels.

While leadership is needed at many levels and may occur at the teacher level in individual schools, idiosyncratic integration patterns sometimes prove difficult to replicate across systems. A particular teacher or small group of teachers (for example, the mathematics department or science department) may take the initiative to explore and implement 21st-century technology in their classrooms. These efforts are often driven by genuine conviction about the efficacy of the innovation, and they build momentum as a result of individual teacher experiences. This type of spontaneous bottom-up leadership requires careful nurturance to develop beyond the limited interests of the smaller group into a systemwide community (Kearsley and Lynch 1992).

The complexity of school reform efforts coupled with the enlarging community of stakeholders has hastened the shift from traditional leadership roles in education. Rather than identifying the "right" educational

Table 1. Technology leadership skills (adapted from Kearsley and Lynch 1992)	
Level	**Skills**
State	Identify a common format for computing across districts
	Statewide networks
	Funding for hardware/software
	Regional technology centers
	Professional development initiatives
	School-level evaluations
	Copyright policy
District	Funding sources for district-related purchases
	Districtwide administrative networks
	District-level objectives
	Inservice training schedules
	Attend to district-level needs
Schools	Funding sources for building-related purchases
	School-level networks and use priorities
	Access and opportunity for use within the building
	Technology training time and professional development
	Ethical use policies
	Highlight exemplary use
Teachers	Effective and appropriate classroom use
	Encourage student and parent involvement
	Interdisciplinary curriculum fit
	Improve personal efficiency
	Articulate and monitor ethical use policies
Technology specialists	Technology support to teachers/staff/administrators
	Develop new applications
	Fit applications to curriculum
	Information source for teachers/staff/administrators
	Articulate and monitor ethical use
	Recommend products for purchase
	Troubleshoot

technology, leaders work to promote change in their systems through people development and collaboration (Valdez 2004). Fullan identified five characteristics of effective leaders: "A strong sense of moral purpose, an understanding of the dynamics of change, an emotional intelligence as they build relationships, a commitment to developing and sharing new knowledge, and a capacity for coherence making" (2002, p.2). Transformative leaders create environments that nurture communities to implement creative and innovative integration of modern educational technologies.

Supporting Teachers and Students in the School Building

Specifically, how can educational leaders create a successful community for integration of educational technology in 21st-century classrooms? The ISTE National Educational Technology Standards (NETS) and Performance Indicators for Administrators address this issue and provide concrete suggestions (ISTE 2002, 2009). In addition to articulating and communicating their vision for technology use, leaders can create and implement a long-term, data-driven plan for achieving their vision. They can serve as local, state, and national advocates for research-based effective policies for technology integration that support relevant national and state standards and promote student learning and effective teaching. ISTE NETS recommend bringing stakeholders together to develop and plan implementation of their shared vision. Leaders can encourage and reward their communities, thereby sustaining an educational culture that both values and rewards instructional innovation that meets the needs of a diverse student body. By establishing, supporting, and modeling a robust and intentional use of educational technology in their own professional practice, individual teachers can establish a norm for others.

Transformative leadership allocates resources, including time and access to quality professional development related to the effective use of educational technology. Training for technology integration can occur through schools of education, state, and local agencies; through professional communities such as the National Science Teachers Association (NSTA) or the National Council of Teachers of Mathematics (NCTM); or directly through vendors. Webinars represent a recent addition to the professional development arena. A webinar (from *web* and *seminar*) is a type of live meeting or presentation conducted via an internet connection.

An important aspect of technology training is the career-long nature of the enterprise. Single-shot summer workshops or after-school technology training rarely provides sufficient knowledge to serve teachers in their technology integration efforts. Research on professional development indicates that successful programs begin with a commitment to a vision that includes identified and articulated educational standards, an analysis of student learning data, goal setting to address critical issues, group planning to select appropriate and effective strategies, implementation, evaluation, and reflection (Loucks-Horsley et al. 2003). Leaders can provide common planning time, release time, stipends, and funding to support sustained educational technology integration efforts (Zhao and Frank 2003). Recognizing the long-term nature of the commitment is a critical aspect of successful technology integration.

Learning communities of teachers, students, parents, administrators and staff that welcome innovation and 21st-century teaching methods need supportive collegial and administrative climates to flourish (Irving, Sanalan and Shirley 2009). Critical evaluation of technologies and careful fitting to meet schoolwide goals and curriculum requirements help teachers implement educational technology in pursuit of student learning. Timely information on educational trends and emerging technology can spark innovative strategies. The variety of classroom technologies that can be used to support and enhance learning encompasses a wide selection ranging from simple word processing programs to two-way audio and video links between learning spaces. The range and diversity can be overwhelming. Three broad distinctions about ways that the technology will be used can help to provide clarity and guidance: (1) students can learn *from* technology; (2) students can learn *with* technology; and (3) teachers and students can monitor classroom learning progress *through* use of technology.

Knowledge transmission provides the paradigm for learning *from* technology. Students receive knowledge from the information source; the technology serves as an electronic information delivery system (Reeves 1998). Examples include intelligent tutors, integrated learning systems (ILS), computer-assisted instruction (CAI), and computer-based instruction (CBI). These types of applications have found a place in classrooms for more than 20 years (Becker, Ravitz, and Wong 1999).

Construction of knowledge provides a useful paradigm for learning *with* technology. Technology serves as a tool to engage students with real-world problem solving, conceptual development and critical thinking (Ringstaff and Kelley 2002). Students can engage in authentic inquiry, explore communication systems such as synchronous conferencing or interactive simulations, construct items such as robots or remote controlled devices, and express themselves with interactive video, animation software packages, or music composition software (Honey, Culp, and Spielvogel 2005).

Electronic audience response system (ARS) technologies have found a place in classrooms to help students and teachers track learning progress. ARS technology connects teachers and students with a networked system of handheld devices using software specifically designed for the classroom (Fies and Marshall 2006; Roschelle, Penuel, and Abrahamson 2004). Teachers and students receive timely and targeted information regarding learning progress when these devices are thoughtfully used during instruction. Studies with ARS technology have shown improved student achievement when coupled with constructivist-based pedagogical strategies (e.g., Owens et al. 2007; Hake 1998).

Supporting Teachers and Students Beyond the School Building

While educational technology integration efforts persist within the school building, virtual educational opportunities continue to grow at a record pace. Research consistently demonstrates that online schooling has the potential to be as good as or better in terms of student achievement than classes taught face-to-face in brick-and-mortar settings (e.g., Cavanaugh et al. 2004). A 2008 survey of U.S. School District Administrators conducted by the Sloan Consortium and Hunter College (CUNY) revealed that 75% of the respondents reported one or more students enrolled in a fully online or blended course (with both online and face-to-face components). The Sloan report estimated that during the 2007–2008 school year, about 1,030,000 K–12 students enrolled in online courses. The most commonly cited reasons for district administrators to offer online courses included (a) specialized needs for particular student groups; (b) broadening the course offering selections; (c) offering Advanced Placement or college level courses; (d) credit recovery (allowing students to retake a course they previously failed to "recover" credit); and (e) resolving scheduling conflicts

(Picciano and Seaman 2009). In 2006, Michigan was the first state to require students to complete an online course for high school graduation. Alabama has created a web-based professional development program for inservice teachers to promote increased content knowledge, improved teaching practice, and student achievement. In addition to students in traditional school settings, home-schooled students represent a potentially large and lucrative market for online learning. The online movement provides increased educational opportunities for students by removing or minimizing barriers that may exist in brick-and-mortar schools.

A variety of providers have entered the online learning field, including school districts, state-sponsored groups, charter schools, and for-profit vendors. The wide variety of e-learning courses introduces into the educational arena the element of competition for students. The potential for districts to lose per-pupil funding to online learning entities has attracted the attention of policy makers and budget directors. A critical issue is the difference between providers that *complement* existing schools versus providers that *compete* with them for student enrollment. Some cyber schools offer full-time enrollment opportunities and compete head-to-head with local school districts for students and funding over a broad geographic region. Other supplemental providers offer individual course opportunities that create new learning choices for students enrolled in traditional brick-and-mortar schools (Watson, Winograd, and Kalmon 2004).

Oversight of program quality for online learning represents an important challenge for school leaders. Many of the same characteristics of quality learning apply to e-learning and face-to-face instruction: course organization, curriculum design, instructional design, and student/teacher interactions. Technology and course delivery aspects are unique for e-learning environments and require special attention (McPherson and Nunest 2008). Statewide online offerings may benefit from quality oversight at the state level. Online courses offered by districts are subject to "local control" oversight similar to brick-and-mortar schools. Differences in program rigor may put some online courses at a competitive disadvantage with lower-quality courses offered by competing providers. One approach to providing oversight for quality, equity, and accountability is the establishment of and requirement for internal compliance mechanisms. Online programs formulate their own policies and goals, develop processes to meet these goals and submit reports to state, district, or other oversight groups. Internal compliance mechanisms require education agencies to have sufficient staffing to provide meaningful oversight. Although virtual schools are expected to meet state content standards, mechanisms to check for alignment are often lacking. In some cases, state-generated end-of-course examinations serve as useful quality-control indicators for online courses (Watson, Winograd, and Kalmon 2004).

In addition to program quality, online learning raises the issue of teacher quality. While most states require online teachers to meet state licensure or certification standards, some (such as Michigan) recognize that the teacher may be licensed in another state. In this case, Michigan requires a certified teacher to be assigned to students as an on-site mentor. To protect student access to teachers, some states mandate that teachers of virtual courses be online and available for students on a daily basis during specified hours. Student-to-teacher ratios raise additional concerns in the virtual learning environment. Minnesota has set 40:1 as a limit for student-to-teacher ratios for online learning classes. California has mandated that the student-to-teacher ratio in the online world be substantially the same as in the "real classroom" (Watson, Winograd, and Kalmon 2004).

Student support for learning in an online world varies considerably. If the student attends a brick-and-mortar school and uses online courses as a supplemental learning opportunity, then student support can easily be provided through the school. A school online learning coordinator can help students with technical issues, check up on course progress, and monitor homework completion. For a cyber-school environment where a student enrolls in the entire educational program through an online learning vendor or state agency, no physical location may be available to provide students with this type of support. Parents, e-mail, or telephone calls may serve as a secondary support system (Watson, Winograd, and Kalmon 2004).

Providing a Reliable Technology Infrastructure

The task of providing reliable and compatible educational technology for schools requires leaders to consider both initial purchase plans as well as the often hidden costs of ownership. Compatibility with existing equipment, sufficient memory and adequate operating systems, manufacturer reliability, warranties, and performance record should be considered in addition to price when making a purchase decision. Initial costs include not only hardware, software and peripherals, but also installation and professional development so that teachers are able to integrate the new technology into their instructional programs. Ongoing costs include routine maintenance, upgrades for hardware and possibly memory, repairing broken equipment, troubleshooting, technical support, and supplies such as batteries for handheld devices, printer cartridges, or projector bulbs (Brooks-Young 2006). One study estimated that ongoing costs may total one-third to one-half of the initial investment (Rothstein and McKnight 1996).

Technology-ready instructional spaces require careful planning. The work of teachers and students can be supported when consideration is given to both electrical and software requirements as well as the work patterns of the people who will actually work in the room. Sightlines, space for collaborative working groups, maintenance issues (can you easily pull out the computers to work on them?), access to USB ports for peripheral devices, and glare from classroom windows, if ignored, can render even the most expensive workspace inefficient for teaching and learning. Conversation with teachers and students regarding design of classroom technology rooms can provide architects and planners with valuable knowledge to design useful and productive spaces. An Internet connection on a wall opposite from the classroom computer creates a practical problem. Tech-ready facilities include appropriate furniture, thoughtfully planned traffic patterns, lighting that allows students to read digital displays, HVAC, and having electrical and network drops in convenient and usable locations (Brooks-Young 2006).

Software and network concerns can create headaches for both administrators and teachers. Denying teachers administrator rights to add and delete software from individual computer stations seems prudent in light of incidences when individuals have crashed entire networks by installation of incompatible or virus-infected programs. However, if technical support personnel are stretched thin, teachers may experience unnecessarily long wait times before the tech guy attends to their request. Sometimes software standardization policies require teachers to stop using older programs they have been previously using successfully in their classroom instruction. Frustration and discouragement might lead the teacher to stop any further technology integration efforts. Balancing the competing goals of providing safe and secure computing resources for teachers, students, and staff with the cost of maintaining a network requires collaboration and active involvement of all stakeholders (Brooks-Young 2006). A reliable infrastructure is a necessary condition for a 21st-century school.

Conclusion

In summary, citizens in the 21st century live in a digital age in which the advance of electronic technologies in all aspects of life continues at an astounding rate. Transformational leadership in the educational community is critical for effective and appropriate infusion of educational technology as a fundamental part of K–12 education. Leaders who value quality teaching and learning can harness the power of strong communities of school-based and community-based leaders to direct the future of educational technology as a force in education. In the 21st century, educational opportunities at brick-and-mortar schools as well as through virtual learning communities will broaden opportunities for students of all ages.

References

Becker, H. U., J L. Ravitz, and Y. Wong. 1999. *Teacher and teacher-directed student use of computers and software, report #3.* Irvine, CA: University of California, Center for Research on Information Technology and Organizations.

Brooks-Young, S. 2006. *Critical technology issues for school leaders.* Thousand Oaks, CA: Corwin Press.

Cavanaugh, C., K. Gillan, J. Kromrey, M. Hess, and R. Blomeyer. 2004. *The effects of distance education on K–12 student outcomes: A meta-analysis.* Naperville, IL, Learning Point Associates.

Davis, M. R. 2009. Breaking away from tradition: E-Learning opens new doors to raise achievement. *Education Week* 28 (26): 8–9.

Fies, C., and J. Marshall. 2006. Classroom response systems: A review of the literature. *Journal of Science Education and Technology* 15 (1): 101–109.

Fullan, M. 2002. Leadership and sustainability. *Principal Leadership* 3 (4): 1–9.

Gurr, D. 2004. ICT, leadership in education and e-leadership. *Discourse: Studies in the Cultural Politics of Education* 25 (1): 113–124.

Hake, R. 1998. Interactive engagement versus traditional methods: A six-thousand student survey of mechanics test data for introductory physics courses. *American Journal of Physics* 66 (1): 64–74.

Honey, M., K. Culp, and R. Spielvogel. 2005. *Critical issue: Using technology to improve student achievement. www.ncrel.org/sdrs/areas/issues/methods/technlgy/te800.htm*

International Society for Technology in Education (ISTE). 2002. *ISTE NETS for Administrators, 2002. www.iste.org/Content/NavigationMenu/NETS/ForAdministrators/NETS_for_Administrators.htm*

——. 2009. *ISTE NETS for Administrators 2009. www.iste.org/Content/NavigationMenu/NETS/ForAdministrators/NETS_for_Administrators.htm*

Irving, K. E., V. A. Sanalan, and M. L. Shirley. 2009. Physical science connected classrooms: Case studies. *Journal of Computers in Mathematics and Science Teaching* 28 (3): 247–275.

Kearsley, G., and W. Lynch. 1992. Educational leadership in the age of technology: The new skills. *Journal of Research on Computing in Education* 25 (1): 50–60.

Ladyshewsky, R., I. Geoghegan, S. Jones, and B. Oliver. 2008. A virtual academic leadership program using a blend of technologies. *The International Journal of Learning* 14 (12): 53–62.

Loucks-Horsley, S., N. Love, K. E. Stiles, P. W. Hewson, and S. Mundry. 2003. *Designing professional development for teachers of science and mathematics*, 2nd ed. Thousand Oaks, CA: Corwin Press.

Lyman, P., and H. R. Varian. 2003. *How much information? www2.sims.berkeley.edu/research/projects/how-much-info-2003*

McPherson, M. A., and J. M. Nunest. 2008. Critical issues for e-learning delivery: What may seem obvious is not always put into practice. *Journal of Computer Assisted Learning* 24: 433–445.

Owens, D. T., K. E. Irving, S. J. Pape, L. Abrahamson, V. Sanalan, and C. K. Boscardin. 2007. The connected classroom: Implementation and research trial. In *Proceedings of the ED-MEDIA world conference on educational multimedia, hypermedia and telecommunications*, eds. C. Montgomerie and J. Seale, 3710–3716. Chesapeake, VA: Association for the Advancement of Computing in Education.

Parsad, B., and J. Jones. 2005. *Internet access in U. S. public schools and class-*

rooms: *1994–2003 (NCES 2005-015)*. U.S. Department of Education. Washington, DC: NCES.

Picciano, A. G., and J. Seaman, eds. 2009. *K–12 online learning: A 2008 follow-up of the survey of U.S. school district administrators*. Needham, MA: Sloan-C.

Reeves, T. C. 1998. *The impact of media and technology in schools: A research report prepared for the Bertelsmann Foundation*. http://it.coe.uga.edu/~treeves/edit6900/BertelsmannReeves98.pdf

Ringstaff, C., and L. Kelley. 2002. *The learning return on our educational technology investment: A review of findings from research*. San Francisco: West Ed RTEC.

Rogers, E. M. 2003. *Diffusion of innovations*, 5th ed. New York, NY: Free Press.

Roschelle, J., W. R. Penuel, and L. Abrahamson. 2004. The networked classroom. *Educational Leadership* 61 (5): 50–54.

Rothstein, R. I., and L. McKnight. 1996. *Technology and cost models for connecting K–12 schools to the national information infrastructure*. Washington DC: National Science Foundation.

Schein, E. H. 1985. *Organizational culture and leadership*. San Francisco: Jossey Bass.

Turkle, S. 1984. *The second self: Computers and the human spirit*. New York: Simon and Schuster.

Valdez, G. 2004. *Critical issue: Technology leadership: Enhancing positive educational change*. Naperville, IL: North Central Regional Educational Laboratory.

Watson, J. F., K. Winograd, and S. Kalmon. 2004. *Education evolution: The need to keep pace with development of K–12 online learning* (No. 17). Napierville, IL: Learning Point Associates.

Zhao, Y., and K. Frank. 2003. Factors affecting technology uses in schools: An ecological perspective. *American Educational Research Journal* 40 (4): 807–840.

Chapter 10

The Role of Leadership in Fostering Inquiry-Based Learning and Teaching

Emily van Zee

Personal concepts of leadership, like concepts of teaching, evolve. As a first-year middle school science teacher, I accepted my role without question: I stood in front of rows of students and delivered information. Now, as an experienced educator of science teachers, I perceive my role differently: My intent is to foster a community of inquiry. Even at conferences, I move chairs out of rows into circles so that all can see one another and participate in the conversation. My ideas about leadership also have evolved. I originally thought that a leader was the person who decides what to do and when, how, and why to do it. Now I realize that a leader is someone who nurtures the informed decisions, actions, and understandings of others. These shifts in my personal beliefs and practices have been deeply influenced by experiences I have had with individuals and institutions while attempting to carry out changes advocated in science education reform documents.

In this chapter, I first comment upon concepts of inquiry and leadership presented in the *National Science Education Standards* (NRC 1996).

Then I present examples of leaders who foster inquiry-based learning and teaching within the context of classrooms, local communities, schools and districts, college science classrooms, teacher preparation programs, and professional development experiences. Quotes from their writings provide evidence of leadership in these diverse settings. I also note ways in which I have used many of these examples in courses designed to prepare prospective and practicing teachers to (a) foster inquiry-based learning and teaching and (b) become active researchers in their own classrooms.

Concepts of Inquiry and Leadership in the *National Science Education Standards*

The National Research Council declared in Teacher Standard A of the *National Science Education Standards* that "teachers of science plan an inquiry-based science program for their students" (1996, p. 30). A description of inquiry included engaging students in

asking questions, planning and conducting investigations, using appropriate tools and techniques to gather data, thinking critically and logically about relationships between evidence and explanations, constructing and analyzing alternative explanations, and communicating scientific arguments (p. 105).

Recommendations included shifts in emphases toward "providing opportunities for scientific discussion and debate among students" (p. 52) and toward "science as argument and explanation" (p. 113). Inquiry approaches are more than just hands-on activities; they should involve students in discussing what they think and why, including citing evidence from observations to support claims. Professional Development Standard A declared that teachers, as well as students, should learn science content "through the perspectives and methods of inquiry" (p. 59).

The *National Science Education Standards* also recommended changing emphases from "teacher as follower" toward "teacher as leader" and from "teacher as target of change" toward "teacher as source and facilitator of change" (p. 72). This expanded concept of the leadership role for teachers included recognizing the potential for teachers to be legitimate generators of knowledge. Professional Development Standard C stated "Professional development activities must... provide opportunities to learn and use the skills of research to generate new knowledge about science and the teaching and learning of science" (p. 68). Science Program Standard E declared that "schools must work as communities that encourage, support, and sustain teachers as they implement an effective science program.... An effective leadership structure that includes teachers must be in place" (p. 222). The implication is that teachers should be centrally involved as leaders in shifting science instruction toward inquiry-based practices.

Leadership in Fostering Inquiry Within the Classroom

What does it mean to provide an inquiry-based science program? How does a teacher lead students in engaging in and reflecting on inquiries into natural phenomena? This chapter draws heavily on writings and websites by teachers who have documented their approaches to inquiry-based teaching and learning. By writing about their own teaching practices and students' learning, these teachers have provided many examples of the role of teacher as an "intellectual leader" (Dewey 1933, p. 337) for their students. In *How We Think*, Dewey noted

> The problem of the pupils is found in the subject matter; the problem of the teacher is *what the minds of the pupils are doing with that subject matter* [italics in the original].... Flexibility, ability to take advantage of unexpected incidents and questions, depends upon the teacher's coming to the subject with freshness and fullness of interest and knowledge. There are questions that he (sic) should ask.... What do the minds of pupils bring to the topic from their previous experience and study? How can I help them make connections? What need, even if unrecognized by them, will furnish a leverage to move their minds in the desired direction? What uses and applications will clarify the subject and fix it in their minds? How can the topic be individualized; that is how shall it be treated so that each one will have something distinctive to contribute while the subject is also adapted to the special deficiencies and particular tastes of each one? (pp. 338–340).

Recent examples of ways that teachers have addressed such elements of inquiry-based teaching and learning are presented on the following pages.

In *Doing What Scientists Do: Children Learn to Investigate Their World*, Ellen Doris (1991) discusses ways in which she creates an environment for science in the primary classroom, encourages students to share their findings during class meetings, facilitates student observations during work periods, interprets children's writings and drawings, and prepares her students for field trips. Throughout her book, she presents transcripts of conversations with her students as well as copies of their work. In addition, she explicitly comments upon the role of the teacher during science meetings:

> As teacher, I determined when we would start our science work but the children helped to define what that work would be, and what procedures or rules would help us carry out the work in our room. Similar collaboration is critical in this first sharing meeting (p. 72). The teacher can help children articulate or demonstrate their discoveries. She can also help keep track of observations, ideas, or questions.... In science it is important to articulate what you have seen, what connections you are making, what questions you have. Teachers can help children do this (p. 75).

Doris also provides an example of the teacher as a "source and facilitator of change" (NRC 1996, p. 72) in the closing chapter on making changes. Here she reports on problems and possible solutions articulated by teachers participating in a summer science workshop. This book does not look like an elementary science-teaching-methods textbook. However, I have used it that way to provide vivid images of inquiry-based learning and teaching for prospective teachers.

In *Talking Their Way Into Science: Hearing Children's Questions and Theories, Responding With Curricula,* Karen Gallas (1995) presents transcripts for a series of "science talks" with elementary children, in which she opens up topics for discussion. She discusses the "cacophony" that sometimes occurs as excited children all start talking at once. This is a phenomenon that teachers commonly encounter when they try shifting toward more open-ended discussions. In commenting upon a student's contribution to a discussion, Gallas wrote

> In the process of a vociferous correction of that idea, many voices broke out in excitement. The tape at this point recorded so much concurrent talk that it was impossible to transcribe, but cacophony in the Science Talks always signals that a break is going to be made in the children's thinking. Although Molly had made an incorrect statement,

her further elaboration of Allen's and Brandy's ideas, and her changing of Allen's vague use of the word "attracted to" to "blown" (a term that Shelly had used in the first minute of that talk) triggered the next leap of thought, and that is what produced the rush of voices (p. 37).

Rather than trying to repress such outbursts, Gallas shares her perception that these seem to be times when the children are making extraordinary conceptual progress. This book can help teachers envision alternatives to maintaining tight control over who says what in class. We have used it, for example, as a prelude to introducing interpretative practices to teachers in a summer institute. In follow-up meetings during the academic year, we then engaged participants in watching videos of conversations about science in their own classrooms. With transcripts in hand, they could identify student utterances by particular lines and discuss with one another these specific instances of student thinking (Hammer and van Zee 2006).

In *Nurturing Inquiry: Real Science for the Elementary Classroom*, Charles Pearce (1999) provides detailed examples and handouts designed to initiate and sustain inquiry in his fifth-grade classroom. He introduces these with a comment elucidating a teacher's role in structuring inquiry:

> Inviting inquiry science into the classroom does not mean chaos will follow. For inquiry to be manageable and beneficial, structure must be planned and implemented. Formal activities at the start of the year will give way to less controlled and restricted activities later. Trusting each student as a scientist also means expecting clearly defined outcomes. Students must understand that as scientists they are expected to question and probe; to design fair tests; to gather data and clearly record discoveries; to compare findings with one another as they search for patterns and connections; and to assess the validity of their own research and the research of others. The following chapters describe a philosophy and range of ideas that will help guide students from the first day of the school year and help sustain inquiry to the very last (pp. 6–7).

By presenting and discussing such ways of encouraging student-to-student engagement, Pearce provides many specific examples for teachers that are interested in shifting toward more inquiry-based practices but are unsure of how to go about doing so. One chapter focuses upon the Kids' Inquiry

Conference, during which students present their results to one another and engage in spirited discussions about their findings. This contrasts with science fairs in which students stressfully perform before adult judges. Reading about the Kids' Inquiry Conference inspired teachers in a teacher research group that I facilitated (Lay 2000). They initiated a Science Inquiry Conference that evolved into a countywide process engaging students from many diverse communities in discussing their findings with one another. This is an example of teachers serving as facilitators of change, based on knowledge generated and communicated by other teachers.

On the website *Feeling at Home in the Science Classroom* (*http://feelingathome.org*), Claire Bove presents video clips, copies of student work, and her own reflections about establishing a community in her middle school classroom, fostering a playful approach to experimentation, talking and arguing about science, and explaining and questioning to develop understanding. These are all elements of her approach to inquiry-based learning and teaching that she has chosen to share via the internet. Her website includes her responses to questions asked by prospective teachers who perused her website in my science teaching methods courses. One viewer left a message on her comment page that read:

> You gave words to everything I have been thinking and feeling as I try, in my second year as a teacher, to make my 6th and 7th grade science classes meaningful and productive for my students. I love all your ideas and will start using some of them when I return to the classroom after spring break next week. Your student body and observations of minority students exactly mirrors my experience in my Philadelphia middle school. Since I began teaching as a mid-life career change I feel a sense of urgency to become the best teacher I can as fast as I can. I don't have 20 years to become the master teacher I strive to be. I want to be there in 5 years! You will help me reach that goal! Thank you so much for this most valuable, instructive and supportive website! (website comment, March 16, 2008).

Such comments are evidence of the leadership teachers can provide to distant and unknown colleagues by sharing findings via the internet from research on their own teaching practices and students' learning.

The *Diagnoser* (*www.diagnoser.com*) is an example of an extensive internet resource developed by a high school physics teacher, Jim Minstrell, and colleagues. This web-based assessment system evolved from the questions Minstrell asked his students in order to diagnose their thinking. He organized their responses into "facets" of knowledge. He then used these to simulate the diagnostic process of a teacher listening closely to students and responding in ways that lead students to the next steps in thinking (Minstrell 2000).

In *Connecting Girls and Science: Constructivism, Feminism, and Science Education Reform*, Elaine Howes (2002) shares her experiences in teaching a high school biology course in which she studied a question that she had formulated: "What can intensive listening to students tell us about their thinking and beliefs concerning their images of science as a social enterprise?" (p. 2). In reflecting upon the vigorous conversations she recorded and interpreted, Howes wrote:

> As a feminist critical teacher, I wanted students to talk, for three basic reasons: I believe that talking is vital to good learning, because students achieve deeper understanding by describing, explaining, and making connections between their lives and scientific concepts; I want them to express their opinions, as a political choice; and, I want to learn what they are thinking in order to teach them the science better. These ideas overlap, particularly in the sense of connecting self to content. Throughout this unit, especially when students were saying exceptionally interesting things, with lots of people talking at once, I am reminded of Karen Gallas's (1995) hypothesis that when students are making a conceptual breakthrough, they get very excited, which often results in lots of students talking at the same time. Unfortunately, this is usually considered disruptive behavior—we continue, even in this enlightened time, to think that children should be seen and not heard (p. 140).

This author is engaging in a professional conversation via published literature. The leadership that Gallas (1995) provided by publicly sharing her ideas about science talks influenced the positive way that Howes perceived and valued her own students' behavior. Aware that some observers might view such "cacophony" negatively, Howes drew support from reading Gallas's analyses, and she offers similar support to others by publicly writing about this phenomenon in her own context.

Leadership Within the Local Community

How can teachers and students extend their inquiries into their local communities? With support from the Carnegie Foundation for the Advancement of Teachers, a group of teachers developed websites documenting their teaching practices and students' learning (*http://gallery.carnegie foundation.org/gallery_of_tl/castl_k12.html*). Among these are studies in which teachers and their students made substantial contributions to their local communities.

In a website entitled *Looking Beyond Themselves: Preparing Students to Become Invested Members of Their Community*, Anne Pfitzner describes how she involved her sixth-grade students in a local issue:

> This classroom project had to do with a piece of riverfront property that was recently acquired by our community. How could we help to ensure that this piece would be different from the strip mall, Arby's, and tire shop that already lined the banks of Alaska's famous Kenai River? Initially, after many discussions my students and I worked to create a survey that was distributed randomly throughout the community. Together we worked to analyze, create a scale model, and present the results of this survey to the community in several different settings. This web page will give you a sense of the journey my sixth grade students and I experienced as we began to address this need in our community.... I now see a group of students who have a continued interest in working with city planners on other issues. They are truly invested in improving the living standards in our community. Seeing the responses of community members and leaders to their hard work, they knew they had made a direct impact and this showed in their daily attitudes. This authentic, project based learning helped to inspire me as well as my students as together we looked beyond the needs of our everyday life to become invested citizens in our own community. Through this web page, I hope to share the integral pieces of this journey. (*http://gallery.carnegiefoundation.org/collections/castl_k12/apfitzner/introopeningessay.html*)

Pfitzner's leadership as a teacher not only provided useful input for her community, but it also communicated via the website the strategies she used so that other interested teachers can learn from her experiences.

In *Pio Pico Student Researchers Participatory Action Research: From Class-*

room to Community, Transforming Teaching and Learning, Emily Wolk describes ways in which she and a group of elementary students collected data, developed interpretations, and lobbied officials to get a traffic light installed at a dangerous intersection near their school. She quotes a student's reflection about this process:

> I joined this group because I wanted to have a better and safer community than it is. I like to come to our meetings, because the more time I have to work on this, the better my community will be.... I have changed a lot because I was very shy and now I'm really loud. I've done presentations in San Diego in front of 300 people. I've also talked to reporters from newspapers and television. I've talked to dignitaries from the city. I think I've changed because of my friends because they're really loud too. And, I'm getting a lot of friends and my voice is getting louder. (*http://gallery.carnegiefoundation.org/collections/ castl_k12/ewolk/index.html*)

The website includes video of the children using radar guns to document the speed of passing vehicles and videos of interviews with the students about their community-based action research.

I use these and other teacher writings and websites in courses for prospective and practicing teachers (van Zee n.d., 2007). After perusing Wolk's website, for example, one prospective teacher posted the following reflection on our electronic bulletin board in response to the prompt: "What have you learned from exploring this view into the world of this teacher and these students?"

> I have learned what a large impact one teacher and her class can make on the community. I think that this website was very motivating and made me realize that each one of us can make a difference in the communities that we teach in.

Another prospective teacher wrote:

> This website and activity have gotten me very excited to teach science. For me, it is a subject that has never really interested me, but I feel like I will be a much more beneficial teacher if I can come up with a way to make science pertain to real life situations so students want to get involved.

This shows that reflecting on websites such as these can contribute to positive shifts in attitude about teaching and learning science. Such comments provide confirming evidence of the Standards' stance that teachers can contribute to knowledge about teaching and learning and serve as a source for changing attitudes and practices.

Leadership Within the School and District

The previous examples have illustrated ways in which individual teachers have served as intellectual leaders (Dewey 1933) in their own classrooms while enacting inquiry-based approaches to learning and teaching. A close reading of these writings and websites indicates that these authors typically have had access to resources garnered by university faculty and/or foundation officials in projects that draw participants from a variety of settings. Thus, these projects have provided the authors with groups of colleagues who, although dispersed throughout different schools and sometimes even different states, supported one another with questions, comments, and ongoing encouragement to teach and reflect upon new methods being advocated in reform documents.

What issues do teachers who assume leadership roles encounter while fostering reforms within their own schools and districts? In *Teacher Research for Better Schools*, Mohr et al. (2004) reflect upon their experiences leading a teacher researcher network within one district. In the opening chapter, entitled "Our Journey: Supporting Teacher Research in Schools," they describe the vision for this project as follows:

> We also believed that knowledge is built collaboratively within schools. We wanted to shape the project to give teachers support as they conducted research with their colleagues and used the resulting knowledge to inform decisions about classroom teaching and learning, curriculum and school programs, and, ultimately, school policies. It would be a project led by teacher researchers themselves, transforming classrooms and schools from the inside out. The role of the central office would be one of support and facilitation rather than of direction and mandate (p. 4).

In a later chapter, entitled Teacher Researcher Leadership, they discuss some of the challenges the teacher researcher leaders encountered in their new roles in their schools as "teachers who lead and follow. They are peer researchers who facilitate the learning of others. They lead by asking questions, at times exposing their uncertainty and vulnerability, characteristics often not associated with leadership" (p. 128). Although not focused specifically on reforming science instruction, these reflections offer many insights relevant for teachers undertaking leadership of colleagues in their own schools.

In *Creating Scientific Communities in the Elementary Classroom*, Reddy et al. (1998) provide an example of collaboration among two teachers and two university researchers during the long-term development of a newly formed school as a science magnet where children learn through questioning, exploring, and discussing. In their acknowledgments, they explicitly comment on the essential role of a supportive principal: "As principal of the Goddard School of Science and Technology, she often speaks about 'inviting children into learning.' Her belief that a school can be a community of inquiry, for adults and children alike, has also invited us into learning" (p. ix). This principal had been instrumental in designing and implementing the school/university partnership that underlay the collaboration among these teachers and researchers.

Leadership Within College Science Classrooms

Teachers' attitudes toward science are affected by their experiences learning science, often negatively if they have been taught science as passive recipients of information in large lecture-based courses. One teacher in our projects stated, for example, "My experience in science has been quite negative.... Physical science in college was a nightmare" (van Zee et al. 2005, p. 1008). How have college science departments responded to the Standards' recommendation that prospective teachers learn science in a different way, through the methods and perspectives of inquiry?

In *Reform in Undergraduate Science Teaching for the 21st Century*, Sunal, Wright, and Day (2004) echo Reddy et al.'s recognition of the importance of a supportive administration:

> Administrative leadership is critical. There must be an identifiable administrator who is highly respected and willing to counter all aspects of institutional resistance to change. The person must aggressively and faithfully represent the planning team's proposal with peers,

central administration, students, the public schools and alumni. This leader, supported by the planning team as a whole, must also have a vision for establishing the proposed new program as a long-term endeavor (p. 39).

Chapter authors report on reform of college science courses led by interdisciplinary collaborative teams of science and education faculty, students, administrators, and public school personnel with support by grants from a government agency, the National Aeronautics and Space Administration, through the NASA Opportunities for Visionary Academics (NOVA) program (*http://education.nasa.gov/nova*).

An example of leadership by professional societies is the Physics Teacher Education Coalition, a national network of over one hundred institutions committed to developing and promoting excellence in physics and physical science teacher preparation with support from the National Science Foundation and corporate sponsors. Its website, *www.phystec.org*, offers extensive resources, including strategies for physics course transformation, information about interactive curricula and methods, and links to institutions that have implemented reforms.

Individual instructors also have contributed insights and findings by conducting research in the context of their efforts to offer inquiry-based courses for teachers. In *Learning to Teach Physics Through Inquiry: The Lived Experience of a Graduate Teaching Assistant*, for example, Volkmann and Zgagacz (2004) reflect upon ways in which the instructor (Volkmann) mentored his graduate assistant (Zgagacz) in understanding and shifting from traditional to reform-based practices in a physics course for prospective elementary school teachers.

In *Professional Development Enhanced: Who Is Responsible for Preparing Science Teachers?*, Otero et al. (2006) describe an innovative program that puts undergraduates in leadership positions as learning assistants who assist college science faculty in making their courses more student-centered, interactive, and collaborative. Outcomes included not only increased student performance but also recruitment of learning assistants into certification programs for science teachers.

Leadership Within Teacher Preparation Programs

What will increase the likelihood that graduates of a science teacher preparation program will choose to engage their students in inquiries into natural phenomena? Windschitl (2003), a leader in designing longitudinal research to examine this issue, reports some of his findings in *Inquiry Projects in Science Teacher Education: What Can Investigative Experiences Reveal About Teacher Thinking and Eventual Classroom Practice?* He documented prospective teachers' conceptions of inquiry and ways they enacted inquiry-based projects during a science teaching methods course and later during student teaching. Those who used guided and open inquiry during student teaching had had significant undergraduate or professional experiences with authentic science research. He advocates that "independent science investigations be part of preservice education and that these experiences should be scaffolded to prompt reflection specifically about the nature of inquiry and conceptually linked to ways in which inquiry can be brought into the K–12 classroom" (p. 112). In the Teachers' Learning Trajectories Project, Windschitl and colleagues currently are documenting the ways that novice teachers engage secondary students in inquiry across four contexts: their teacher education coursework, student teaching, sessions of analysis of their pupils' work, and their early years as practicing teachers.

In an entire issue of *Science Education*, Hewson and colleagues provide an outstanding example of research on a teacher education program. In *Educating Prospective Teachers of Biology: Findings, Limitations, and Recommendations*, Hewson et al. (1999) summarize a series of articles in order to form a comprehensive report on efforts to shift prospective teachers' conceptions of teaching from transmitting facts toward eliciting and refining students' conceptions. In addition to attention to the on-campus components of the program, they commented upon the importance of leadership by the cooperating teacher: "The cooperating teacher is a powerful role model, whether positive or negative; his or her beliefs and teaching approaches can significantly influence the direction of a prospective teacher's development" (p. 381).

Most research on such field experiences has been conducted in the context of student teaching. Abell (2006), however, calls for research on field experiences in conjunction with science teaching methods courses in *Challenges and Opportunities for Field Experiences in Elementary Science Teacher Preparation*: "Ethnographies and phenomenological studies of teacher apprenticeships could help to examine what happens as students of science teaching become teachers of science, and what facilitates and constrains their learning" (p. 85).

In *The Continuum of Secondary Science Teacher Preparation*, Collins and Gillespie (2009) present reviews of the literature and calls for research in chapters composed by working groups of scientists, science teacher educators, and teachers who examined multiple aspects of secondary science teacher preparation. This is an example of leadership by a foundation through the sponsoring of a conference and the issuance of an invitation to participants to summarize research findings and articulate new directions for research that could improve teacher preparation programs.

Leadership Within Professional Development Experiences

How can national, state, district, school, and teacher leaders organize and deliver professional development that enhances teachers' interest and ability to engage their students in inquiries into natural phenomena? National leadership from government agencies such as the National Science Foundation has prompted systemic initiatives and a vast array of programs providing professional development for teachers. A goal of the Math Science Partnerships (MSP), for example, is to "develop mathematics and science teachers as school- and district-based intellectual leaders and master teachers" (*www.nsf.gov/ehr/MSP/nsf05069_3.jsp*). Our MSP project culminates in participants' developing, facilitating, and evaluating professional development experiences for colleagues within their own schools.

In *Designing Professional Development for Teachers of Science and Mathematics*, Loucks-Horsley et al. (2003) call for professional development "placing learning and student thinking at the center ... and as a result ... adopt(ing) many practice-based strategies such as examining student work and using cases of student learning to deepen understanding of content and how children learn it" (p. 44).

An example of such professional development is described by Flick (2005) in *Developing Understanding of Scientific Inquiry in Secondary Students*:

After a year of concentrated work, these teachers developed broad concepts of classroom implementations of inquiry. Descriptions of classroom inquiry reflected attention to learning goals that went beyond task completion. Improved classroom discourse was directly influenced by increased cognitive engagement of students such that teachers developed skills for listening and interpreting student thinking (p. 168).

In *Teaching Nature of Science Through Inquiry: Results of a 3-Year Professional Development Program*, Akerson and Hanuscin (2007) reflected on the processes that they would retain about the monthly workshops they had facilitated at a school:

We would lead teachers through specific explicit activities designed to help them see how to use such explicit activities with their own students. The monthly workshops should be retained also to give teachers a venue for discussing their instruction—the activities they are trying, and to provide feedback to one another. The monthly workshops also can serve as a venue for teachers to raise questions and refine their ideas (p. 676).

A possible outcome of such professional development programs is an increased sense of confidence by the participants and their emergence as leaders in their schools and communities. In *From Science Teacher to Teacher Leader: Leadership Development as Meaning Making in a Community of Practice*, Howe and Stubbs (2003) identified four characteristics of such a program: (1) mutual respect between participating scientists and teachers, (2) challenging tasks, (3) creation of a community of practice, and (4) opportunities for teachers to assume leadership roles. Such roles included planning and facilitating activities for other teachers in their schools and districts, leading program workshops, writing and field-testing curriculum, and participating in and presenting at local, state, and national meetings.

Conclusion

The examples presented here have been drawn from literature that celebrates teachers as active participants in inquiries into science learning and teaching. The National Science Teachers Association has recognized the importance of such inquiries through Teacher Researcher Day at national conferences. During a full day of activities, teachers and teacher educators share their insights and findings. We invite you to join us there!

References

Abell, S. 2006. Challenges and opportunities for field experiences in elementary science teacher preparation. In *Elementary science teacher education: International perspectives on contemporary issues and practices*, ed. K. Appleton, 73–89. Mahwah, NJ: Lawrence Erlbaum.

Akerson, V., and D. L. Hanuscin. 2007. Teaching nature of science through inquiry: Results of a 3-year professional development program. *Journal of Research in Science Teaching* 44 (5): 653–680.

Collins, A., and N. Gillespie, eds. 2009. *The continuum of secondary science teacher preparation: Knowledge, questions and research recommendations*. Boston: Sense Publications.

Dewey, J. 1933/2008. *How we think*. In *The later works of John Dewey, Volume 8, 1925–1953: 1933, Essays and how we think, revised edition*, ed. J. A. Boydston. Carbondale, IL: Southern Illinois University Press.

Doris, E. 1991. *Doing what scientists do: Children learn to investigate their world*. Portsmouth, NH: Heinemann.

Flick, L. 2005. Developing understanding of scientific inquiry in secondary students. In *Scientific inquiry and nature of science: Implications for teaching, learning, and teacher education*, eds. L. Flick and N. G. Lederman, 157–172. New York: Springer

Gallas, K. 1995. *Talking their way into science: Hearing children's questions and theories, responding with curricula*. New York: Teachers College Press.

Hammer, D., and E. H. van Zee. 2006. *Seeing the science in children's thinking: Case studies of student inquiry in physical science*. Portsmouth, NH: Heinemann.

Hewson, P. W., B. R. Tabachnick, K. M. Zeichner, and J. Lemberger. 1999. Educating prospective teachers of biology: Findings, limitations, and recommendations. *Science Education* 83: 373–384.

Howe, A. C., and H. S. Stubbs 2003. From science teacher to teacher leader: Leadership development as meaning making in a community of practice. *Science Education* 87 (2): 281–297.

Howes, E. V. 2002. *Connecting girls and science: Constructivism, feminism, and science education reform*. New York: Teachers College Press.

Lay, D. 2000. Science Inquiry Conference—a better way! In *Inquiring into inquiry teaching and learning in science*, eds. J. Minstrell, and E. H. van Zee. Washington, DC: American Association for the Advancement of Science.

Loucks-Horsley, S., N. Love, K. E. Stiles, S. Mundry, and P. W. Hewson. 2003. *Designing professional development for teachers of science and mathematics*, 2nd ed. Thousand Oaks, CA: Corwin Press.

Minstrell, J. 2000. Student thinking and related assessment: Creating a facet assessment-based learning environment. In *Grading the nation's report card: Research from the Eevaluation of NAEP*, eds. J. Pellegrino, L. Jones, and K. Mitchell, Washington DC: National Academy Press.

Mohr, M. M., C. Rogers, B. Sanford, M. A. Nocerino, M. S. MacLean, and S. Clawson. 2004. *Teacher research for better schools*. New York: Teachers College Press.

Otero, V., N. Finkelstein, R. McCray, and S. Pollock. 2006. Professional development enhanced: Who is responsible for preparing science teachers? *Science* 313 (5786): 445–446.

Pearce, C. 1999. *Nurturing inquiry: Real science for the elementary classroom*. Portsmouth, NH: Heinemann.

Reddy, M., P. Jacobs, C. McCrohon, and L. R. Herrenkohl. 1998. *Creating scientific communities in the elementary classroom*. Portsmouth, NH: Heinemann.

Sunal, D. W., E. L. Wright, and J. B. Day, eds. 2004. *Reform in undergraduate science teaching for the 21st century*. Charlotte, NC: Information Age Publishing.

van Zee, E. H. n.d. Exhibition: Studies in science contexts. *www.cfkeep.org/html/snapshot.php?id=88988139749494*

van Zee, E. H. 2007. Reflections on fostering teacher inquiries into science learning and teaching. In *Teacher research: Stories of learning and growing*, eds. D. Roberts, C. Bove, and E. H. van Zee, 138–155. Arlington, VA: NSTA Press.

van Zee, E. H., D. Hammer, M. Bell, P. Roy, and J. Peter. 2005. Learning and teaching science as inquiry: A case study of elementary school teachers' investigations of light. *Science Education* 89 (6): 1007–1042.

Volkmann, M. J., and M. Zgagacz. 2004. Learning to teach physics through inquiry: The lived experience of a graduate teaching assistant. *Journal of Research in Science Teaching* 41 (6): 584–602.

Windschitl, M. 2003. Inquiry projects in science teacher education: What can investigative experiences reveal about teacher thinking and eventual classroom practice? *Science Education* 87: 112–143.

Chapter 11

Bending the Professional Teaching Continuum

How Teacher Renewal Supports Teacher Retention

Mistilina Sato, Gillian Roehrig, and Joel D. Donna

Introduction

This chapter is built on the premise that science teachers develop their practice along a professional continuum that consists of recruitment, preparation, new teacher induction, ongoing professional development, and advanced certification or master teacher opportunities (NCTAF 1996). Teachers need professional learning opportunities that are specifically designed to meet their differentiated needs as they progress along the continuum. We argue that science leadership from local districts, state policymakers, and providers of higher education can keep science teachers in the classroom and the larger educational system by providing professional learning opportunities that meet these particular needs. We also propose that by intentionally providing opportunities for teachers who have advanced along the career continuum to interact with early-career teachers, leaders can leverage the knowledge and wisdom of practice of experienced teachers to support the development of beginning teachers.

Why We Are Concerned About Keeping Science Teachers

Nationally, we need to recruit and retain more science teachers in our classrooms (Ingersoll and Preda 2006). Some analyses of the potential shortage of science teachers have gone as far as using national economic concerns to emphasize the strategic and immediate concerns we face in science teacher recruitment and preparation (NAS 2006; National Commission on Mathematics and Science Teaching for the 21st Century 2000).

Research clearly shows that current teacher shortages are not due to lax recruitment efforts or an insufficient supply of teachers, but are created by high attrition rates within the profession. We lose teachers at all stages of the professional continuum, and attrition is particularly significant in the early career years. Overall teacher attrition rates of up to 50% within the first five years create an alarming amount of teacher turnover (Smith and Ingersoll 2004), and the annual turnover of science and mathematics teachers is slightly higher than that of the teacher population as a whole (Ingersoll 2003). While teacher attrition lessens with more experience, projections for the next decade show that teacher retirements from the baby boom generation will create a need to replace over one-third of science and mathematics teachers in the United States (Behrstock and Clifford 2009; NCTAF 1996). Ingersoll and Preda (2006) suggest that, if it were not for preretirement loss, the current rate at which colleges and universities graduate science and mathematics teachers would be sufficient to meet future demands.

However, with science education losing both its new entrants as well as its seasoned veterans, there is a definite need to develop better strategies for breaking the cycle of attrition in order to keep science teachers in our schools. This creates an educational system in which students are more likely to have inexperienced teachers who, on average, are less effective (Rivkin, Hanushek, and Kain 2005). High turnover also creates instability within schools, making it more difficult to sustain curricular and instructional programs. The high turnover of teachers is especially acute in high-poverty schools that struggle to close the student achievement gap (U.S. Department of Education 2007). When resources are spent constantly hiring, training, and supporting teachers new to the school and new to the profession, schools are less able to invest in developing collaborative teams and a culture of learning.

In examining the reasons that teachers leave schools or the profession altogether, several predictable reasons rise to the top. Broadly, limited job satisfaction accounts for most of the attrition of teachers (Ingersoll 2001). This includes issues such as poor working conditions, low professional status, lack of control over policies in the workplace, and little access to colleagues during the regular working day. Salaries are a factor in teacher retention and also create recruitment challenges, especially in mathematics and the sciences, due to competition from better paying professional occupations (Hansen et al. 2004). Fortunately there is much that science leaders can do to break the cycle of attrition of both early career and experienced teachers. Possible measures include quality preparation, induction supports for beginning teachers, raising salaries, and improving working and professional teaching conditions (Darling-Hammond and Sato 2006).

We argue that in addition to improving workplace conditions and salaries, school, district, and state leaders can potentially increase the retention of science teachers by providing professional and personal growth opportunities, especially ones in which the wisdom of experienced teachers can be passed on and shared with beginning and novice teachers. If experienced teachers are given opportunities for sharing reform-based teaching practices and new roles that are related to instruction and learning, including new responsibilities for inducting beginning teachers, they are more likely to remain in the profession (Fulton, Yoon, and Lee 2005). We identify ways that educational systems can redistribute the skills that highly accomplished teachers have learned through their years of practice, thus providing professional opportunities for advanced teachers that will support the induction and development of their novice colleagues. The simultaneous attention to creating career development opportunities for teachers advanced in their practice and to developing the practices of beginning teachers can create a professional career cycle of retention and renewal while strengthening classroom instruction and learning.

Professional Teaching Continuum

A professional teaching continuum can be viewed as a structural sequence for career progression or as a development or learning progression for teachers. Structurally, we can envision teaching as a trajectory that is based on requirements within the educational system, as well as experience and the advancement of teacher knowledge. The National Commission for Teaching and America's Future (NCTAF 1996) proposed a structural continuum that consists of recruitment to a teacher education program, preservice preparation, initial license, new teacher induction, continuing license requirements, ongoing professional development, and advanced certification (see Table 1). Each of the stops along the continuum is specified with a professional benchmark that would allow for the continuous support and assessment needed to move teachers along the career trajectory.

Table 1. Professional Continuum for Teacher Development (NCTAF 1996, p. 67)	
Recruitment to a teacher education program	based on academic background and ability to work with children
Preservice preparation	in an NCATE-accredited school of education
Initial intern license	based on Interstate New Teacher Assessment and Support Consortium (INTASC) tests of subject matter and teaching knowledge
New teacher induction	1–2 years of early career mentoring and evaluation
Continuing license	based on INTASC performance assessments, including a portfolio of classroom artifacts (video, student work) and written evaluations
Ongoing professional development	in and out of the classroom
Advanced certification	based on National Board for Professional Teaching Standards performance assessments and examinations

Feiman-Nemser (2001) introduced a professional learning continuum for teachers from initial preparation through the early years of teaching. This continuum was intended to provide a curricular framework that identifies the central tasks of learning to teach during preservice preparation, induction, and early career professional development. By laying out these central tasks along a continuum, Feiman-Nemser argued that we can build a set of experiences that will address the special challenges experienced at each of these points along the continuum and also enable teacher educators to establish a more seamless process of development. For example, the author identified the preservice teacher learning needs as performing a critical examination of prior beliefs about teaching and learning, developing subject matter knowledge, understanding learning and learners, developing a beginning repertoire of practice, and developing an understanding of the processes of learning from practice. Professional development needs after the induction years include extending and deepening subject matter knowledge as well as repertoires of curriculum, instruction, and assessment; strengthening skills and dispositions of inquiry; and expanding responsibilities and leadership skills (2001, p. 1050).

In both of these examples of professional teaching continua, the image created is one of a linear progression from unlicensed to licensed, from novice to master, from preservice to inservice, from developing to expanding (see Figure 1).

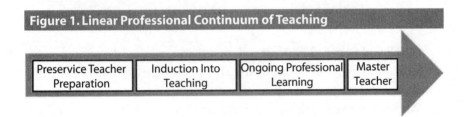

Figure 1. Linear Professional Continuum of Teaching

Preservice Teacher Preparation | Induction Into Teaching | Ongoing Professional Learning | Master Teacher

If, however, we imagine that once teachers become experienced professionals in need of ongoing professional learning opportunities, master practitioners, and/or National Board Certified Teachers, they are able to impart their wisdom of practice and expertise by working with their lesser-experienced colleagues; this linear continuum does not fully capture the possibilities of teachers' professional work and development. The linear continuum does not explicitly help us see how the knowledge and experience of the seasoned veteran can be recaptured and used by others within the profession. Instead, we need to imagine how the continuum bends itself from the experienced end of the progression to wrap back around and feed the preservice and induction years (see Figure 2).

Chapter 11

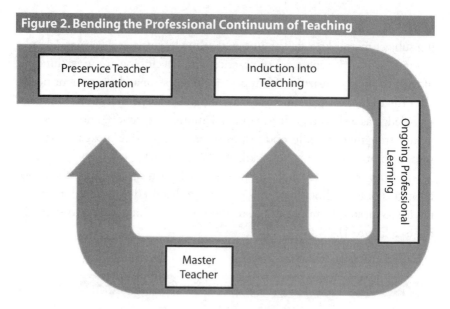

Figure 2. Bending the Professional Continuum of Teaching

Preservice Teacher Preparation

Induction Into Teaching

Ongoing Professional Learning

Master Teacher

Caroll and Foster (2008) imagine this wraparound of the continuum as a shift toward teachers working together in cross-generational learning teams.

> We need to re-imagine the teaching career to sustain the growth of teams of educators over time. The tradition of hiring young teachers in their twenties and expecting them to do essentially the same job for the next 30 years is a thing of the past. Sustaining teachers' growth throughout their careers calls for the creation of new roles and opportunities to support intern and apprentice teachers who develop their skills alongside more accomplished educators (p. 13).

In the following sections, we argue that intentionally bending the professional continuum can create opportunities for renewal of experienced teachers while simultaneously creating mechanisms for retaining beginning teachers. We also provide examples of ways that school, district, higher education, and state leadership can provide opportunities for experienced/master teachers to support the development of preservice and beginning teachers.

Preservice Teacher Preparation

Typically, colleges and universities take responsibility for teacher preparation and school districts provide ongoing professional development for teachers they employ. This tradition places a clear boundary between the experience-base of practicing teachers and the preparation of preservice teachers. Preparation programs try to overcome these boundaries by giving preservice teachers access to authentic practice through short-term practicums and student teaching placements in schools. During these field-based experiences, cooperating teachers host student teachers and, in a best-case scenario, the two work alongside each other in a mentoring or coaching relationship. Under the current system, typically, the selection of cooperating teachers is not predictable or based on clear criteria, the relationship between novice and veteran lasts only for a few weeks, and the level of engagement that the cooperating teacher has with higher education preparation program varies widely. In our bending of the professional continuum model, the role of experienced teachers in preparing new teachers would be become more intentional and systematic while also being based on the experienced teachers' expertise and readiness to assume additional responsibilities.

Partnering to Prepare Teachers

Teacher preparation programs built on the professional development model address the idea of bending the professional continuum more systematically through ongoing partnerships between schools and colleges or universities, and they emphasize the mentoring, coaching, and instructor roles that teachers play in the preparation of beginning teachers (Teitel 2004). Recently developed urban teacher residencies in Chicago, Boston, and New York embed teacher preparation and continuous professional development into schools. In these models, the preservice teacher "resident" learns to teach alongside an experienced, trained, and compensated mentor during a yearlong internship. Host schools serve as the location for preparing the resident in classrooms of teachers who have demonstrated high-quality, effective teaching practices. After completing the residency, the beginning teacher is placed in another school within the same district as a first-year licensed teacher and continues to be supported by the school district during the induction years. Recruiting and developing highly skilled mentors and teachers who serve as teacher educators is a core design principle of the urban teacher residency model. Colleges and universities work in partnership with the school district sponsoring the residency program to provide graduate course work that is wrapped around the daily practice of the resident working in the school. As this model becomes more widespread, colleges and universities will have to rethink the methods they use to conduct and support teacher preparation. Teaching experts from within schools may find more opportunities to serve as teacher educators in joint appointment roles with their school districts and the degree-granting institution (Berry et al. 2008), thus creating a predictable and sustained career path for experienced teachers.

Induction Into Teaching

Over the past decade, policy makers have focused much attention on the preservice and induction phases of the professional continuum due to concerns related to teacher supply and demand discussed earlier. These concerns about attrition of early career teachers have lead to the development of mentoring and induction programs across the nation. National data suggests that up to 90% of teachers receive some form of local induction support (Smith and Ingersoll 2004). Unfortunately, the nature and quality of this support varies widely and is often limited to participation in district-run mentoring programs. Smith and Ingersoll found that this basic level of support had minimal impact on teacher retention rates.

Based on their studies of induction programs in several countries, Britton and Raizen (2003) argued that induction programs for science teachers must shift from limited focus on orientation, emotional support, enculturation, and retention toward a comprehensive and multifaceted approach that provides differentiated support for beginning teachers while promoting career-long learning processes and enhancing overall teacher quality. Research has shown that meeting the unique needs of secondary science teachers is best done through content-specific induction support that bridges content-specific teacher preparation and professional practice (Luft, Roehrig, and Patterson 2003; Roehrig and Luft 2006). By focusing on science content–specific induction, induction programming can support the development of a repertoire of practices that are needed if we are to achieve the vision of science instruction identified in national reform documents (Wang, Odell, and Schwill 2008).

In order to provide science teacher induction, several systems must be in place to support beginning teacher professional development that is specific to the courses and students they teach. Subject-specific induction requires mentors who have both content expertise and the skills of mentoring beginning teachers in critical reflective practice and how to best support student learning of the content that is being taught. This form of mentoring requires systems that enable communication and collaboration between these teachers for a sustained period of time, perhaps through models that provide time for mentors and beginning teachers to engage in ongoing subject-specific development. This form of induction support also requires professional development of mentors so that they are able to provide science-specific support for the beginning teachers they serve. In rural and low-population areas where fewer teachers are hired, schools or districts may not have the capacity for subject-specific support, because beginning science teachers may not have experienced peers who teach similar subjects within their district. In these cases, regional consortium models or electronic networks need to be created to provide content-specific support (Donna 2009). Enacting the level of science specific induction support called for here requires collaboration and leadership among colleges and universities, school districts, and the guidance of state policy to develop and sustain effective programs.

Higher Education Supporting Induction

Higher education institutions can play a significant role in the development and coordination of induction programs. In most school districts, there are not enough new teachers in secondary science to allow for professional development targeted toward beginning teachers in subject-specific cohorts. However, colleges and universities have the expertise in subject-specific teacher education and research to develop and sustain regional models of support for science teachers. While school districts are best positioned to coordinate on-site mentoring that provides logistical, emotional, and general instructional support, colleges and universities can supplement this with professional development that focuses on reform-based practices in science.

One such program is the Science Teacher Induction Network—(S)
TIN. TIN was developed as a collaborative effort between the University of
Minnesota and the Minnesota Department of Education to provide online
induction support for STEM teachers throughout the state. Each beginning teacher was matched with an experienced science mentor according
to content area and grade level. Mentors were identified from the Teacher
Quality Network run by the Minnesota Department of Education in
order to provide beginning teachers with access to mentors who exemplify
reform-based science teaching. By identifying mentors at the state level
rather than at the local level, TIN is better able to provide beginning teachers with mentors who demonstrate leadership skills and expertise in their
specific content area (e.g., physics, chemistry, biology).

TIN was designed to meet the induction needs of beginning secondary science teachers by supplementing, not supplanting, existing mentor
programs available in larger school districts and enhancing content-specific
support for beginning teachers in outlying rural areas that have fewer science teachers. Beginning teachers and mentors used online web conferences a minimum of twice a month. Conversations were expected to address
the immediate needs of the beginning teacher and also provide structured
opportunities to focus on planning for and reflecting on reform-based
science lessons. These structured conversations focused on inquiry-based
instruction and were embedded in professional development modules
developed at the university.

As a program designed to provide subject-specific mentoring, TIN was
successful in that it provided opportunities for experienced science teachers to share their expertise in planning and implementing reform-based
science lessons with beginning teachers. As a research project at the university, TIN was also successful because it allowed several experienced science
teachers to draw on their classroom teaching experiences while engaged in
doctoral studies at the university. Many experienced and master teachers
want to continue their professional development by entering advanced
degree programs. From our experience, we have learned that teachers often
find advanced degree programs a better fit for keeping in touch with issues
of instruction and learning than administrative credential programs. For
advanced degree students with content and pedagogical expertise from
years of classroom teaching, development and research projects such as
TIN can provide opportunities to incorporate that expertise back into the

educational system. Several working teachers enrolled in graduate degree programs were provided with opportunities to learn about mentoring and induction not only as a theoretical construct, but also through applied and facilitated practical experiences working with beginning teachers, as well as through research. TIN not only enriched the beginning teacher's experience, but also provided ways for the "teacher" graduate students to contribute their own expertise to the professional learning continuum.

Collaborative Leadership to Support Induction

In order to support this bending of the professional continuum, state-level leadership that both informs and supports implementation of high-quality induction programming is needed. If logistical and technical support for districts is not provided by state-level leadership, the system's overall capacity to induct beginning teachers and to prepare experienced teachers to support these teachers is diminished. State-level leadership can enable collaboration between higher education, local education associations, state education agencies, and state-science teacher organizations to enact and sustain these efforts and inform legislation.

Minnesota provides an example of this kind of partnership. Minnesota's Teacher Support Partnership (TSP) comprises members from the higher education community, the Minnesota Department of Education, and Education Minnesota (the state teachers' union). TSP advocates subject-specific support for all secondary teachers, and, as such, it does not focus specifically on science, but it has developed general guidelines for local development of educator induction systems within Minnesota. These guidelines include recommendations for content-specific professional development activities, formative assessment of beginning teachers, and mentor preparation. These guidelines will be used to inform state-level policy and legislation that connects induction to other education policies such as licensure and teacher advancement initiatives. State leaders will also need to develop a stable and consistent form of funding to support district induction. This funding could support statewide technical, logistical, and oversight support for district and regional programs.

Ongoing Professional Learning and Master Teachers

In a review of research on the current status of professional learning opportunities for teachers in the United States, results of national teacher surveys consistently showed that teachers felt that their professional development opportunities were inadequate, inappropriate, and ineffective for meeting their needs (Darling-Hammond et al. 2009). The same study compared professional development and ongoing learning opportunities of teachers in the United States with those of other countries. The study concluded

> Comparisons of American teachers' participation in professional development with that of teachers in the international community also demonstrate that the United States is substantially behind other OECD [Organization for Economic Cooperation and Development] nations in providing the kinds of powerful professional learning more likely to build teachers' capacity and have significant impact on student learning. While American teachers participate in workshops and short-term professional development at similar levels as teachers in OECD nations, the United States is far behind in several respects. The nation lags in providing public school teachers with chances to participate in extended learning opportunities and productive collaborative communities in which they conduct research on education related topics; to work together on issues of instruction; to learn from one another through mentoring or peer coaching; and collectively to guide curriculum, assessment, and professional learning decisions. (p. 27)

Unfortunately, in the United States, packaged professional development opportunities that are "delivered" to teachers continue to dominate, while research and teacher reports support professional learning that is built on a model of "activating" teachers to learn in their local instructional contexts (Wilson and Berne 1999). Similarly, Ball and Cohen (1999) argue that teacher learning should be embedded in practice and draw upon opportunities for critical analysis, reflection, and development of new understandings that take place in the daily practices of the teacher.

State, district, and higher education leaders have much to learn about keeping science teachers in the profession from these perspectives on professional learning. First, we must find ways to make professional development an engaging and rewarding process for teachers so that ongoing learning is not viewed as a bureaucratic hoop, as a tacit way to control teachers' professionalism, or as misaligned programming that wastes valuable time and resources. Second, we must find ways to support the professional learning of science teachers that allows experienced teachers who have demonstrated effective practices or high-quality instruction to play more significant roles in the professional learning of their colleagues.

Supporting Authentic Professional Learning

One example of a professional learning opportunity that has clearly demonstrated a practice-embedded approach while being a rewarding process for experienced teachers is the National Board Certification Process. National Board Certification offers teachers an opportunity to examine their practice through the lens of a rigorous set of teaching standards established and vetted by the professional teaching community. Many teachers who have completed the assessment regard the process as a professional development opportunity rooted in their everyday work in classrooms. This comment from an interview study with National Board candidates illustrates a common perspective on the certification process:

> When I started doing the National Board assessment, reading their standards was the first thing. I thought, "Yes, I agree." This is what I want to be as a teacher and I think I do pretty much most of this. But when you really start picking apart your work, you can really see those big gaps . . . it was professional development in that I got to analyze and really take apart my work and see where I was, where I felt successful, and where I felt I needed to something different or something more. It really woke me up to some things that I had sort of let slip by. (Sato 2004)

Linking professional standards to an examination of their own day-to-day teaching practice through a study of teaching artifacts (e.g., video, unit plans, and student work samples) allows teachers to focus on incorporating these standards into their practice. As a result of participating in the National Board Certification process, teachers have reported increased disciplinary content knowledge, expanded teaching repertoires, greater attention to individual students, greater personal awareness, and the ability to articulate their tacit professional knowledge (Sato 2004). In an observation-based study that examined the impact of the National Board Certification process on the classroom assessment practices of science and mathematics teachers, teachers who engaged in the certification process showed more improvement in their assessment practices than teachers who did not pursue National Board Certification (Sato, Wei, and Darling-Hammond 2008). Participants reported that the teaching standards provided a set of clear goals for practice as well as a practical sense of the components of those goals. They also reported that the portfolio entries required them to engage in reflection that brought assessment into sharper focus, which helped them become more aware of the ways that assessment operated in their classrooms. One teacher noted that the portfolio prompts consistently asked for evidence of learning and promoted specific, systematic attention to individual elements of comprehension. This emphasis was critical for her because, by distinguishing between "hard evidence" and anecdotal evidence, she was able to develop tools to evaluate her teaching practices and students' learning outcomes. Similar results for science teacher learning through National Board Certification were identified in a quasi-experimental research study that investigated learning outcomes for high school science teachers who pursued National Board Certification (Lustick and Sykes 2006).

School and district leadership can take advantage of the professional learning opportunities embedded in the National Board assessment processes. Local candidate support groups provide opportunities for certified teachers to become coaches and support providers for future and current candidates. In these support roles, National Board Certified Teachers not only provide emotional and technical guidance, but also help their colleagues understand how to examine their own practice for evidence of the teaching standards, share their own classroom practices that led to National Board Certification, and engage groups of teachers in analyses of the ways in which instruction is linked to student learning. An interview study of 14 teachers showed that the teacher-to-teacher interactions preceding National Board Certification enhanced reflection on teaching practice, established a professional discourse community, raised standards for teaching performances, and facilitated teacher collaboration (Park et al. 2007).

In some areas, National Board candidate support happens on an ad hoc basis and in other areas there is a systemic process in place that draws on the expertise of master teachers to support future candidates (Freund

2005). Schools and districts can invest their professional development dollars wisely by making the processes that comprise National Board Certification more widely available to teachers and by employing master teachers in mentor and coaching roles. A recent study on the cost of the National Board Certification process by the Finance Project (Cohen 2005) found that National Board Certification as a model of teacher professional development is no more expensive than alternative professional development programs, and is less costly than some. This study showed that even in comparison to well-established, well-funded, high-quality professional development programs in which teachers in the non–National Board group were engaged during the study, the National Board Certification process had a large and consistent influence on teachers' practices. The findings of this research study support previous findings that the National Board Certification experience is a powerful form of professional development and a potentially high-yield investment. It is especially important that administrative leaders consider this information when making funding decisions, because other professional development initiatives may be unproven in their effectiveness.

State incentives and support for National Board Certification would not only contribute to increasing the quality of the teaching workforce, but it would also address the teacher retention problem. While research on the connection between National Board Certification and teacher retention is relatively new, some studies have documented that National Board Certified Teachers consider staying in the classroom longer than non–National Board Certified Teachers (Sykes et al. 2006). These teachers report that, as a result of going through the certification process, they have gained new understanding, enthusiasm, and renewal for their professional work, especially with regard to pedagogy and instructional leadership. Schools that capitalize on the authentic professional growth opportunities afforded by the National Board Certification process—including the promotion of collaboration among teachers and the creation of new opportunities for experienced teachers to take on leadership roles—are better able to address the core concerns that teachers consider when deciding whether to continue their work or leave education. Finally, the combination of local policy that supports National Board Certification with state incentives for teaching in underperforming schools has the potential to recognize and distribute accomplished teachers more equitably across schools, as is happening in Los Angeles Unified School District in California (Humphrey, Koppich, and Hough 2005).

Diversifying the Roles of Experienced Teachers

A second strategy that local and state leadership can use to purposefully bend the professional continuum by empowering experienced teachers to support early career development for beginning teachers is through programs that offer greater diversity in professional development roles accompanied by salary advancement. For example, the Teacher Advancement Program (TAP), developed and established by the Milken Family Foundation and now coordinated by the National Institute for Excellence in Teaching, provides opportunities for highly qualified and effective teachers to take on roles as master or mentor teachers, receive salary compensation for these roles, and advance professionally without leaving the classroom. School districts that use the TAP strategy commit to providing multiple career paths for teachers through master teacher roles such as mentors, coaches, and curriculum leaders. Professional development in the TAP model takes place during the regular working day through collaborative structures, which results in a design that is ongoing and directly linked to instructional practice. These professional growth opportunities are designed to meet teachers' instructional needs with the ultimate goal of improving student learning. Teachers' compensation is linked to their roles and responsibilities, their performance in the classroom, and the performance of their students.

In Minnesota, state legislation established the Quality Compensation for Teachers (Q Comp) program in 2005. Q Comp was built from the TAP model to establish a comprehensive, systemic model for teacher professional development and compensation in order to address issues of teacher retention through differentiated career ladders and compensation for performance. Participation in Q Comp is voluntary within the state. Districts that choose to participate are given design parameters for their Q Comp programs and then have the flexibility to supplement these programs to address local needs. Districts decide how to support and measure teacher performance, how to structure their salary schedules, and which career opportunities to afford their teachers. While still early in its implementation, an evaluation of Q Comp reported that districtwide implementation led to onsite professional development that was integrated into teachers' schedules in such a way that it provided a unifying focus as well as a framework for collaboration on issues of instruction, planning, and professional development. Some schools also experienced an overall shift from administrative decision making to teacher decision making along with the development of career ladder systems for teachers. A related finding indicated that, when Q Comp is implemented in schools, one of the conditions that predicts increases in student achievement is the addition of multiple career paths to the school, likely due to the effect this has on encouraging teachers to remain in the profession longer (Hezel Associates 2009).

Conclusion

Science educators have long recognized that teacher professional development needs to be continuous and allow for a more seamless process that moves from preservice, through induction, into inservice, and this process must be differentiated to address the unique needs of teachers at different places along the continuum while maintaining a focus on reform-based practices in science education (Adams and Krockover 1997; Emmer 1986; Loughran 1994; Luft, Roehrig, and Patterson 2003; Simmons et al. 1999). We have argued that district, higher education, and state leadership need to design professional learning opportunities for teachers that purposefully provide teachers who demonstrate exemplary practices the opportunity to share their expertise and wisdom with their colleagues. By supporting teachers to pursue master teacher and leadership opportunities, districts can leverage the expertise that exists within their own system and provide a differentiated path for teachers who are seeking ways to expand their work and influence outside of their own classrooms while staying close to the work of teaching.

A recent study by the Finance Project (Miles et al. 2005) of investment in professional development in five large school districts found that the average annual spending of these districts ranged from 2.2%–6.9% of their operating budgets ($2,100–$7,900 per teacher). The study also found that numerous efforts were sometimes aimed at the same targets, but that these were often uncoordinated, resulting in duplication or conflicting goals. We can no longer afford this waste of resources within school districts or across the professional development continuum. Wasley (2007) calls for "mutual accountability links between and among those who are responsible for teachers' capacity to serve all their students" (p. 6). We have suggested ways that leadership can support the preparation, induction, and ongoing professional development of teachers along a professional continuum that is owned collaboratively by all partners (see Figure 3). There remains a lot of work to do to build stronger collaborative systems between colleges and universities, school districts, unions, and state departments of education, including recognition of differentiated expertise, better information flow, joint development of programs, sharing resources and data systems, and collaborative policy development.

Figure 3. Collaborative Leadership Within the Professional Continuum of Teaching

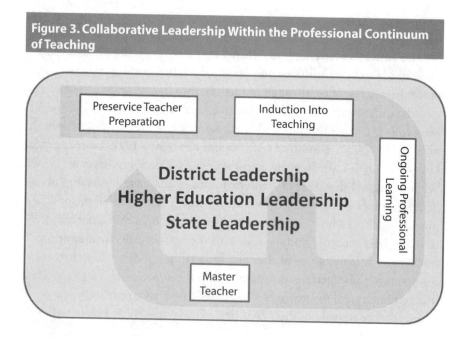

Finally, we have argued that we must become explicit and intentional about building a seamless professional career and development continuum that begins with preservice and residency teaching, bridges to induction, and then extends to multiple roles for accomplished teachers. We must find ways to capture the expertise of veteran teachers and redistribute this knowledge throughout the profession through instructional coaches, mentors, online education providers, curriculum designers, residency hosts, adjunct instructors, coteachers in higher education, professional development designers, learning community facilitators, and National Board–support providers. If we envision a future educational community that encourages and retains experienced or master teachers, we need to be explicit and intentional about enacting a professional continuum that bends back around in such a way as to continuously contribute to the development of early career teachers.

References

Adams, P. E., and G. H. Krockover. 1997. Concerns and perceptions of beginning secondary science and mathematics teachers. *Science Education* 81: 29–50.

Ball, D., and D. Cohen. 1999. Developing practice, developing practitioners: Toward a practice-based theory of professional education. In *Teaching as the learning profession: Handbook of policy and practice*, eds. L. Darling-Hammond and G. Sykes, 3–32. San Francisco, CA: Jossey-Bass.

Behrstock, E., and M. Clifford. 2009. Leading Gen Y teachers: Emerging strategies for school leaders (TQ Research and Policy Brief). Washington, DC: National Comprehensive Center for Teacher Quality. *www.tqsource.org/publications/February2009Brief.pdf*

Berry, B., D. Montgomery, R. Curtis, M. Hernandez, J. Wurtzel, and J. Snyder. 2008. Creating and Sustaining Urban Teacher Residencies: A New Way to Recruit, Prepare, and Retain Effective Teachers in High-Needs Districts. Washington, DC: The Aspen Institute. *www.teachingquality.org/legacy/AspenUTR.pdf*

Britton, E., and S. Raizen. 2003. Comprehensive teacher induction in five countries: Implications for supporting U.S. science teachers. In *Science teacher retention: Mentoring and renewal*, eds. J. Rhoton and P. Bowers, 13–21. Arlington, VA: National Science Education Leadership Association and NSTA Press.

Carroll, T. G., and E. Foster. 2008. *Learning teams: Creating what's next.* Washington, DC: National Commission on Teaching and America's Future.

Cohen, C. 2005. *National board certification as professional development: Pathways to success.* Washington, DC: The Finance Project.

Darling-Hammond, L., and M. Sato. 2006. Keeping good science teachers in the classroom: What science leaders can do. In *Issues and trends in science teaching and learning for the 21st century*, ed. J. Rhotan, 177–196. Arlington, VA: NSTA Press with National Science Education Leadership Association.

Darling-Hammond, L., R. Wei, A. Andree, N. Richardson, and S. Orphanos. 2009. *Professional learning in the learning profession: A status report on teacher development in the United States and abroad.* Dallas, TX: National Staff Development Council and The School Redesign Network at Stanford University.

Donna, J. 2009. Surviving and thriving as a new science teacher: Exploring the role of comprehensive online induction Unpublished doctoral dissertation. Minneapolis, MN: University of Minnesota–Twin Cities.

Emmer, E. T. 1986. Academic activities and tasks in first year teachers' classes. *Teaching and Teacher Education* 42: 386–399.

Feiman-Nemser, S. 2001. From preparation to practice: Designing a continuum to strengthen and sustain teaching. *Teachers College Record* 103 (6): 1013–1055.

Freund, M. 2005. A study of the role of mentoring in achieving certification by the national board for professional teaching standards. Washington, DC: The George Washington University Graduate School of Education and Human Development.

Fulton, K., I. Yoon, and C. Lee. 2005. *Induction into learning communities,* Washington DC: National Commission on Teaching and America's Future.

Hansen, M. L., D. S. Lien, L. C. Cavalluzzo, and J. W. Wenger. 2004. *Relative pay and teacher retention: An empirical analysis in a large urban district.* Alexandria, VA: The CNA Corporation.

Hezel Associates, LLC. 2009. *Quality compensation for teachers: Summative evaluation.* Syracuse, NY: Hezel Associates.

Humphrey, D. C., J. E. Koppich, and H. J. Hough. 2005. Sharing the wealth: National board certified teachers and the students who need them most. *Education Policy Analysis Archives* 13 (18): 1–50.

Ingersoll, R. M. 2001. Teacher turnover and teacher shortages: An organizational analysis. *American Educational Research Journal* 38 (3): 499–534.

———. 2003. Turnover and shortages among math and science teachers in the United States. In *Science teacher retention: Mentoring and renewal,* eds. J. Rhoton and P. Bowers, 1–12. Arlington, VA: National Science Education Leadership Association and NSTA Press.

Ingersoll, R. M., and D. Preda. 2006. What the data tell us about shortages of mathematics and science teachers. Paper presented at the National Commission for Teaching and America's Future Symposium on the Scope and Consequences of K–12 Science and Mathematics Teacher Turnover, Racine, WI.

Loughran, J. 1994. Bridging the gap: An analysis of the needs of second-year science teachers. *Science Education* 78: 365–386.

Luft, J. A., G. H. Roehrig, and N. C. Patterson. 2003. Contrasting landscapes: A comparison of the impact of different induction programs on beginning secondary science teachers' practices and beliefs. *Journal of Research in Science Teaching* 40: 77–97.

Lustick, D., and G. Sykes. 2006. National board certification as professional development: What are teachers learning? *Education Policy Analysis Archives* 14 (5): 1–46.

Miles, K. H., A. Odden, M. Fermanich, and S. Archibald. 2005. *Inside the black box: School district spending on professional development in education. Lessons from five urban districts.* Washington, DC: The Finance Project.

National Academy of Sciences (NAS). 2006. *Rising above the gathering storm.* Washington, DC: National Academies Press.

National Commission on Mathematics and Science Teaching for the 21st Century. 2000. *Before it's too late.* Washington, DC: Government Printing Office.

National Commission on Teaching and America's Future, The (NCTAF). 1996. *What matters most: Teachers for America's future.* New York: NCTAF.

Park, S., J. S. Oliver, T. S. Johnson, P. Graham, and N. K. Oppong. 2007. Colleagues' roles in the professional development of teachers: Results from a research study of National Board certification. *Teaching and Teacher Education* 23: 368–389.

Rivkin, S., E. Hanushek, and J. Kain. 2005 Teachers, schools, and academic achievement. *Econometrica* 73 (2): 417–458.

Roehrig, G. H., and J. A. Luft. 2006. Does one size fit all?: The induction experience of beginning science teachers from different teacher preparation programs. *Journal of Research in Science Teaching* 43 (9): 963–985.

Sato, M. 2004. National board for professional teaching standards: Teacher learning through the assessment process. Paper presented at the meeting of the American Educational Research Association, San Diego, CA.

Sato, M., R. C. Wei, and L. Darling-Hammond. 2008. Improving teachers' assessment practices through professional development: The case of national board certification. *American Educational Research Journal* 45 (3): 669–700.

Simmons, P.E., et al. 1999. Beginning teachers: Beliefs and classroom actions. *Journal of Research in Science Teaching* 36: 930–954.

Smith, T. M., and R. M. Ingersoll. 2004. What are the effects of induction and mentoring on beginning teacher turnover? *American Educational Research Journal* 41 (3): 681–714.

Sykes, G., D. Anagnostopoulos, M. Cannata, L. Chard, K. Frank, R. McCrory, and E. Wolfe. 2006. National Board Certified Teachers as an organizational resource. Final report to the national board for professional teaching standards. Arlington, VA: NBPTS.

Teacher Advancement Program. *www.tapsystem.org*

Teitel, L. 2004. *How professional development schools make a difference: A review of research*, 2nd ed. Washington, DC: National Council for Accreditation of Teacher Education.

U.S. Department of Education. 2007. *Teacher attrition and mobility: Results from the 2004–05 teacher follow-up survey.* Washington, DC: U.S. Department of Education.

Wang, J., S. Odell, and S. A. Schwill. 2008. Effects of teacher induction on beginning teachers' teaching: A critical review of the literature. *Journal of Teacher Education* 59 (2): 132–152.

Wasley, P. 2007. *The strengthening and sustaining teachers initiative 1998–2007.* Seattle, WA: College of Education, University of Washington.

Wilson, S. M., and J. Berne. 1999. Teacher learning and the acquisition of professional knowledge: An examination of research on contemporary professional development. *Review of Research in Education* 24: 173–209.

Chapter 12

No Boundaries

The Role of Mobility in Recruiting New
Teachers and Developing New Leaders

Ruth Heuer, Karen Charles, and Courtney Burns

*I start with the premise that the function of leadership is to produce more
leaders, not more followers.*

—Ralph Nader

*Teachers who become leaders experience personal and professional satisfac-
tion, a reduction in isolation, a sense of instrumentality...all of which spill
over into their teaching.*

—Roland Barth

At the core of the National Science Education Leadership Association's
(NSELA) mission and commitment is the development and maintenance
of the science leadership community. With a combination of formal and
informal support, each generation has nurtured the development of the
next. There has always been a selfless and almost invisible passing of the
torch of leadership that ensures a seamless transition from the outgoing
veterans to the incoming stars. However, this process that has been an
unwritten rite of passage in many educators' careers might be in danger of
extinction. The science education community has more mentors available
than mentees.

The Recruitment Challenge

As the number of science teachers continues to dwindle (Hirsch 2001), the obvious associated problem is the dwindling pool of candidates for science leadership positions. School districts and professional organizations are challenged to develop and nurture leadership skills for all current and potential leaders. The development of teacher leaders in any discipline is hindered when the pool of available candidates is shallow, and developing science leaders—whether at the classroom, district, state, or national level—depends largely on having a rich and robust pool of candidates.

The looming dilemma is that we cannot develop what we do not have. Before we can develop strong science leaders, we must develop strong science teachers. Some of the questions that the science education community must help principals and district leaders to answer are: What do the new young science teachers look like, what are the key employment decisions they are making, and how do these decisions impact districts?

New Teacher Profiles: What's the Same

In many ways, the next generation of teachers shares a number of characteristics with previous generations. As evidenced over the years, the majority of graduates entering the workforce are still women. The difference is that fewer female graduates are entering the teaching profession. The decline, from 50% in 1960 to 10% in 1990, can be attributed to the fact that many more opportunities have opened up for women in other areas of the job market (Guarino et al. 2006). The majority of individuals entering the teaching field tend to be of white non-Hispanic descent. However, over the years, the number of minority individuals in the field of teaching has doubled in public schools and quadrupled in private schools.

Like their predecessors, new teachers are drawn to the profession for personal satisfaction as well as the desire to contribute to society and help others (Guarino et al. 2006). Teaching also allows more time for family. Unfortunately, students with a higher level of measured ability and intellectual proficiency tend to enter the teaching profession at a lower rate than other college graduates (Allen 2005), and this tendency is even greater for elementary teachers than for secondary teachers. Further depleting a school's ability to invest in and develop teacher leaders is that fact that teachers of high ability are more likely to leave the teaching profession, and those who remain are more likely to move to another school. It is this increased mobility of young college graduates that is creating new challenges for schools and districts vying for the best young teachers.

New Teacher Profiles: What's Different

Mobility affects the pool of potential teachers in any district and presents challenges to employment recruiters, principals, and district leaders. It contributes to and results in the inequitable distribution of human resources. Recent studies on teacher mobility (U.S. Department of Education 2005) examine the movement of teachers between schools and out of the workforce, but the role of mobility in the decisions of first-year teachers to explore, accept, or reject employment opportunities in certain districts is rarely a part of these studies. "Why don't they come?" is a different question from "Why do they leave?"

Young adults in their 20s are the most mobile segment of the population. This stage in life is associated with leaving home, entering college, and starting a career, which often requires long-distance moves. While the migration literature shows a general trend away from urbanization in the United States during the last four decades, young, educated adults are attracted to cities and are settling there at a higher rate than the general population. They are attracted by the wealth of employment opportunities in urban areas relative to those in rural areas, and they are, perhaps, also attracted by the "bright lights"—the abundance of social activities and tolerance of diversity equated with urban areas—and are repelled by the lack of relevant work opportunities (related to their education) as well as perceived lifestyle restrictions and closed-mindedness associated with rural areas.

Urbanization—the migration of people from rural, agricultural areas, to urban, industrial centers—is largely the result of the mechanization and industrialization associated with a developing country. This was the trend in the United States from at least the time of the first census in 1790 through the 1950s. Since the 1950s, however, first suburban and, more recently, rural areas have grown faster than urban areas. This rather unexpected phenomenon has been dubbed the nonmetropolitan turnaround or rural renaissance, and it is generally thought of as middle-class whites fleeing central cities.

The net flow for all age groups except young adults is currently from urban to rural counties, with the highest rural in-migration occurring among young families and persons in their early career years. Johnson and Fuguitt (2000) hypothesize that lifestyle factors may exert a stronger influence on this age group, because rural areas appeal to adults with children as good places to raise a family. Commuting counties are particularly popular among young families because they offer access to the urban labor market in addition to the rural environment, whereas recreational counties are popular with retirees.

Even before being faced with the decision of where to work, young adults are faced with the decision of where to go to college. Postsecondary institutions are located disproportionately in urban areas, biasing college-related migration in the direction from rural to urban areas more often than the reverse. The highly uneven distribution of postsecondary schools across small towns and rural areas and the lack of postsecondary institutions in most rural areas force rural college-bound students to migrate or commute long distances to school (Gibbs and Cromartie 1994). This affects subsequent migration, as those who migrate to college are much more likely to migrate again.

In the past, education has been regarded as better suited to the needs of urbanites than to those of rural people. Urban jobs generally have higher educational requirements than rural jobs, which frequently causes college graduates in rural areas to be underemployed (Swanson and McGranahan 1989). Consequently, those leaving rural areas have tended to be more highly educated than those who stay, resulting in a "brain drain" (Kosinski 1975). This rural outmigration of the educated is attributed to the lure of better job opportunities and higher salaries available in urban areas (Swanson and McGranahan 1989).

Personal preferences play an increasing role in migration behavior. Until recent times, people had to live in close proximity to their workplace. The national highway system and recent advances in technology allow people to live greater distances from their workplace. This increased freedom to live where one desires has fueled a debate over whether economic or quality-of-life factors are the primary motivation for migration.

Economic factors, including high wages and diverse occupational opportunities typically associated with urban employment, are important to young adults (Mueser, White, and Tierney 1988). One would expect the importance of the labor market in migration decisions to increase as young people invest time and money in their education. Furthermore, some of the detractors of city life, such as high crime rates, are less of a concern for young adults who tend to be less risk-averse than older adults.

The Baccalaureate and Beyond: a 2000/2001 study tracked individuals who completed their bachelor degrees during the 1999–2000 academic year and interviewed them approximately one year after college graduation (U.S. Department of Education 2003). The interview included a small number of items to capture migration behavior, including location of residence at both high school graduation and at the time of the interview (one year after college graduation). The location of residence (zip codes) responses was recoded into Rural Area Commuting Codes to provide geographic details (U.S. Department of Agriculture 2002). For those living more than 50 miles from where they lived in high school, their reason for moving to where they currently live was collected.

Approximately one-half of the pool of recent college graduates was living more than 50 miles from where they lived when they completed high school. Those who migrated were living, on average, about 450 miles from where they attended high school. Of the recent graduates who migrated, 84% settled in urban areas, 9% in large towns, 4% in small towns, and 2% in rural areas. Compared with where they lived while attending high school (72% urban, 11% large town, 9% small town, and 8% rural area), this represents a shift toward urban residence. Certain characteristics (e.g., older graduates, those who are married, those who have children, and those who grew up in a rural area or small town) are associated with migration to small towns and rural areas. Employment reasons for migrating were cited twice as often as quality-of-life reasons for these recent college graduates, although those in certain high-demand fields (e.g., engineering), those currently enrolled in additional schooling, singles, males, and younger graduates were more likely than their counterparts to cite quality-of-life reasons (Heuer 2004).

Information about college major and current occupation (one year after college graduation) was collected in the Band B: 2000/2001 interview. Among those who were education majors and who were working in an education-related job (i.e., potential teachers), just over one-third (36%) were living more than 50 miles from where they lived in high school, so the majority ended up in the same area where they lived when they graduated high school. Also, 92% of potential teachers who lived in urban areas in high school lived in urban areas after college. Roughly half of those from large and small towns resided in a similarly sized town after college, but only one-third of those from rural areas settle in a rural area.

Of those potential teachers who moved more than 50 miles from where they lived in high school, the tendency was to migrate to urban areas (but less so than among recent college grads as a whole): 72% settled in urban areas, 16% in large towns, 9% in small towns, and 4% in rural areas. Of these potential teachers, a greater proportion cited quality-of-life reasons (47%), rather than work-related reasons, for moving compared to the recent college graduate population. Quality-of-life reasons were most often cited by those who settled in large towns. One-half of potential teachers who lived in rural areas in high school migrated (primarily to urban areas, 56%; and large towns, 30%) and over three-quarters of them cited employment-related reasons for the move.

How Mobility Impacts Districts

Because of increased mobility, new young teachers can be selective about their employment opportunities. New science teachers can be even more selective since they are highly sought. Mobility results in an uneven distribution of potential science leaders and rural and urban districts are most likely to experience this drain.

The percentage of out-of-field teachers varies by school poverty indicators and minority enrollment (U.S. Department of Education 2004). As a result, "hard-to-staff" rural and urban districts and schools will experience a lack of highly qualified teachers from which to draw their faculty leaders. The Education Commission of the States (ECS) presents the harsh reality of the attraction and retention difficulties of hard-to-staff schools:

> Hard-to-staff and at-risk schools have difficulty attracting and retaining qualified teachers. These schools tend to have higher concentrations of lower-performing and lower income students, hire more inexperienced and beginning teachers, and suffer higher teacher attrition. In addition, these schools generally serve higher concentrations of minorities, are located in inner city or rural areas, and have lower graduation rates than other schools. The students in hard-to-staff schools are often considered the ones who are most in need of a high quality education from experienced veteran teachers, yet research shows that

this population is the most under-served by public education. Studies show disparities between at-risk or hard-to-staff schools and schools that provide higher salaries and better working conditions. The problem continues to grow as schools lose highly qualified teachers to safer, wealthier and less challenging environments. (ECS 2009, website)

Rural schools and districts struggle to attract young, highly qualified teachers for a number of reasons. Socially, they cannot offer the excitement and entertainment of the big city. Potluck suppers and church socials cannot compete with skyscrapers and a beckoning nightlife. Young teachers with spouses often find few appropriate employment prospects for their spouse in rural areas, and young single teachers may find a limited dating pool. In addition, rural districts do not draw down the federal funding necessary to offer signing bonuses or competitive salaries. Even the funding available through the new federal stimulus spending bill, the American Recovery and Reinvestment Act of 2009, will be distributed with a Title 1 formula that favors large districts, regardless of the percentage of impoverished students (Howley 2009).

While all districts face recurring shortages of mathematics and science teachers, the major impact of the current and continuing teacher shortage falls on the urban school districts. These are the teaching positions that many traditionally prepared teachers are unwilling to take. Urban teachers are still predominantly women, but they are usually over 30 years of age, have attended urban schools themselves, have completed a bachelor's degree in college but not necessarily in education, have worked at other full-time jobs, and are parents themselves. This successful pool also contains a substantially higher number of individuals who are African American, Latino, and male. These teachers are also more likely to be underqualified and teaching out-of-field (Hirsch 2001).

Attracting Quality Science Teachers

School districts may not be able to overcome the attractions that influence the mobility decisions of young graduates, but knowing that this generation of teachers is more mobile than previous ones can inform hiring practices and district policies. The recruitment conversation typically focuses on recruiting students into the teaching profession, not on the recruitment of teachers by a district. This issue is one of attraction—a sort of competition among districts. Like birds preening before potential mates, districts compete to attract new hires.

In order to retain science teachers within the school system, strategies and incentives must first be put into place in order to attract them. Skilled science teachers tend to work in environments with better resources and with higher-performing students, which results in difficult recruitment situations for those lower-performing schools with fewer resources and programs. So what can low-performing schools do to find these highly qualified teachers and keep them? Several incentive programs can be put into place, such as mentoring programs, scholarships and signing bonuses (NCTQ 2009). These types of programs can help to attract teachers and then keep them by offering development programs and support.

In order to have a larger pool of talented science teachers, school districts can identify those students that tend to do very well in mathematics and science and encourage them to pursue a teaching career. Doing so might help to "grow" students from within the very community in which they are being taught. Districts can also look at those paraprofessionals who are already helping in science classrooms and provide them incentives like a higher base salary or signing bonuses. Parents and community leaders can also be sought; especially those with a background in science and those looking for a career change (NCTQ 2009).

Given the mobility findings cited above, the tendency of potential teachers to settle in places close to where they lived in high school, and the fact that those who do move are less drawn to urban areas and more likely to cite quality-of-life reasons for moving when compared to other recent college graduates, the following additional recommendations come to mind for hard-to-staff school districts: First, target recent graduates who grew up or have family geographically close to the school district. Second, make a determined effort to showcase the quality-of-life factors that are important to your community, whether it be recreational features like lakes and greenways; community gatherings like fairs and festivals; or school functions like sports, science fairs, and talent shows. Districts must sell not just the teaching position to job candidates, but also the reasons why people choose to live and stay in the area.

Who Stays, Who Leaves, Who Moves

In the spring and summer of 2000, public and private schools experienced a 16% teacher turnover rate (U.S. Department of Education 2005). This turnover, however, does not represent the loss experienced by the teaching profession. In this instance, about half were transfers (movers) and the other half were true leavers. Both, though, do represent an opportunity for a principal to infuse the school faculty with new thinking, new ideas, and new leadership potential. For principals, carefully choosing new hires can increase the likelihood of leader-capable teachers being infused into a needy situation.

Schools have always dealt with the leavers, the stayers, and the movers (Learning Points Associates 2001), but never before has the teacher shortage, particularly in science and mathematics, been more critical. The leavers are attracted away from teaching by better paying, more satisfying jobs, and this migration impacts the overall quality of the science education community. The movers are attracted to better districts with fewer problems, and this migration results in an uneven distribution of high-quality science teachers and leaders.

Leavers leave for predictable reasons: jobs outside teaching, further education, and family reasons. The distressing news is that those who leave the profession are more likely to be highly capable but, also, more likely to have been teaching out of field (U.S. Department of Education 2005). In particular, science teachers are significantly more likely to leave, because their skills are in high demand in the general workplace (Learning Point Associates 2009). This negatively impacts the science leadership pool. Those leaving to pursue further education include highly qualified teachers, and retention of these teachers should be a district priority. Districts need to make it easy and desirable for these teachers to return to their positions or to continue working while in school. With over three-fourths of the teacher profession being female, it is not surprising that significant attrition related to the birth of children is frequently cited.

Transfers are more likely to be teaching out-of-field than continuing teachers. They also tend to be younger and less experienced than stayers (U.S. Department of Education 2005). This is not surprising when one considers that some districts hire young teachers who will accept any conditions in order to secure employment. It is quite possible that movers are offered positions in their preferred field and take the opportunity to do so.

Developing Leaders

Research indicates that mathematics and science at the middle and high school grades continue to lead the list of academic disciplines taught by out-of-field teachers (Seastrom et al. 2002). Coupled with findings that suggest that high school students learn less in mathematics and science from out-of-field teachers, these trends speak loudly for the need for strong teacher leaders in these areas. Young, eager, and inexperienced teachers need faculty mentors and colleagues who will guide them through the maze of curriculum and instruction decisions they must make every day.

Creating an environment in which students can succeed goes hand-in-hand with creating an environment in which teachers can succeed. Teachers will stay in an environment where they can see themselves growing, contributing, and succeeding. The school principal is at the heart of setting the tone of a school. Principals shape the school atmosphere and are critical to the successful development of all teacher leaders. Strong principals realize that teachers do not view themselves as official leaders, nor do many of them aspire to be building or district administrators. They will, however, emerge as valuable school leaders when they are included in problem-solving, decision-making, and informal leadership opportunities. Teacher leaders emerge in an environment that empowers them. Good principals make this happen routinely.

Teacher leaders have long been a reliable and necessary segment of the science education continuum that forms the bridge between the reality of the classroom and the expectations of the district. No longer are leaders only those in positions of authority. Some leaders are designated by position and title, while others assume informal leadership positions in their schools. Teacher leaders are educators who want to make a difference in practical and fundamental ways (Cowdery 2004). Recognizing that leadership in science education comes in many forms, NSELA opens its membership to science leaders in all phases of leadership and at all stages of their careers and supports, encourages, and nurtures the development of science education leadership. Join us!

References

Allen, M. B. 2005. *Eight questions on teacher recruitment and retention: What does the research say?* Denver, CO: Education Commission of the States.

Cowdery, J. 2004. Getting it right: Nurturing an environment for teacher-leaders. *Kappa Delta Pi Record:* Spring.

Education Commission of the States (ECS). 2009. *Teaching Quality: Hard to Staff Schools. www.ecs.org/html/issue.asp?issueid=129&subIssueID=61*

Gibbs, R., and J. Cromartie. 1994. Rural youth outmigration: How big is the problem and for whom? *Rural Development Perspectives* 10 (1): 9–16.

Guarino, C. M., L. Santibanez, G. Daley, and D. Brewer. 2006. A review of the research literature on teacher recruitment and retention. *Review of Educational Research* 76 (2) 173–208.

Heuer, R. 2004. Migration of recent college graduates. *Dissertation Abstracts International* 65 (01): 296 (UMI No. AAT 3120230).

Hirsch, E. 2001. Teacher recruitment: Staffing classrooms with quality teachers. The SHEEO project. Denver, CO: State Higher Education Executive Officers.

Howley, C. 2009. Federal formula skews against rural schools. *Daily Yonder: Keep it Rural. www.dailyyonder.com/federal-formula-skews-against-rural-schools/2009/04/21/2072*

Johnson, K., and G. Fuguitt. 2000. Continuity and change in rural migration patterns, 1950–1995. *Rural Sociology* 65: 27–49.

Kosinski, L. 1975. Education and international migration. In *Education and Population: Mutual Impacts*, ed. H. Muhsam. Dolhain, Belgium: Ordina Editions.

Learning Points Associates. 2001. Teacher turnover in the midwest: Who stays, leaves, and moves? *Policy Issues* 10 (December).

———. 2009. *Teacher quality: Teacher mobility. www.learningpt.org*

Mueser, P., M. White., and J. Tierney. 1988. U.S. Migration: Age patterns and spatial differentiation. *Canadian Journal of Regional Science* 11: 57–76.

National Comprehensive Center for Teacher Quality (NCTQ). 2009. *Recruiting quality teachers in mathematics, science, and special education for urban and rural schools. www.nctq.org*

Seastrom, M., K. Gruber, R. Henke, D. McGrath, and B. Cohen. 2002. *Qualifications of the public school teacher workforce: Prevalence of out-of-field teaching 1987–88 to 1999–2000 (NCES 2002-603).* U.S. Department of Education, National Center for Education Statistics. Washington, DC: U.S. Printing Office.

Swanson, L., and D. McGranahan. 1989. Nonmetro youths lagging in education. *Rural Development Perspectives* 5 (3): 36–37.

U.S. Department of Agriculture. 2002. *Measuring rurality: Rural-urban commuting area codes.* www.ers.usda.gov/Briefing/Rural/Data/desc.htm

U.S. Department of Education. 2003. *Baccalaureate and beyond longitudinal study: 2000/01 methodology report.* Washington, DC: U.S. Department of Education.

——. 2004. *The Condition of Education: 2004.* Washington, DC: U.S. Government Printing Office.

——. 2005. *Special analysis, 2005: Mobility in the teacher workforce.* http://nces.ed.gov/programs/coe/2005/analysis/sa02.asp

Section Four

School Improvement Processes and Practices: Professional Learning for Building Instructional Capacity

Chapter 13
Professional Learning Communities
School Collaboration to Implement Science Education Reform

Lois Brown Easton

Teacher One

Jeremy returned from a weeklong summer science institute full of great ideas. At the first science department meeting in his middle school, Jeremy shared with his colleagues what he had learned. "This is so good, guys," he exulted. "We've got to do this. It'll make such a difference in how our students learn!" His colleagues all nodded agreement, but Betsy was engaged in putting names into her grade book, and Norm was thumbing through the teacher's manual of the textbook, marking pages with yellow tabs. Carolina and Brad were listening, but when Jeremy asked them to stay to talk about the new program, they excused themselves in order to check supplies in the science lab.

"Oh, well," Jeremy said to himself. "I'll just do it by myself." And, he tried. He really did, but somehow other responsibilities invaded his purpose. He had to get ready for Back-to-School Night. He had to prepare units, lessons, and assessments, and he couldn't figure out how to apply the new strategies he'd learned to the needs of his students. When he did try out a new technique, he found himself wondering if he was doing it "right" and was very critical of himself. The students were wary about Mr. Johnson's new strategies; they were so different from what they had become used to at Montfort Middle School. They resisted, and Jeremy—feeling quite alone and isolated in the department—eventually gave up, returning to the tried-and-true techniques he'd used for the last few years.

Teachers Two, Three, and Four

Belinda, Warren, and Trent came back from their weeklong summer science institute full of great ideas they wanted to share with their colleagues and implement in their high school science classrooms. Their colleagues had participated in summer learning activities as well, so the first department meeting of the school year, before school started, was focused on sharing their experiences. The essential question driving the dialogue was "How can we improve student comprehension of our science objectives this year?" The department worked all day to come up with some key changes they wanted to make during the coming year, including some of the ideas that Belinda, Warren, and Trent had shared.

On the basis of data concerning details and results of science instruction at Rose High School, the science department decided on its top three priorities for the year. The data included not only test scores, but also observations, anecdotal information, reviews of student portfolios, and other student work. Then, they decided what they needed in order to implement these priorities.

Belinda suggested that the group start by engaging students in the effort. "Let's interview them," she said, "and find out what they think about what we want to do. We should continue with focus groups throughout the year as we change our classrooms."

Another teacher, Kyla, suggested that they approach the changes through action research. "Let's identify our research questions, establish baseline data, and then collect information that tells us whether what we're doing is working or not."

"I think we should collect student work as we go and analyze it using tuning protocols," Warren suggested. "That will tell us exactly when we're making progress."

The group concurred. Then, Isaac said, "I think I'll really need problem-solving meetings. I'll need sessions during which I can discuss what's happening in my classroom and get help."

"How about doing a problem-solving protocol?" Belinda asked.

The group continued to plan the professional learning they would need in order to implement their top three priorities. They had one and a half hours of Professional Learning Community time every other week, and they decided to supplement that by devoting every other department meeting to professional learning, rather than the usual business. They also hoped they could talk the district into releasing them on district staff development days to work specifically on learning and growth related to their departmental priorities.

By the end of the school year, despite a few bumps along the way and getting bogged down in February (who doesn't get bogged down in February?), at the end of the school year, when they reviewed the data, they were pleased with the degree to which they had made change and the degree to which their changes improved student achievement.

The Big Difference

While Jeremy stood alone both in his department and in his school, Belinda, Warren, and Trent stood with their colleagues in a Professional Learning Community (PLC). Jeremy struggled to change and, eventually, gave up. Members of the Rose High School Science Department struggled with change, too, but did not give up. The chief difference between the two efforts is the context. One environment was conducive to change while the other environment was uninterested in change—or even averse to it.

It has never been more important for teachers to work together. We must learn from each other, open up our classrooms, share student work, serve as mentors and coaches, and work with mentors and coaches. Not only is the world more complex and the student population more diverse, but also, educators now know much more about how people learn. We are derelict if we do not apply this exciting new knowledge in the classroom.

Schools are slow to change. Yet, change they must, and soon. Poor high school retention rates are the shame of this nation. We must teach in ways that these young people find engaging and relevant. Even students that do graduate sometimes complete only minimal requirements, and it has been said that far too few of them have learned to use their minds effectively (Sizer 2004).

There are many projects, initiatives, and programs designed to aid in changing primary and secondary education. We know what to do to make school more hospitable for young people, but we suffer an implementation gap. The distance between a good idea for school change and its effect on student learning is vast. Like all systems, school systems strive for homeostasis; they easily (and with a sigh of relief, perhaps) revert to the familiar when change becomes challenging.

Until recently, training and professional development were the only mechanisms for building a bridge between good ideas and implementation in the classroom. Teachers and principals were trained or developed, often by an expert who visited just long enough to tell them about the basics of the new system. When this person left, despite the best of intentions, trained or developed educators found it very difficult to follow through. They were insecure because, without access to experienced coaches or mentors, they were unsure if they were correctly implementing the new strategies. They did not know how to deal with peripherals, such as curriculum, that must be adapted any time any aspect of the classroom changes. How might assessment change? Instruction? What about grading, record keeping, and reporting, for example?

What Is a PLC?

A Professional Learning Community can be defined in a single three-part sentence.

A PLC is

- a group of educators who meet regularly to engage in professional learning. . .
- for the purpose of enhancing their own practice as educators. . .
- in order to help all students succeed as learners.

All three parts of this definition are critical. Although PLCs can vary in many ways, they must focus on adults learning together to improve their technique in the classroom in order to benefit student learning. PLCs share the following characteristics:

- Team learning

- Shared vision, values, and beliefs
- Reflective dialogue
- Deprivatization of practice
- Collective focus on student learning
- Collaboration
- Supportive and sustaining leadership
- Supportive conditions
- Action orientation and experimentation
- Results orientation
- Collection and use of effective data

Although most of these elements of a PLC are straightforward, the fourth one, deprivatization, deserves some discussion. Classrooms have been characterized as side-by-side caves or egg cartons. Each classroom is an individual, privatized enterprise. Teachers in such classrooms seldom volunteer to share their students' work or ideas about their own practice, and they rarely speak with other teachers about their student work or practices. In order to meet the challenges of working with young people in today's complex world, educators need to share effective techniques and work together on improving other, less effective strategies. Educators must come out of their classrooms and deprivatize in order to reach this objective.

Do PLCs Work?

Professional Learning Communities are not new, even to the world of education. As far back as the 1950s, Deming had developed the idea of Quality Circles and Theory Z (2000). Additionally, Peter Senge listed team learning (1990) as one of five disciplines inherent to effective organizations, including schools. According to Senge, team learning is united through systems thinking with the additional disciplines of personal mastery, mental models, and building shared vision. In a later book *The Fifth Discipline Fieldbook: Strategies and Tools for Building a Learning Organization* (1994), he and his colleagues described how the disciplines might be implemented in schools and school districts.

The Coalition of Essential Schools initiated Critical Friends Groups in the 1980s. This was the first known formal application of the idea of team learning in schools (Cushman 1998). Many have written about and have studied PLCs, including Kruse, Louis, and Bryk (1994), Hord (1997), Hord and Sommers (2008), DuFour and Eaker (1998, 2008), and Blankstein (2004).

Shirley Hord's 1997 research on PLCs showed effects for both students and teachers. Among the results for teachers are

- Reduction of isolation of educators;
- Increased commitment to the mission and goals of the school and increased vigor in working to strengthen the mission;
- Shared responsibility for the total development of students and collective responsibility for students' success;
- Powerful learning that defines good teaching and classroom practice and that creates new knowledge and beliefs about teaching and learners;
- Increased meaning and understanding of the content that educators teach and the roles they play in helping all students achieve expectations;
- Higher likelihood that educators will be well informed, professionally renewed, and inspired to inspire students;
- More satisfaction, higher morale, and lower rates of absenteeism;
- Significant advances in adapting teaching to the students, accomplished more quickly than in traditional schools;
- Commitment to making significant and lasting changes; and
- Higher likelihood of undertaking fundamental, systemic change.

Hord's research found the following effects for students:

- Decreased dropout rate and fewer "cut" classes;
- Lower rates of absenteeism;
- Increased learning that is distributed more equitably in the smaller high schools;
- Larger academic gains in math, science, history, and reading than in traditional schools; and
- Smaller achievement gaps between students from different backgrounds.

Lew Smith (2008) closely studied 8 of 48 schools that were given National School Change Awards. He studied four elementary and four secondary schools that went from being "considered a failure or a major disappointment," to being exemplary according to a number of factors, including achievement (p. 6). His work, based on "an eight year national research project, which looked at data and documentation from 44 states" and "16 criteria that measure significant school change," helped him identify four constants for change (pp. 5–6). These elements, which were present in the eight schools he studied extensively, as well as most of the other 48 that won awards, are context (culture, climate, message, and environment), capacity (to plan, to assess, to teach, to work in teams, and to learn), and conversations.

The last two elements—capacity (to work in teams) and conversations—are the heart of PLCs. All eight closely studied schools (and most of the others) had teams dedicated to breaking down the isolation typical in schools. They engaged in professional conversations—not just the convivial sort that characterizes faculty lounges—but substantive, collegial, problem-solving conversations that were focused on learning.

Roberts and Pruitt (2009) report on a number of studies that link teacher learning and teacher practice (what teachers do in the classroom) with student achievement. Ancess (2000) discovered that high school teachers influence graduation and college admissions rates, as well as success in higher education. Roberts and Pruitt tell the story of Dr. Peter McFarlane, leader of the Hugo Newman College Preparatory School in New York City, who transformed the school from "one of the poorest performing schools" to an "A" school and winner of the Panasonic National School Change Award (p. 15). How did he do it? As Roberts and Pruitt explain, the change happened because "teachers and leaders work collaboratively to accomplish the learning goals they have established for their students" through "structured opportunities for collaboration" (p. 16). The teachers made use of PLCs, in other words.

Other researchers have also explored the effects of collaboration and teaming, and they have found that PLCs have significant effects on professional learning. A list of some of these references can be found in the Resources section of this chapter.

What Do PLCs Look Like?

PLCs take many different forms. They are usually school-based, although PLCs can also be formed across schools as well. A whole school can become a PLC if the school is small enough. "Air time" becomes a problem when a school is too large. PLCs usually function most effectively with groups of 10 teachers or fewer, so many schools have grade-level or department PLCs. Other schools choose to have PLCs made up of teachers from adjacent grade levels, also called vertical teams, or they may form interdisciplinary PLCs. Some educators belong to more than one PLC, but it's important for each educator (and each school employee) to belong to at least one PLC.

PLCs can be mandated, but they tend to work better when they are initiated by teachers or when teachers and administrators work jointly to start them. Often PLCs come about because one or more teachers hear of them and decide to get together to share what they are doing and learning. They let the principal know what's happening and share their news regularly at faculty meetings or in a blog. Others hear about the initial group and are invited to participate, and so the group grows, or new PLCs are formed.

Sometimes, PLCs work on a school goal, such as reading across the curriculum, through a variety of professional learning experiences. Some members may do action research, while others do a book study and another group interviews students or surveys teachers. Periodically, members of the PLC meet to share what they are learning and to revise their goals and objectives.

In terms of other characteristics, PLCs can vary greatly. The size of the group, as well as its name and membership, can be adjusted along with the frequency of meetings or the duration over which the meetings take place in order to meet the specific objectives of the group. However, the defining characteristic of a PLC is that members of the group engage collaboratively in professional learning. PLC meetings are not faculty, department, or grade-level meetings, but it can be very effective to reinvent those meetings for the purpose of acting as a PLC. Care should to taken to separate routine reporting and decision making from time scheduled for discussing and reflecting on the themes selected by the PLC. The focus must be on the actions that educators take, the ways those actions affect their classrooms, and ways that educators can improve their practice. By concentrating on these goals, educators can truly focus on the ultimate objective of helping all students to succeed.

Professional Learning

Teacher education used to be called professional development or training. However, the phrase "professional learning" better conveys the process of discovering how to implement worthwhile school change initiatives. Professional learning is ongoing, embedded, and peer-to-peer. It is characterized by the following (Easton 2008):

It arises from and returns benefits to the real world of teaching and learning. Professional learning is based on providing educators with the knowledge that they need in order to help students learn, and these techniques are then applied in the classroom. The process begins by identifying strategies that have been shown to be effective in helping young people to learn and separating these ideas from outdated or untested techniques.

It requires the collection, analysis, and presentation of real data. Data, which includes but is not limited to test scores, descriptive/anecdotal data, and analysis of student work, is used by educators to identify the needs of their students and, therefore, the content knowledge and supports for learning that teachers need to provide.

Powerful professional learning results in application in the classroom. Teachers, with the help of their peers, try out the techniques that they are learning and report results, solve problems, and address issues together.

Powerful professional learning experiences may not formally end. Few educators can say, "Been there, done that. I am developed!" Learning raises more questions and leads to more learning.

Powerful professional learning honors the professionalism, expertise, experiences, and skills of staff. Someone outside the system can jump-start the learning with new ideas, but implementation requires the skills of those inside the system.

Powerful professional learning is content-rich. The content of professional learning is what teachers study, including the school or district itself, its staff, and its learners. This is content that matters to the people engaged in the experience.

Powerful professional learning is collaborative or has collaborative aspects.

Powerful professional learning establishes a culture of quality. As educators reflect on their current teaching and learning, they gradually begin to discuss methods of improving their performance.

Powerful professional learning leads to "buy-in" because it utilizes the talent within. When an initiative comes from outside, its supporters worry about how to get "buy-in." When an initiative comes from within, "buy-in" is easier to attain because the people responsible for implementing the initiative are the same people who designed it.

Powerful professional learning slows the pace of schooling. A key component of professional learning is reflection.

Powerful professional learning takes a variety of forms, including the following:

Accessing Student Voices

Action Research

Assessment as Professional Development

Book Study

Case Discussions

Classroom Walkthroughs With Reflective Inquiry

Critical Friends Groups

Curriculum Design

Data Analysis

Differentiated Coaching

Immersing Teachers in Practice

Journaling

Lesson Study

Mentoring

Portfolios for Educators

Protocols, a Variety of

School Coaching

Shadowing

Standards in Practice (Assignment Analysis)

Study Groups

Training the Trainer

Tuning Protocol

Using Video to Change Practice

Visual Dialogue

Powerful professional learning designs provide the activities that make professional learning communities (PLCs) more than just a structure. Although structure is an important aspect of PLCs, it is the way that the members function within that structure that is critical to the productiveness and effectiveness of the PLC.

Some Professional Learning Opportunities for Science Educators

The Tuning Protocol to Look at Student Work

Science educator Dave Hoskins brought his students' science portfolios to a tuning protocol. He asked his colleagues to help him fine-tune these portfolios so that he could encourage higher-level thinking. The group silently took notes while he presented the portfolios to his group. Then the group had an opportunity to ask questions, and he responded to clarify some remaining uncertainties. After everyone seemed to have a clear understanding of the process, they all wrote about the two key questions he had brought before the group. Dave had asked: "What evidence of higher-level thinking skills do you find?" and "How can I encourage higher-level thinking through use of portfolios?"

Next, it was Dave's turn to listen. He took notes as his colleagues discussed the material that he had presented. During their 15-minute dialogue, they made both warm (praise) and cool (critique) comments. Their cool comments were phrased as ideas to be investigated, such as "I wonder what would happen if students were asked to reflect on what they had done right after they finished an activity." The group was impressed with the portfolios, but they found that students had written more describing what they had done, rather than what they had learned. They recommended that Dave institute a reflection time after the conclusion of an activity. After Dave's tuning protocol group had finished their discussion, Dave reflected aloud on their comments. His group listened and then engaged with him in an open discussion. As a result of the tuning protocol, this closing discussion reached a much deeper level than it would have if they had tried to discuss the topics without ensuring that everyone had had an opportunity to clearly formulate their own thoughts and understand the thoughts of other members of the group.

The protocol protected Dave. It can be daunting for teachers to share student work, but because the protocol provides different times for speaking and listening, Dave knew he wouldn't be interrupted and lose his train of thought. He knew also that he wouldn't be defensive, because he stayed out of his colleagues' initial discussion. Dave was able to do this comfortably, because he knew that after they finished, he would have time to further the discussion and clarify his own intentions or seek clarification of his colleagues' ideas concerning his techniques. The combination of warm and cool feedback was effective in maintaining Dave's interest because the constructive suggestions lent validity to the praise and encouragement while, at the same time, these positive remarks also served to prevent the helpful suggestions from becoming a litany of things Dave was doing wrong.

The protocol also served to prepare the group for a more involved conversation. With each turn to speak, participants built on what had already been said. The alternate speaking and listening steps prevented debate over any particular pro/con statement from stalling the discussion.

The Tuning Protocol to Look at Educator Practice

The same protocol can be used to examine a particular aspect of an educator's teaching practice. For example, a science teacher can bring a unit plan, an assessment, a rubric, a design for project-based learning, other material, or a combination of any of these to be discussed and honed by the group. By the time the protocol has been completed, the educator presenting the artifact of practice to the group has learned how to refine it, and the colleagues have also learned about their own practice. One of the exciting aspects of the tuning protocol is that, while it may initially seem to be about one teacher (or one teacher's student), throughout the process all teachers benefit from the opportunity to reflect on themselves and the ways their materials and techniques do or could affect their students.

Lesson Study

Catherine Lewis of Mills College writes about the Japanese practice of lesson study (2008), which she and others brought to the United States. In Japanese lesson study, teachers with a common grade level and subject work together over at least a year on both an academic and a personal development focus. They bring lessons related to these foci before the group. Teachers work over one of the lessons until they are satisfied with it. Then one or more of the participants uses the revised lesson design in their classroom while the others collect on-the-spot data. The data could be the types of questions that the students ask, lists of common points of confusion or misconception, or ratings of student engagement. Then the group holds a colloquium. The teacher that presented the lesson design talks about the experience, paying particular attention to aspects that didn't seem to be working, and then the data collectors share their information. The whole group then decides whether to continue refining the lesson or to proceed with work on another lesson. As the group becomes more experienced, they are able to use the learning from previous lesson designs to improve new lesson designs.

In the United States, lesson study proceeds much as it does in Japan. Some variations are possible, however. For example, a rich professional discussion occurs when educators get together to dissect and improve a lesson, whether or not they teach it. Although Japanese lesson study participants usually work with already prepared lessons, groups can design a lesson together, from scratch, and then teach it. Participants can have a follow-up lesson study by using a tuning protocol to examine student work that resulted from that lesson.

Assignment Analysis

This process originally comes from the Education Trust, and it is known as Standards in Practice (Mitchell and Kennedy-Salchow 2008). Assignment analysis can also be used to evaluate assessment prompts and instructional tasks. In this process, a teacher brings in an assignment, prompt, or task that is workable. *Workable* means that the assignment is substantive, with more than one right answer, rather than a worksheet with specific, definitive answers.

- The group engages in a variety of activities related to the workable assignment, prompt, or task:
- They try it themselves, if possible.
- They describe what it requires of students in terms of knowledge, skills, and behaviors (perhaps also attitude and aspirations).

- They analyze the lesson in terms of levels of thinking required.
- They analyze the rigor of the lesson, using a variety of descriptors of rigor.
- They determine a set of criteria that could be used in a rubric to evaluate student work resulting from the assignment, prompt, or task.
- If student work is available, they use the set of criteria to review that work.

If the assignment has not yet been given, the group might help the teacher think about instruction related to the assignment, going back to step two: What formative assessments will help teachers determine the current knowledge and abilities of their students? What scaffolding is needed? What instructional strategies that have proven to be effective can the teacher use to convey these concepts? How can the teacher differentiate?

If the assignment has been given and the teacher has student work, the group might do a tuning protocol on the work.

Accessing Student Voices

Of all of the stakeholders in education who need to have a say in educational improvement, students are the least consulted. Their voices can be powerful, and science teachers and teacher leaders might want to engage in professional learning by formally talking to students. Focus groups can help teachers to identify and concentrate on the areas of support that students need to succeed in science (Hord and Robertson 2008). Teachers can also benefit by observing students work through a problem and encouraging them to talk aloud about what they are doing and why. Recently, in New Jersey, teachers in a math consortium actually involved students in designing a lesson. Science educators can also formally interview students—indeed, all stakeholders—about science education. Informally "hanging out" with students and asking them to talk about their own learning needs can also be effective.

Protocols for Discussion

A variety of protocols for discussion regarding problems, issues, and understanding of text comes from The National School Reform Faculty and the Coalition of Essential Schools. They have been collected by the author (Easton 2009) and have been published by the Association of Supervision and Curriculum Development. The tuning protocol described earlier is the best-known protocol, and the others derive from it.

Protocols, in general, are processes that help groups achieve deep understanding through dialogue, which may lead to effective decision making, although decision making and problem solving are not typically the end-goals of protocols. Protocols provide structures for groups that allow them to explore ideas deeply through student work, artifacts of educator practice, texts relating to education, or problems and issues that surface during the day-to-day lives of educators.

A good discussion protocol is called the triad protocol. After reading the selected text, the group breaks into triads and decides who in each group will be A, B, and C. In the first round, A presents an idea, B responds to A, and C summarizes what A and B have said and may add comments as well. In rounds two and three, the roles change. A becomes B, B becomes C, and C becomes A. At the end of the protocol, all three members of the triad will have played all three roles, and they will have a deeper understanding of the text.

Another protocol, the Success Analysis Protocol, asks each member of a group to write a case about something that worked well in science classrooms or other professional contexts. In groups of three to four, each person presents a case and then listens silently as the rest of the group analyzes it for factors that led to its success. After all members of the small groups have presented a case and had it analyzed by others, the small groups summarize the success factors and post them for others to examine.

A third protocol, which is sometimes known as Peeling the Onion, helps people address issues related to curriculum, instruction, assessment, or any other aspect of teaching science. The person bringing the issue to a group is not necessarily the person who has the issue, just someone who wants to have it addressed. The presenter describes the issue fully while participants take notes and then ask one or two key questions. Then, everyone does a short free-write on the issue and key questions. As in the tuning protocol, the presenter then becomes an observer as the group discusses the issue. The first part of the discussion focuses on understanding with statements such as these:

- "What I heard [the presenter(s) say] is..."
- "One assumption that seems to be part of the problem/dilemma is..." OR, "One thing I assume to be true about this problem is... "
- "The heart of this issue is. . . ."
- "A question this raises for me is...“
- In additional rounds, the group asks and discusses probing questions such as these:
- "What would happen if. . . ?"
- "How would X be different if. . . ?"
- "What's another way you might. . .?"
- "What do you assume to be true about. . .?"

Then, the presenter reflects aloud, without interruption by the participants, about the points discussed by the group. Effort should be taken to avoid a defensive rebuttal. Instead, the goal is to thoughtfully build on the ideas that were generated. Finally, the whole group debriefs the content and the process.

There are many protocols not discussed in this chapter that science teachers can use effectively in PLCs. Some of these include the slice, the descriptive review, the collaborative assessment conference, the consultancy, the text-based (Socratic) seminar, and the last word protocol.

Conclusion

Jeremy's experience at the beginning of this chapter was disappointing. His ideas for improving science education for all students were exciting, but, without support, they died a slow death. What a difference a supportive environment can have on improving a school or department! As a member of a community of leaders in science education, and with access to a variety of professional learning strategies, his innovation might have seen the light of the classroom—and the light in his students' eyes.

Science educators who see themselves as part of a professional learning community relentlessly search for new and better ways of helping students learn science. They find the work of a PLC infinitely more energizing than the business-as-usual meetings that characterize faculty and department meetings. They engage in a process—inquiry—that is essential for them in their field. The way that teachers learn affects how students learn. What could be a more natural way for science educators to learn than inquiring into teaching and learning through professional learning strategies in their PLCs? What could be a more natural way to teach science?

References

Ancess, J. 2000. The reciprocal influence of teacher learning, teaching practice, school restructuring, and student learning outcomes. *Teachers College Record* 102 (3): 560–619.

Blankstein, A. 2004. *Failure is not an option: Six principles that guide student achievement in high-performing schools.* Thousand Oaks, CA: Corwin Press.

Cushman, K. 1998. How friends can be critical as schools make essential changes. *Horace* 14 (5): 1–20.

Deming, W. E. 2000. *The new economics for industry, government, education,* 2nd ed. Boston: MIT Press.

DuFour, R., R. DuFour, and R. Eaker. 2008. *Revisiting professional learning communities at work: New insights for improving schools.* Bloomington, IN: Solution Tree.

DuFour, R., and R. Eaker. 1998. *Professional learning communities at work: Best practices for enhancing student achievement.* Bloomington, IN: Solution Tree.

Easton, L. B. 2009. *Protocols for professional learning.* Alexandria, VA: Association for Supervision and Curriculum Development.

———, ed. 2008. *Powerful designs for professional learning.* Oxford, OH: National Staff Development Council.

Hord, S. M. 1997. *Professional learning communities: Communities of continuous inquiry and improvement.* Austin, TX: Southwest Educational Development Laboratory.

Hord, S. M., and H. M. Robertson. 2008. Accessing student voices, in *Powerful designs for professional learning,* ed. L. B. Easton, 53–62. Oxford, OH: National Staff Development Council.

Hord, S. M., and W. A. Sommers. 2008. *Leading professional learning communities: Voices from research and practice.* Thousand Oaks, CA: Corwin Press and the National Staff Development Council.

Kruse, S., K. S. Louis, and A. S. Bryk. 1994. Building professional community in schools. *Issues in restructuring schools* 6 (spring).

Lewis, C., and R. Perry. 2008. What is successful adaptation of lesson study in the U.S.? *Journal of Educational Change* (March 14).

Mitchell, R., and S. Kennedy-Salchow. 2008. Standards in practice, in *Powerful designs for professional learning*, ed. L. B. Easton, 229–242. Oxford, OH: National Staff Development Council.

Roberts, S. M., and E. Z. Pruitt. 2009. *Schools as professional learning communities: Collaborative activities and strategies for professional development*, 2nd ed. Thousand Oaks, CA: Corwin Press.

Senge, P. 1990. *The fifth discipline: The art and practice of the learning organization*. New York: Doubleday.

Senge, P., A. Kleiner, C. Roberts, R. B. Ross, and B. J. Smith. 1994. *The fifth discipline fieldbook: Strategies and tools for building a learning organization*. New York: Doubleday.

Sizer, T. R. 2004. *Horace's compromise*. New York: Mariner Books.

Smith, L. 2008. *Schools That Change*. California: Corwin Press.

Resources

Annenberg Institute for School Reform. 2004. Professional learning communities: Professional development strategies that improve instruction. *www.annenberginstitute.org/images/ProfLearning.pdf*

Cochran-Smith, M., and S. L. Lytle. 1999. Relationships of knowledge and practice: Teacher learning in communities. In *Review of research in education*, eds. A. Iran-Nejad and P. D. Pearson, 24. Washington, DC: American Educational Research Association.

Darling-Hamond, L., S. Orcutt, and D. Martin, D. 2003. Pulling it all together: Creating classrooms and schools that support learning. In *The learning classroom: Theory into practice 1–5, 25–27*. Stanford, CA: Stanford University School of Education.

Darling-Hammond, L., R. C. Wei, A. Andree, N. Richardson, and S. Orphanos. 2009. *Professional learning in the earning professional: A status report on teacher development in the United States and abroad*. Oxford, OH: National Staff Development Council.

Duke, D. L. 2006. What we know and don't know about improving low-performing schools. *Phi delta kappan* 87 (10): 728–734.

DuFour, R., R. DuFour, R. Eaker, and G. Karhanek. 2004. *Whatever it takes: How professional communities respond when kids don't learn.* Bloomington, IN: Solution Tree.

DuFour, R., R. DuFour, R. Eaker, and T. Many. 2006. *Learning by doing: A handbook for professional learning communities at work.* Bloomington, IN: Solution Tree.

Eaker, R., R. DuFour, and R. DuFour. 2002. *Getting started: Reculturing schools to become professional learning communities.* Bloomington, IN: Solution Tree.

Erb, T. O. 1995. Teamwork in middle school education. In *Teamwork models and experience in education,* ed. H. G. Garner, 175–198. Boston: Allyn and Bacon.

Fal, J., B. E. Drayton, and S-Y. Lee. 2004. The pivotal role of teacher collaboration in sustaining systemic reform efforts. Paper presented at the Annual Conference of the American Education Research Association, San Diego, CA.

Goddard, R. D., W. K. Hoy, and H. A. Woolfolk. 2000. Collective teacher efficacy: Its meaning, measure and impact on student achievement. *American Educational Research Journal* 37: 479–508.

Hausman, C. S., and E. B. Goldring. 2001. Sustaining teacher commitment: The role of professional communities. *Peabody Journal of Education* 76 (2): 30–51.

Hord, S. M., ed. 2004. *Learning together, leading together: Changing schools through professional learning communities.* New York: Teachers College Press.

Inger, M. 1993. *Teacher collaboration in urban secondary schools.* New York, NY: ERIC Clearinghouse on Urban Education. (ERIC/CUE Digest No. 93).

Keating, J., R. Eaker, R. DuFour, and R. DuFour. 2008. The journey to becoming a professional learning community. Bloomington, IN: Solution Tree.

Little, J. W. 2002. Locating learning in teachers' communities of practice: Opening up problems of analysis in records of everyday work. *Teaching and Teacher Education* 18 (8): 917–946.

Little, J. W. 2003. Inside teacher community: Representations of classroom practice. *Teachers College Record* 105 (6): 913–945.

Little, J. W., and I. S. Horn. Forthcoming. Normalizing problems of practice: Converting routine conversation into a resource for learning in professional communities. In *Professional learning communities: Divergence, detail and difficulties*, eds. L. Stoll and K. S. Louis. London: Open University Press.

Louis, C. C. 2008. Lesson study, in *Powerful designs for professional learning*, 2nd ed., ed. L. B. Easton, 171–184. Oxford, OH: National Staff Development Council.

Marks, H. M., and K. S. Louis. 1997. Does teacher empowerment affect the classroom: The implications of teacher empowerment for instruction practice and student academic performance. *Educational evaluation and policy analysis* 19: 245–275.

McLaughlin, M. W., and J. E. Talbert. 2001. *Professional communities and the work of high school teaching*. Chicago: University of Chicago Press.

Wilson, S. M., and J. Berne. 1999. Teacher learning and the acquisition of professional knowledge: An examination of research on contemporary professional development. *Review of Research in Education* 24: 173–209.

Chapter 14

Leading Through Collaboration
Historically Black Colleges and Universities Preparing Future Teacher Leaders in Science Education

Helen Bond and Izolda Fotiyeva

Introduction

This chapter will address how to create a community of minority science teacher leaders who are not only committed to teaching in urban schools, but also to helping close the achievement gap, especially in the area of science education. One method is to incubate them in a learning community with special expertise in producing science, technology, engineering, and mathematics (STEM) graduates. Historically Black Colleges and Universities (HBCUs) have been the main producers of minority STEM graduates. This chapter explores the role of HBCUs and their collaborators in cultivating a leadership network to implement science education. The National Aeronautics and Space Administration (NASA) sponsored Pre-Service Teacher Program (PSTP) and Pre-Service Institute (PSIT) will be highlighted as effective examples of this effort.

Effective Instruction

Science leadership begins with good teaching. Good teaching is enriched through collaboration, effective preparation, and professional development. Preparing preK–12 students for careers in science, technology, engineering, and mathematics cannot be accomplished without competent teachers leading the way. Teachers that are strong in both science content and inquiry-based pedagogy are a critical component of the foundation upon which continuing science education is built. They lead through competence and a willful desire to raise student achievement. While science leadership is needed at every level within school systems, teacher leaders bridge the policy and political gaps by connecting students with effective instruction (Rhoton and McLean 2008).

Leaky Pipeline

This loss of potential leaders is especially true in urban settings where well intended bureaucracy may hamper change efforts. Many urban schools are plagued by low levels of academic achievement that hamper minority students' future prospects in STEM careers (NACME 2008). This is often referred to as the "leaky pipeline" where students drip from the pipe before they have a chance to pursue degrees in STEM fields (LPFI 2005). The National Action Council for Minorities in Engineering (NACME) identified a section of this leaky pipe as the "four percent problem" (2008). The four percent problem is the painfully low percentage of minority students that leave high school eligible to pursue an engineering degree. In 2002, approximately 690,000 minority students were awarded graduation diplomas. Of this number, a mere 28,000 had the necessary courses in mathematics and science to even enroll in an engineering program of study in college (NACME 2008). According to ACT (2005), some students who have taken STEM coursework are still ill-prepared for college-level work in the subjects of English, mathematics, and science, and the percentage of minority students prepared for these critical college preparatory subjects is even lower than that of the population as a whole.

NACME refers to this lack of college readiness as the "new American dilemma" (2008, p. 3). A report published by the National Academies describes it as a national security problem, and the general public knows it as the achievement gap (The Committee on Prospering in the Global

Economy of the 21st Century 2007). Leadership at all levels is critically important in science education and other STEM fields, but without effective instruction in the classroom, even the best leadership efforts will likely fail.

Role of Teacher Leaders

This is where teacher leadership comes in. Katzenmeyer and Moller (1996) emphasize the importance of teachers as the critical link in sustaining leadership, especially in the area of improved professional practice. They define teacher leaders as those "who lead within and beyond the classroom, influence others toward improved educational practice, and identify with and contribute to a community of teacher leaders" (p. 6). Teacher leaders consistently demonstrate the following traits: expertise in instruction, collaboration with others, a lifelong commitment to learning, reflexive practice skills, ability to take reasonable risks, and commitment to being active in the professional community, such as by participating in the preparation of preservice teachers (Katzenmeyer and Moller 1996; Maton and Hrabowski 2004).

Role of HBCUs

The key question is how to create a community of minority science teacher leaders who are knowledgeable and committed to serving an urban or minority population. One way is to grow and nourish these future teachers in learning communities. This technique has a nearly 200-year history of producing successful graduates. HBCUs are institutions founded for the education of African Americans, but they do not exclude others from attending. Cheyney University of Pennsylvania was established in 1837, making it the first HBCU. Then in 1867, shortly after the end of the Civil War, Howard University opened its illustrious doors. For minority students, HBCUs have been the main producers of STEM graduates and graduates in general.

In 2000, HBCUs produced almost 40% of all bachelor degrees in the natural sciences earned by African Americans (SEF 2005). There are a total of 105 HBCUs in the United States. Despite comprising only 3% of the higher education community, they collectively enroll 14% of all African American students (Gregory et al. 2008).

What do HBCUs have to offer that other schools do not in producing a strong community of minority science teacher leaders? HBCUs have special tools at their disposal. These tools include a wealth of minority faculty, positive campus climates, less assimilating pressure, higher levels of interaction between faculty and peers, familiar community and culture, and many opportunities to demonstrate leadership. Leadership opportunities flourish at HBCUs (NACME 2008; Maton and Hrabowski 2004). Preservice teachers have numerous opportunities at their disposal to increase their science knowledge, and by building this knowledge, they increase their capacity to lead.

Katzenmeyer and Moller's (1996) definition of a teacher leader is one who identifies with and contributes to a larger community. It is important that minority preservice teachers of science see themselves as part of a larger science community. One way to accomplish this is to enrich and expand the learning community through collaboration. While HBCUs offer a warm and welcoming environment, collaborating with Traditionally White Institutions (TWI), Tribal Colleges and Universities (TCUs), Hispanic Serving Institutions (HSIs), and formal and informal science organizations (like NASA) enables preservice teachers at HBCUs to further expand their science knowledge and sense of community. Minority preservice teachers working with others benefit from mutual association.

Pre-Service Teacher Program

The Pre-Service Teacher Program (PSTP) at NASA Langley Research Center in Hampton, Virginia, is one example of such collaboration. Since its development in 1994, PSTP has collaborated with a number of HBCUs to organize 13 years of science conferences specially designed to enhance the development of science teachers. TWIs, HSIs, TCUs, and HBCUs are invited to participate. The PSTP initiative is funded by the Minority Universities Research and Education Division in the Office of Equal Opportunities. The basic premise behind the PSTP program is to enhance the training of preservice K–8 teachers in mathematics, science, and technology. One unique aspect of the PSTP program is the way that HBCUs work together to create leadership and learning opportunities for future minority teachers.

In 2008, a new emphasis on engineering was included in the PSTP. This changed the PSTP to the Pre-Service Teacher STEM Program (PSTSP). The annual conference's program offers a wide variety of activities, including keynote speakers, workshops, a judged educational poster competition, talent show, and more. For example, the 2007–2008 program included an annual three-day conference for preservice teachers in Washington D.C., a two-week Pre-Service Teacher Institute (PSTI) held at the Langley Research Center, and a two-day Pre-Institute Professional Development session for faculty participating in the institute.

In addition to the conference, the PSTI was developed because of the need to provide a more in-depth experience for preservice teachers. At the PSTI, preservice teachers spend two weeks being exposed to problem-based learning, mathematics, and other science and technology–based activities. Preservice teachers are able to interact with NASA personnel and tour NASA facilities. These preservice teachers learn to incorporate NASA's cutting-edge research into lesson plans for elementary and middle school teachers. The institute culminates with preservice teachers developing and teaching problem-based lessons to children from local schools.

Howard University School of Education

Howard University preservice teachers have been participating in the program since 1997. The coauthor of this chapter, Dr. Fotiyeva, served as an advisor for the Howard University team for three consecutive years. In 2008, for the first time, the Howard University team won first place in the very competitive Poster Competition. The title of the prize-winning poster and corresponding lesson was *Why Did Pluto Get Kicked Out of the Planet Club?*

The 2008 conference guests included approximately 350 students, faculty advisors, and ambassadors from more than 50 colleges and universities across the United States. It was an eye-opening opportunity for many of the preservice teachers, some of whom had never had a chance to attend a professional conference. The popular keynote speaker for the opening session was Dr. Calvin Mackie, President of the Channel Zero Group, an organization committed to maximizing the effectiveness and potential of individuals and organizations. Dr. Mackie—speaker, author, educator, and inventor—was honored in 2003 by President Bush with the

Presidential Award for Excellence in Science, Mathematics, and Engineering Mentoring.

The diverse workshop offerings covered a wide range of STEM and STEM-related topics, such as NIA/NASA Future Forums—Supporting STEM Education; CSI = Creative Science Inquiry; Innovative Strategies for Leveraging Technology to Engage Young Students; Inspiring Future Engineers; and Earth Counts: Integrating Math and Human Ecology.

Six Howard University preservice teachers participated in the NASA Pre-Service Teacher Conference in 2008. The group, led by Dr. Fotiyeva, began working on the poster and lesson plan competition in October 2007. The first task was to choose an innovative and creative science topic that the judges, most of whom are NASA scientists, would appreciate and consider competitive. Strong integration of mathematics and technology in the lesson plan was critical.

An important aspect of the program at Howard University is that preservice teachers choose a topic that is outside their comfort zone, meaning a topic that is not plant-, animal-, or weather-related. As part of the topic development phase, the preservice teachers were treated to a tour of the National Air and Space Museum. A guide standing near the model of the solar system informed the team about Pluto being demoted from the status of planet to dwarf planet. The students became very interested in how this happened. The question clearly etched across their faces was "How could the planet that we know and love suddenly become a non-planet?" This became the topic for the lesson plan and the poster. The group continued to meet weekly throughout the fall and spring semesters. They developed an integrated lesson plan and a very imaginative poster. The lesson "Why Did Pluto Get Kicked Out of the Planet Club?" engages fifth-grade students in discovering why Pluto is no longer classified as a planet in our solar system. The constructivist 5-E lesson plan model was used to demonstrate the ways in which the science lesson would achieve its objectives of modeling and promoting the use of scientific inquiry among fifth graders. The 5-E lesson plan consists of the following parts: *Engage* in planetary science; *Explore* and become "experts" of the planets through technology-based research; *Explain* findings about the research through the creation of a comic strip; *Elaborate* on knowledge through a mathematical connection of mass, gravity, and graphing of their weights and ages on Pluto; and *Evaluate* comprehension of planetary science through the use of several standards-based rubrics. The rubrics assessed the legibility, precision, and accuracy of the classroom data represented through graphs. In addition, another rubric assessed the illustration of the importance of construction, creativity, theme, time, and effort within the planetary comic strips, which was included for creativity. The lesson designed for fifth-grade students consisted of exploring the modern phenomenon of a nine-planet solar system converting into an eight-planet solar system through planetary science, technology, and mathematics. The Howard University team presented the lesson plan to a panel of judges, followed by a question-and-answer session. The criteria included were strong content knowledge of astronomy, as well as the inclusion of mathematics, technology, and language arts. In addition to ranking high in all of these areas, the judges commented that the lesson was the most enthusiastic and interesting. The Howard University team of preservice teachers was awarded first place in the competition. The team met for a final reflection about the knowledge and experience they had gained from the conference. A sample of their reflections is provided below. This material does not consist of exact quotes, but it represents the general themes embodied in the reflections.

- The conference enhanced my knowledge, skills, and strategies for teaching mathematics and science.
- I became more enthusiastic and self-confident in teaching science and mathematics.
- The conference provided me with relevant curricula and resource materials for teaching mathematics and science at the elementary and middle school levels.
- The conference helped me to develop more positive attitudes about teaching science, mathematics, and technology.

Conclusion

The lesson presented by the Howard University team of preservice teachers was designed to create a sense of wonder and discovery for elementary school students. However, the fifth graders were not the only beneficiaries. The activity helped the preservice teachers understand the work of scientists and the nature of science. One aim of the NASA preservice teacher conferences and institutes is to promote the use of scientific inquiry.

Leadership cannot be developed or sustained in the absence of knowledge, and knowledge is enhanced through collaboration. By collaborating with NASA's preservice teacher programs, HBCUs and other colleges and universities are taking beneficial steps toward the development of teacher leaders in science education.

References

ACT. 2005. Crisis at the core: Preparing all students for college and work. *Activity* 43 (Winter).

Committee on Prospering in the Global Economy of the 21st Century. 2007. *Rising above the gathering storm: Energizing and employing America for a brighter economic future.* Washington, DC: The National Academies.

Gregory, S., W. Dianne, P. Tawan, and R. Charlisha. 2008. Historically black colleges and universities: Caretakers of precious treasure. *Journal of College Admission* (fall): 24–29.

Katzenmeyer, M., and G. Moller. 1996. *Awakening the sleeping giant: Leadership development for teachers.* Thousand Oaks, CA: Corwin Press.

Level Playing Field Institute (LPFI). 2005. *Increasing the representation women and people of color in science, technology, engineering, and math (STEM).* Washington, DC: LPFI.

Maton, K. I., and F. A. Hrabowski III. 2004. Increasing the number of African American PhDs in the sciences and engineering: A strengths-based approach. *American Psychologist* (59): 547–556.

National Action Council for Minorities in Engineering (NACME). 2008. Confronting the "new" American dilemma. Underrepresented minorities in engineering: A data-based look at diversity. *www.nacme.org/user/docs/NACME 08 ResearchReport.pdf*

Rhoton, J., and J. E. McLean. 2008. Developing teacher leaders in science: Catalysts for improved science teaching and student learning. *Science Educator* 17 (2): 45–56.

Southern Education Foundation (SEF). 2005. *Igniting potential: Historically black colleges and universities and science, technology, and engineering, and mathematics. www.sefatl.org/pdf/Igniting-Potential.pdf*

Chapter 15

Assessing Assessment to Inform Science Leadership

Don Duggan-Haas

As science educators, we should hold evidence-backed explanation paramount. Evidence-based assessment of our students' understandings, of
our own understandings, and of our teaching provides the framework to
question and to lead.

What do we try to assess? What actually gets assessed? What should we
assess? Why can students succeed in school without really learning? How
can changing the nature of assessments change the nature and direction
of science teaching? The NSF-funded project Regional and Local (ReaL)
Earth System Science engaged early-career teachers in investigating these
questions. The teacher participants in this network have continued to
wrestle with these questions and helped their colleagues to do likewise,
both in their own schools and through workshops they have led.

Five questions drove the project:
- Why does this place look the way it does? (This is the focus question
  for science instruction.)
- What ideas are essential for understanding the Earth system?

- How should research on the ways that people learn inform the strategies that we use to teach? (This is the focus for engaging in analysis of our teaching.)
- How and why can students succeed in school without really learning? (This is the focus for engaging in the analysis of our assessment.)
- How can we build and sustain a network of teachers who pursue questions like these?

This chapter uses the ReaL Earth System Science project as a metaphor for investigating the landscape of assessment in science education. This framing turns the focus of the five questions away from the Earth system and toward the system of educational assessment. This chapter is as much an assessment of *what* to assess as it is of *how* to assess. The adage "What gets tested is what gets taught" highlights the intertwined nature of these processes. This metacognitive and meta-assessment approach brings forth questions that provide direction for educational leadership.

Evidence Is Paramount

Assessing the system of assessment might reasonably lead to the conclusion that we typically assess the wrong things and assess them badly. Evidence is paramount in science, and yet much, if not most, of what we do in science classrooms is based on tradition and intuition. This problem cuts across the teaching enterprise. Assessment is the collection and evaluation of evidence. It is inquiry. In education, we tend to think of assessment in terms of student understanding, but we should also assess the nature of the system and use that assessment to guide our actions within the system. Unfortunately, assessment intended to inform action frequently misses the mark.

There was, for example, no evidence-based assessment—no *On the Origin of Courses* authored by some educational equivalent of Charles Darwin—that laid down a set of fundamental natural laws on how to structure educational systems. Nor are there any universally agreed upon descriptions of the content that everyone should understand about *any* topic that have been successfully implemented on a large scale, in spite of countless attempts to do just that throughout history. Strategies for the assessment of student understanding fall into the same category. In all of these cases, we most commonly use the techniques that we are comfortable with, rather than practices that are grounded firmly in research. The practice of doing things with which we are comfortable and about which we feel knowledgeable rather than doing what needs to be done is part of what Dietrich Dörner called "the logic of failure" (1996). How can we collect the kind of evidence necessary to better direct our educational endeavors?

Typical assessment, like the curriculum in which it sits, is an inch deep and a mile wide. We assess both too much and not enough—too much content and not enough depth. In order for assessment to be more useful in guiding instruction, it must include more focus on the *how* of science than on the *what*. It is a great and largely unmet challenge to determine what and how to assess, as well as what do with the information gathered through assessment.

Assessment should give us evidence to steer our educational course. Defined broadly, assessment has a history of doing just that. Assessment of our scientific standing in the world led to the Sputnik-inspired reforms in the middle of the last century. Assessment of the dearth of scientific understanding led to Project 2061 and *The National Science Education Standards* (NRC 1996). Assessment and evaluation of the effectiveness of these initiatives are now leading educators to sharpen their focus on bigger ideas over longer stretches of instructional time through the development of learning progressions (Duschl, Schweingruber, and Shouse 2007; Michaels, Shouse, and Schweingruber 2008; Smith et al. 2006) and NSTA's Science Anchors (Mervis 2006; NSTA n.d.). Although the National Science Education Standards (NSES) and state standards derived from the NSES require less content than is traditionally covered in school science, these standards still assume deep understanding of more content than is feasible. Robert Marzano (2003) estimates that schools only have about 9,042 available instructional hours to teach 15,465 hours worth of the standards required in most K–12 state standards documents. Overwhelmed, teachers are forced to make "idiosyncratic decisions regarding what should be covered and to what extent" (p. 23).

This chapter will describe assessment as a type of inquiry and use Regional and Local (ReaL) Earth System Science—a National Science Foundation–funded professional development and curriculum materials project for early career Earth science teachers—as a metaphor for investigating the nature, structure, and role of assessment in science education leadership. Through this lens, we will see that assessment, like Earth system science, is both a form of inquiry and a body of knowledge, and we will consider what constitutes the most important ideas of both Earth system science and educational assessment.

Assessment Is Inquiry

Assessment and *evaluation* are terms used to describe inquiry into student understanding. These terms are frequently used interchangeably, and both act sometimes as nouns and other times as verbs. Assessments and evaluations are instruments or methods used to measure student understanding. There is no clear line between the two, but evaluation tends more toward quantification, whereas assessment more frequently refers to teacher-created materials and approaches. While both of these concepts should be thought of as something used in the service of helping students learn, evaluation tends toward a snapshot taken at the end of a period or unit of instruction. Conversely, assessment, especially when it is labeled as "embedded" or "authentic," is woven into the fabric of instruction, and, most importantly, assessment *informs* instruction. Assessment should be seen as an iterative process. Evaluation can be seen as linear.

Assessment Is Cyclic

Inquiry is commonly viewed as a cyclic process, (Krajcik et al. 1998; AAAS 1993; University of California, Berkeley Graduate School of Education and Lawrence Hall of Science 2009; White and Frederiksen 1998) and cyclic views of assessment have been discussed (Ash and Levitt 2003; Harlen et al. 2000; Harlen, Brand, and Brown 2003). Compare Figures 1 and 2. Both show inquiry cycles, but the first is generic and the second is specific to educational assessment.

Chinn and Malhotra (2002) contrasted school and scientific inquiry. They differentiated between simple inquiry tasks and authentic scientific inquiry tasks. In classrooms with authentic inquiry tasks, elementary students are asked to engage in a kind of inquiry more sophisticated than the kind of inquiry represented by typical school assessment. However, classrooms that utilize authentic scientific inquiry are relatively uncommon.

Most school inquiry falls into one of three categories: simple experi-

Figure 1. One Configuration of the Inquiry Cycle

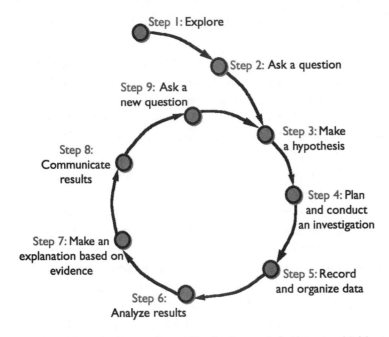

(Adapted from The Seeds of Science/Roots of Reading Inquiry Cycle, University of California, Berkeley Graduate School of Education, and Lawrence Hall of Science 2009.) This configuration is intended for use at the fourth- and fifth-grade levels.

Figure 2. One Form of the Assessment Cycle

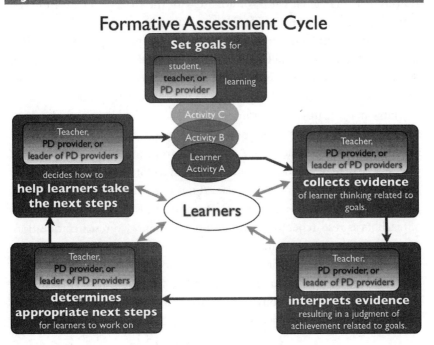

(adapted from Harlen et al. 2000; Harlen, Brand, and Brown 2003)

ments, simple observations, or simple illustrations. In these inquiries, students tend to use a provided research question to investigate one or two variables that have been determined by the teacher. If there are control variables, there is typically only one, and it is defined for the student. Students are told what to measure and observe, as well as how to do so. The complex chains of inference common to authentic science are missing. Observer bias is typically not addressed. Outcomes can typically only be generalized to exactly similar situations. Each of the above limitations differentiates school inquiry from authentic scientific inquiry (Chinn and Malhotra 2002). Parallels to most or all of these limitations also apply to the simple inquiries of most school assessment.

Logically, increasing the complexity of assessment about inquiry will increase the complexity of the inquiry teaching, as is reflected in the common lament, "What gets tested is what gets taught." This may be related to science assessment's fundamental role in leading educational change.

Chinn and Malhotra (2002) evaluated textbook- and researcher-created inquiries in terms of 11 features of authentic inquiry. In the nine textbooks analyzed, activities averaged less than 0.5 of these inquiry features. The 26 tasks developed by researchers faired somewhat better, averaging 2.9 out of 11. Their 11 features resonate with the five essential features of inquiry as defined in the NSES. These features are (1) Learner engages in scientifically oriented questions, (2) Learner gives priority to evidence in responding to questions, (3) Learner formulates explanations from evidence, (4) Learner connects explanations to scientific knowledge, and 5) Learner communicates and justifies explanations to others (NRC 2000).

How many features of inquiry would be identified in an analysis of a typical classroom's assessment over the course of a year? This may seem like an unreasonable question. After all, it can be argued that, in large part, teachers seek very similar outcomes. All devoted teachers desire to help their students improve understandings relevant to their grade or subject. If most teachers are targeting the same ends, is it appropriate to think of teachers as researchers who should pursue their own research questions regarding student understanding?

There are several reasons that teachers should treat their teaching and assessment as areas of research. Every student and every classroom is characterized by a unique combination of factors affecting teaching and learning. Teachers who act as agents of inquiry act as models for their students by showing a scientific attitude. The act of researching student understanding professionalizes the act of teaching and brings deeper understanding of understanding than is likely to be achieved by translating the work of others to your classroom. (See the work of Emily Van Zee for much more on teachers as educational researchers.)

Assessment Is an Inch Deep and a Mile Wide

The first principle is that you must not fool yourself and you are the easiest person to fool.

—Richard Feynman

If the curriculum is an inch deep, then the assessment of the knowledge that students gain from that curriculum is unlikely to be deeper. The shallow depth refers to more than just the content and processes being assessed. It also refers to the superficiality of educator inquiry into student thinking. This is not to say that student understandings don't run deeper—sometimes they do. However, the instruments that are commonly used in this inquiry do not tell us that.

This shallowness invites broad interpretation of the evidence. The now classic *Private Universe* videos showed that students who were remarkably successful (and therefore successful in typical assessments) were largely clueless if the assessment more than scratched the surface of understanding (Harvard-Smithsonian Center for Astrophysics 1995). This highlights one of the ways that assessment can fool educators into believing that understanding is widespread.

Figure 3, page 248, is a modified version of a question asked on New York State's 2008 Eighth-Grade Science Test. What do different kinds of answers to this question tell us? Any science teacher will recognize it as a question about density, and many students will view this question the same way. However, an English language learner who has not seen the demonstration in science class (and where else would anyone see such a thing?) may well answer the question perfectly so long as she recognizes that the numbers in the diagram are in sequence and that the numbers above can be plugged into that sequence.

Figure 3. Modified Version of a Standardized Test Question.

The text of the question was replaced with nonsense. Note that the question is still answerable, and that the only skills needed to answer the question correctly are the abilities to recognize a sequence and place numbers within that sequence.

71 Chicken, chicken, chicken. Chicken chicken chicken chicken. Chicken. Chicken chicken chicken chicken chicken.

Chicken, chicken, chicken.

Chicken	Chicken (ch/kn)
Chicken ♥	8.90
Chicken ☺	1.17
Chicken ☎	1.34
Chicken ⚥	0.71

Chicken, chicken, chicken. Chicken chicken chicken chicken. Chicken. Chicken chicken chicken chicken chicken.

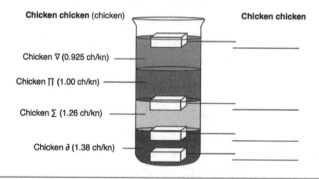

Asking elementary school students to draw a scientist often yields cartoonish and stereotypical representations of wild-eyed, wild-haired men in lab coats (Chambers 1983; Symington and Spurling 1990; Thomas, Henley and Snell 2006). Does that mean kids really believe this is what scientists look like? Probably not, as rephrasing the question to ask for a realistic drawing of scientists yields fairly different results. Just because I draw a smiley face on the Sun in a diagram doesn't mean that I think the Sun has a mouth. While this assessment does provide some insight about elementary students' conceptions regarding the nature of science and scientists, the drawings that these students produce should be considered more indicative of their level of whimsy.

Many assessments will test different abilities for different students, no matter how well designed those assessments are. Virtually all science tests are reading tests first. If all "A" papers look the same, that is an indicator that the assessment does not teach independent thinking and may not be testing the targeted content.

The Components of ReaL and ReaL as Metaphor

ReaL's goals were to help teachers teach about local and regional geology in an inquiry-oriented way through the use of both virtual and actual fieldwork and to build a network of emerging teacher-leaders. A byproduct of this work was the creation of virtual fieldwork experiences. This grant work also included making revisions to *The Teacher Friendly Guide to the Geology of the Northeastern U.S.* in order to include additional pedagogical support for inquiry teaching.

The project asked that teacher participants (1) apply research on how people learn (Donovan, Bransford and Pellegrino 1999; Donovan and Bransford 2005) to the design of instruction; (2) target instruction on the understanding of five profound ideas about the Earth system, how we have come to understand those ideas, and how understanding those ideas should inform our actions; (3) engage students in fieldwork through actual and/or virtual means of the teacher's own design; and, (4) collaborate in a network of other early career Earth science teachers in order to achieve these goals.

Virtual fieldwork experiences (VFEs; see *http://virtualfieldwork.org*) are as much a by-product as a product of the project. They provided a vehicle by which we gave teachers a short, mentored experience in fieldwork (during the workshop that initiated the professional development) and provided a focus point for discussions about inquiry, how students learn, assessment, teaching in the field, and VFE creation. They also provided a reason for teachers to look closely at their local environment. These discussions continued over a two-year period using internet conferencing through Skype. The virtual study groups engaged in an ongoing assessment of pedagogy and content knowledge. Considerable time was spent pondering how students could be successful in classes while clearly not understanding the target content. Mentored field experiences coupled with strong nudges to look closely at geologically interesting local fieldwork sites and produce a representation of those sites for use in instruction are logical steps toward creating opportunities for students to engage in both virtual and actual fieldwork. The four project activities act as parallels to what we should be doing with the use of assessment in the development of educational leadership. In our work as educational leaders, we should:

- apply research on how people learn to the design of our instruction,
- target instruction at the most profoundly important ideas derived from educational research,
- engage teachers in the fieldwork of studying their own students' understanding, and
- build networks of educators to achieve these goals. Curriculum programming should be designed with measurable goals in mind and be driven by engaging questions.

Why Does This Place Look the Way It Does?

This question, directed at physical landscapes, drove student and teacher work in ReaL. The ultimate goal of ReaL was to have students tell the story of local landscapes by drawing evidence from the landscape itself, as well as from external sources, and to integrate big ideas of Earth system science into those explanations. And they did literally draw; teachers worked with students to create geologic maps and stratigraphic columns, as well as illustrated posters designed to explain the story of the landscape. Evidence for these explanations should be drawn from both micro and macro scales, and that evidence should then be stitched together into a coherent story that acknowledges the interaction of Earth systems. Students should be able to describe how a place and its constituent parts came to look the way it does. Ideally, learners use the local landscape to understand the global landscape. The attention to the role of evidence highlights another goal: to be reflective and analytical, as well as to wrestle with the overarching questions, "How do we know what we know?" and "How does what we know inform our decision making?" These are lofty goals.

In educational leadership, we want the educators we work with to be able to tell the story of their local educational landscape by drawing evidence from their surroundings and external sources. Here, too, we want the incorporation of profound ideas of the discipline integrated into explanations of real-life observations. As in ReaL, learners (now the educators rather than the students) should draw evidence from a range of scales and stitch the evidence together into a coherent whole that acknowledges the interaction of the involved systems. In this case, the systems involved are educational and social. We wish to use the local to understand the global, and we wish to have understanding inform action. The important overarching questions are the same in both settings. Again, these are lofty goals. See Table 1.

In the case of either the physical landscape outside our window or the educational landscape, we are interested in a form of forensic inquiry. We want to understand how this place came to be the way that it is; if we do not like what we see, we must figure what we should do to change it and prevent similar problems from occurring elsewhere. Then we must share our understandings with others.

Assessing deep understandings elicits stories. These stories are tales of what led to what and how different actors are connected to one another.

Table 1. Comparing Guiding Questions

	In Earth systems science:	**In educational assessment:**
Driving Questions:	Why does this place look the way it does?	Why does understanding look the way it does?
	In both contexts, "look" is a proxy. We generally want to know why something is the way it is.	
Underlying Questions:	How do you characterize the landscape?	How do you characterize understanding?
	What is the landscape like (at multiple scales and from multiple perspectives)?	What are the understandings like (at multiple scales and from multiple perspectives)?
	What is the available evidence to tell the history of the landscape?	What is the available evidence to tell the history of the landscape?
Predictive and Reflective Questions:	What outcomes are likely?	
	How do we know what we know?	
	In what ways might we be misled? (In what ways might evidence be misinterpreted?)	
	How does what we understand inform what we should do? Why?	

Without a storyline emerging from assessment, we lack the conceptual framework that ties bits of knowledge together, and this is needed to achieve deep understanding.

What to Assess? Big Questions and Big Ideas

What if a high school science course only taught five things? What if teachers understood five things about assessment in such a deep way that they truly understood a great deal? If every American deeply understood a few ideas about the Earth system, what should those ideas be? If every science teacher deeply understood a few ideas about assessment, what should those ideas be? We began our work with early-career Earth science teachers by raising the first of these two questions. Stop reading and consider your answers to both of these questions.

Figure 4 lays out a tentative answer to the first question. These big ideas resonate with Project 2061's Common Themes (AAAS 1989, 1993). This chapter is intended to initiate a discussion about the second question. These questions drew inspiration from Richard Feynman, who asked:

> If, in some cataclysm, all of scientific knowledge were to be destroyed, and only one sentence passed on to the next generations of creatures, what statement would contain the most information in the fewest words? (1963, pp. 1–2)

Working with Sarah Miller, then an MAT student, we first asked a more Earth science–specific version of the question of ourselves and then of our colleagues: "If all understanding of Earth science was lost except for a few paragraphs, what should those few paragraphs say?" and a follow-up question: "What understandings do we want students to hold onto as a result of taking Earth science?" We were in pursuit of the "big ideas" of the discipline. In fact, we sought the *biggest* ideas of the discipline—ideas larger in scope than those identified by many others who use the label, including Wiggins and McTighe (1998, 2005) and their series of Earth system science literacy initiatives (on climate science, atmospheric science, Earth science, and ocean science).[1]

---

1. The Earth Science Literacy Initiative, *www.earthscienceliteracy.org*, includes links to the set of ideas on the "Complementary Projects" page. Taken collectively, these projects identify dozens of big ideas or fundamental principles about the Earth system and cover approximately 200 underlying concepts.

Overarching Questions: How do we know what we know? How does what we know inform our decision making?

The Earth Is a System of Systems.

The Earth system is composed of and part of a multitude of systems, which cycle and interact resulting in a dynamic equilibrium (though the system evolves). The Earth is also nested in larger systems, including the solar system and the universe. However, there is an inherent unpredictability in systems, which are composed of an (effectively) infinite number of interacting parts that follow simple rules. Each system is qualitatively different from, but not necessarily greater than, the sum of its parts.

The Flow of Energy Drives the Cycling of Matter.

The Earth is an open system—it is the constant flow of solar radiation that powers most surface Earth processes and drives the cycling of most matter at or near the Earth's surface. Earth's internal heat is a driving force below the surface. Energy flows and cycles through the Earth system. Matter cycles within it. Convection drives weather and climate, ocean currents, the rock cycle, and plate tectonics.

Life, Including Human Life, Influences and Is Influenced by the Environment.

Photosynthetic bacteria reformulated the atmosphere making Earth habitable. Humans have changed the lay of the land, altered the distribution of flora and fauna and are changing atmospheric chemistry in ways that alter the climate. Earth system processes affect where and how humans live. For example, many people live in the shadow of volcanoes because of the fertile farmland found there, however they must keep a constant vigil to maintain their safety. The human impact on the environment is growing as the population increases and the use of technology expands.

Physical and Chemical Principles Are Unchanging and Drive Both Gradual and Rapid Changes in the Earth System.

Earth processes (erosion, evolution, or plate tectonics, for example) operating today are the same as those operating since they arose in Earth history and they are obedient to the laws of chemistry and physics. While the processes constantly changing the Earth are essentially fixed, their rates are not. Tipping points are reached that can result in rapid changes cascading through Earth systems.

To Understand (Deep) Time and the Scale of Space, Models and Maps Are Necessary.

The use of models is fundamental to all of the Earth sciences. Maps and models aid in the understanding of aspects of the Earth system for which direct observation is not possible. Models assist in the comprehension of time and space at both immense and submicroscopic scales. When compared to the size and age of the universe, humanity is a speck in space and a blip in time.

A big idea is not simply a topic that typically appears in textbooks, but a key concept that cuts across all topics within a discipline. "A big idea can be described two ways: as involving an enduring principle that transcends its origins, subject matter or place in time; and as a *linchpin* idea—one crucial to a student's ability to understand a subject" (Wiggins and McTighe 1998, p. 113). Furthermore, big ideas require uncoverage— a sustained inquiry with breadth and depth. A novice and an expert may both understand a big idea, but they likely understand it in different ways and to different degrees. While big ideas are not the same as the generative topics described by Wiske, they are similar in that they "often have a bottomless quality, in that inquiry into the topic leads to deeper questions" (1998, p. 18).

In both geology and educational assessment, context matters a great deal. To a geologist, a sample that is dissociated from information about its origin is far less useful than a sample for which that information is known. Seeing things in situ often offers insights not evident when the subject of study is taken out of context. That is because context matters. Understanding of the bigger ideas is interdependent (see Figure 5). The interdependency of ideas is both profoundly important and not simply assessed.

In both settings, we need to sort out the signal from the noise. To engage in authentic scientific inquiry, we need to choose our own variables and, often, proxies for those variables. In the real world, there are a huge number of variables. One of the characteristics that distinguish an expert from a novice is the ability to ignore that which is irrelevant.

A defining set of big ideas can be identified that encompasses all that is important to understand within a particular discipline. For any field, this set of ideas should be manageable—perhaps a maximum of seven—in order to ensure that it provides focus and cohesion. This resonates with the NSES, which suggest a change in emphasis related to content from, "covering many science topics," to "studying a few fundamental science concepts" (NRC 1996, p. 113). Further, it harmonizes with the work of the National Academy of Sciences Committee on How People Learn:

> This essential link between the factual knowledge base and a conceptual framework can help illuminate a persistent debate in education: whether we need to emphasize "big ideas" more and facts less, or are producing graduates with a factual knowledge base that is unacceptably thin. While these concerns appear to be at odds, knowledge

Figure 5. Selected Connections Among Big Ideas.

Note that not all important connections are shown, including any connection to overarching questions.

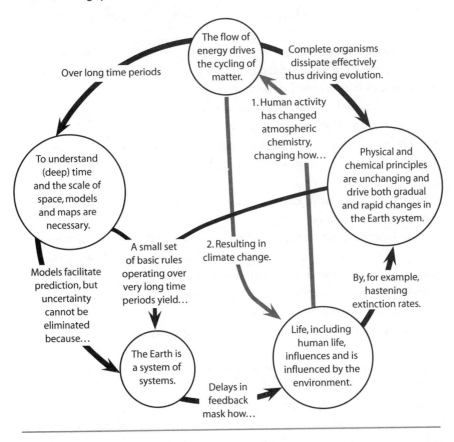

of facts and knowledge of important organizing ideas are mutually supportive. Studies of experts and novices—in chess, engineering, and many other domains—demonstrate that experts know considerably more relevant detail than novices in tasks within their domain and have better memory for these details... But the reason they remember more is that what novices see as separate pieces of information, experts see as organized sets of ideas (Donovan and Bransford 2005, p. 7).

We see big ideas as the pylons of a bridge connecting inquiry and understanding. These big ideas help us to ask and investigate important questions. Without any one of these ideas, the bridge may stand, but it is incomplete and weak. If an individual fails to meaningfully understand any two of the ideas, the bridge does not stand and, we believe, a person without such understandings cannot be said to truly understand Earth science.

Working with many teacher candidates, teachers, and scientists, we derived a set of big ideas for Earth system science. What makes an idea *big*?

- The idea cuts across the Earth science curriculum.
- Understanding of the idea is attainable by students and the understanding holds promise for retention.
- The idea is essential to understanding a variety of topics.
- The idea requires uncoverage; has a bottomless quality.

Furthermore, the entire Earth system science curriculum is represented by this (small) set of ideas.

In order to deeply understand these ideas, whether from Earth system science or from assessment, one must also have some sense from where these ideas were derived. In addition to five big ideas, we identified two overarching questions that are fundamental to understanding:

- How do we know what we know?
- How does what we know inform our decision making?

Understanding of these big, metacognitive questions must be assessed in conjunction with the assessment of ideas.

Science is not only a body of knowledge, but also a way of knowing. Perhaps equally as important, science defines a way of *not* knowing and strategically wondering what to do about what you do not know. These overarching questions go beyond the confines of Earth system science and even beyond the confines of science in general. They apply equally well to the discipline of education and are at the very core of educational assessment.

If one were to identify big ideas about educational assessment or about the science of education more broadly, what would those ideas be? Replace "scientific knowledge" in Feynman's question with "educational research," or, "science education research." How would you answer? If you expanded it to a few paragraphs, what would be identified as the fundamental concepts?

Figure 6 shows some suggested big ideas in science, science education, and in education more generally. Project 2061's common themes clearly

Figure 6. Big Ideas From Biology, *How People Learn*, and Inquiry

	Other Big Ideas
Overarching Questions: How do we know what we know? How does what we know inform our decision making?	**Biology:** E. O. Wilson suggests biology instruction be grounded in two ideas; he describes these as two laws of biology: • All organic processes are ultimately obedient to the Laws of Physics and Chemistry. • All living systems and processes evolved by natural selection.

	How People Learn:
	Donovan, Bransford, and Pelegrino's synthesis of research on how people learn defines three key findings for the teacher (1999):
	1. Students come to the classroom with preconceptions about how the world works. If their initial understanding is not engaged, they may fail to grasp the new concepts and information or they may learn them for the test but revert to their preconceptions outside the classroom.
	2. To develop competence in an area of inquiry, students must:
	  a. have a deep foundation of factual knowledge,
	  b. understand facts and ideas in the context of a conceptual framework, and
	  c. organize knowledge in ways that facilitate retrieval and application.
	3. A "metacognitive" approach to instruction can help students to take control of their own learning by defining learning goals and monitoring their progress in achieving them. (Donovan, Bransford, and Pellegrino 1999)
	These key findings might reasonably be labeled as big ideas for teaching (though not a full set). Simultaneous consideration of Earth science big ideas and these teaching big ideas enhances instruction.

	Five Essential Features of Inquiry: (NRC 2000) 1. Learner engages in scientifically oriented questions. 2. Learner gives priority to evidence in responding to questions. 3. Learner formulates explanations from evidence. 4. Learner connects explanations to scientific knowledge. 5. Learner communicates and justifies explanations to others. These five features of inquiry can be seen as five aspects of the idea of inquiry. The "strands of science" discussed in Ready, Set Science! (Michaels, Shouse, and Schweingruber 2008) and Learning Science in Informal Environments: People, Places and Pursuits (National Research Council (U.S.) 2009) are a different framing of topics underlying inquiry.
	Common Themes From *Science for All Americans* (American Association for the Advancement of Science 1989) • Systems, • Models, • Constancy & Change, and • Scale The common themes were a key inspiration for the development of the Earth system science big ideas shown in Figure 4.

informed the development of ReaL's big ideas and, as common themes, have some potential for generalization to ideas about the system of education. For example, the educational system is also a system of systems. We need maps and models to understand the scale and nature of understanding. That is, we need to represent the complexity of understandings within individuals and across and between populations in order to make sense of it and to inform our actions.

Review and evaluate the big ideas expressed in Figures 5 and 6. Taken collectively, what do they suggest about approaches to instruction? Do any of these ideas suggest that places for learning should look like schools or classrooms? That is, what is there in the nature of science or in the nature of cognition that suggests placing 20 or 30 preadolescents or adolescents in a room together for 40 or 50 minutes at a time repeatedly throughout the day, day after day, and year after year?

Make It Obvious What Matters Most

Peruse several science exams from state departments of education, from textbook publishers, and those created by teachers. Topics will be obvious. Big ideas are typically much more shrouded. If the old adage, "What gets tested is what gets taught," is true, *and* if Henri Poincare was correct when he noted, "Science is built up with facts as a house is with stones, but a collection of facts is no more a science than a heap of stones is a house" (1905, p. 101), then we are not teaching science in the typical science classroom.

Ask students which ideas they judge to be the most important or which concepts they hope to still remember and understand ten years after the class is completed. Consider your own history as a student. How many classes can you identify that had obvious key ideas? How many were science classes?

Some of the teachers associated with ReaL made posters of big ideas that stayed on their walls throughout the year. One included questions linking all labs done during the course of the year to big ideas. Is it clear when you witness teachers in action what the most important ideas of the course or discipline are? Is it clear when you reflect on your own instruction?

Conclusion

If the subjects of our study are viewed *in situ*, they often tell us much more than when they are decontextualized, whether the subject of study is a rock, a child, or a teacher. If we want to understand how something came to be the way that it is, we need to understand its story. This chapter highlights problems of how and what we assess and of what we fail to assess. Assessment, like the curriculum in which it sits, is an inch deep and a mile wide.

What are we assessing? How well are we doing? Assessment is grounded data, yet too often we select data that is not relevant (or as relevant as we think) to our goals, and this causes us to assess the situation poorly. For example, a question may have been written with the intention of assessing student understanding of density, but, in application, that question may be assessing a range of ideas and skills.

This should lead us to be filled with doubt, which in turn leads to leadership by doubters; however, leadership cannot be achieved without commitment. This means that, if we are doing well, we are building commitment to doubt. Skepticism of the current state of affairs is fundamental to leadership for change.

References

American Association for the Advancement of Science (AAAS). 1989. *Science for all Americans*. Washington, DC: AAAS.

———. 1993. *Benchmarks for science literacy*. Washington, DC: AAAS.

Ash, D., and K. Levitt. 2003. Working within the zone of proximal development: Formative assessment as professional development. *Journal of Science Teacher Education* 14 (1): 23–48.

Chambers, D. W. 1983. Stereotypic images of the scientist: The draw-a-scientist test. *Science Education* 67 (2): 255–265.

Chinn, C. A., and B. A. Malhotra. 2002. Epistemologically authentic inquiry in schools: A theoretical framework for evaluating inquiry tasks. *Science Education* 86 (2): 175–218.

Donovan, M. S., and J. D. Bransford, eds. 2005. *How students learn: Science in the classroom*. Washington, DC: National Academy Press.

Donovan, M. S., J. D. Bransford, and J. W. Pellegrino, eds. 1999. *How people learn: Bridging research and practice*. Washington, DC: National Academy Press.

Dörner, D. 1996. *The Logic of failure: Recognizing and avoiding error in complex situations.* New York: Metropolitan Books.

Duschl, R. A., H. A. Schweingruber, and A. W. Shouse. 2007. *Taking science to school: Learning and teaching science in grades k–8.* National Academies Press.

Exploratorium Institute for Inquiry. (n.d.) Assessing for learning. *www. exploratorium.edu/ifi/workshops/assessing*

Feynman, R. P. 1963. *The Feynman lecture on physics.* Reading, MA: Addison-Wesley.

Harlen, W., et al. 2000. Supporting learning as inquiry at the elementary level: The role of formative assessment. Paper presented at the American Educational Research Association Annual Conference. New Orleans, LA.

Harlen, W., J. Brand, and R. Brown. 2003. Enhancing inquiry through formative assessment. San Francisco, CA: Exploratorium.

Harvard-Smithsonian Center for Astrophysics. 1995. *Private universe teacher workshops: Workshop 1. Astronomy: Eliciting student ideas.* DVD. Annenberg/CPB.

Krajcik, J., P. C. Blumenfeld, R. W. Marx, K. M. Bass, J. Fredricks, and E. Soloway. 1998. Inquiry in project-based science classrooms: Initial attempts by middle school students. *Journal of the Learning Sciences* 7 (3): 313–350.

Marzano, R. J. 2003. *What works in schools: Translating research into action.* Alexandria, VA: Association for Supervision and Curriculum Development.

Mervis, J. 2006. Science Education: Doing more with less. *Science* 314 (5804): 1374–1376.

Michaels, S., A. W. Shouse, and H. A. Schweingruber. 2008. *Ready, set, science! Putting research to work in k–8 science classrooms.* Washington, DC: National Academies Press.

National Research Council (NRC). 1996. *National science education standards.* Washington, DC.: National Academy Press.

———. 2000. *Inquiry and the national science education standards: A guide for teaching and learning.* Washington, DC: National Academy Press.

———. 2009. *Learning science in informal environments: People, places, and pursuits.* Washington, DC: National Academies Press.

National Science Teachers Association. (n.d.). Science anchors: The challenge. *http://scienceanchors.nsta.org/Content/TheChallenge/Default.aspx*

Poincaré, H. 1905. *Science and hypothesis.* New York: Science Press.

Smith, C. L., M. Wiser, M., C. W. Anderson, and J. Krajcik. 2006. Implications of research on children's learning for standards and assessment: A proposed learning progression for matter and the atomic-molecular theory. *Measurement: Interdisciplinary Research & Perspective* 4 (1): 1.

Symington, D., and H. Spurling. 1990. The "draw a scientist" test: Interpreting the data. *Research in Science and Technological Education* 8 (1): 75–77.

Thomas, M. D., T. B. Henley, and C. M. Snell. 2006. The draw a scientist test: A different population and a somewhat different story. *College Student Journal* 40 (1): 140–148.

University of California, Berkeley Graduate School of Education, and Lawrence Hall of Science. 2009. Program overview: The seeds of science/roots of reading. Delta Education. *http://seedsofscience.org/papers*

White, B. Y., and J. R. Frederiksen. 1998. Inquiry, modeling, and metacognition: Making science accessible to all students. *Cognition and Instruction* 16 (1): 3–118.

Wiggins, G., and J. McTighe. 1998. *Understanding by design.* Alexandria, VA: ASCD.

——. 2005. *Understanding by design*, 2nd ed. Alexandria, VA: ASCD.

Wiske, M. S., ed. 1998. *Teaching for understanding: Linking research with practice.* San Francisco: Jossey-Bass

Chapter 16

Care to Share?

The Marymount School Science Department Professional Development Program

Eric A. Walters

Background

The Marymount School of New York is an all-female, independent school in New York City, which features an innovative, engaging, and challenging science curriculum for students from preK–12. Our Lower School science curriculum is hands-on and activity-based, with a special focus on scientific literacy viewed through an interdisciplinary lens. In Middle School, the curriculum becomes more inquiry-based, as students develop their critical-thinking and problem-solving skills. The curriculum is further supported by visits to local science museums and research institutions. Students in the Upper School (grades 8–12) engage in a standard science curriculum of biology, chemistry, physics, Advanced Placement electives, and atmospheric science. Science education in the Upper School is further based in real-world applications. Additionally, the school has made a significant commitment to integrate technology into the science curriculum to enhance the learning process.

Why Set Goals and Develop Professionally?

Thomas Hoerr states, "Educators' goals are typically tied to student success. Sometimes our goals are professionally oriented: We want to improve this pedagogical technique, we want to develop that curriculum, or we want to create a new professional development plan." (2004, p. 86) However, having faculty members actually sit down, reflect on instructional strategies, and commit to writing down professional goals is often a challenge. Teachers tend to focus on setting personal/professional goals. These goals focus on the effect that such factors as personality, leadership style, and balance have on our performance at work. (Hoerr 2004, p. 86)

The key question, then, is "How do you have faculty develop goals that are not purely student-centered, and not purely teacher-centered, but instead strike an appropriate balance between the two?" As Hoerr further suggests, "Supporting teachers' progress in achieving their goals fosters a climate of collaboration and collegiality. As a result, everyone in the building benefits. We all gain when we stop to reflect on our interactions with others and consider the influence those interactions have on our performance." (2004, p. 87)

While developing a goal-setting model for faculty members, department chairs and district supervisors need to be mindful of the following:

- Goals should be *relevant*. Will my goals improve my professional practice? Will they help me be a better model for my students? Are they the most important areas in which I need to improve to further promote student learning?
- Goals should be *achievable*. Are the goals realistic? Can my goals be accomplished with the resources available to me?
- Goals should be *measurable*. Is it easy for me to tell when I have accomplished my goals?

Once appropriate, beneficial goals have been selected, administrators must begin to support their faculty in meeting these goals. In order to accomplish this, there must be a consistent, relevant, and understandable framework for goal setting. As Danielson suggests, "By providing an agreed-upon framework for excellence, a framework for professional practice serves to structure conversations among educators about exemplary practice. A uniform framework allows those conversations to guide novices as well as to enhance the performance of veterans" (2007, p. 6). Moreover, "a framework for professional practice has important uses in the service of teaching and learning. These uses demonstrate the framework's power to elevate professional conversations that characterize the interaction of exemplary teachers everywhere" (Danielson 2007, p. 13).

The professional development framework that supports the goal-setting exercise is key for the goal setting and execution to be effective. As noted by Thomas Stigler in his interview with James Willis, "Professional development should be site-based, long-term, grounded in teachers' practice and an ongoing part of the workweek" (Willis 2002, p. 6). An effective professional development program should "engage teachers in reflection on their practice" (Flinn 2002, p. 42) as well as "build a community of learners" (Routman 2002, p. 4). The Marymount School Science Department Professional Development model has been built based on these principles.

The Marymount Model

In our model, teacher goals are matched with professional development opportunities and shared in an online professional learning community. This model effectively promotes innovation in the classroom, in the curriculum, and in the school and involves teachers in the decision-making process for professional development programs, curriculum changes, and other activities that affect their practice. This model has created an educational culture within the science department in which professional development opportunities are both encouraged and supported and has produced a K–12 science curriculum that is innovative, creative, and engaging. As a result, Marymount has a true community of science educators and learners.

As part of the school's culture, faculty is always encouraged to be reflective of their teaching practices. Furthermore, the school's summer professional development requirement includes attendance at a workshop or conference, curriculum work, or summer reading. Over the summer, the science department faculty reflects on instructional practices, successful strategies, and areas for improvement from the previous academic year. These reflections have often served as the seed that develops into goals implemented the following year.

In order to improve on these practices, after considering the insights of Willis, Flinn, and Routman, a conscious decision was made to formalize the goal setting and the professional development program for the science department. In the past year, this program has been supported by an on-line Professional Learning Community. This community is hosted on the Ning Social Networking Site at *www.mynycsience.ning.org*. This Professional Learning Community "creates contexts in which collaborative work can be sustained." (Willis 2002, p. 7) The basic timeline and outline of the plan is shown in Table 1.

Table 1. Goal Setting and Professional Development Timeline	
Target Date	**Component to Be Completed**
Early September	Faculty members determine yearly professional goals.
Mid September	Faculty members meet with department chair to review goals.
Late September	Faculty members receive conference strands for major science education conferences.
Late September	Faculty members review conference strands and develop strand analyses.
Early October	Yearly goals and strand analyses posted on Professional Learning Community.
October to April	Dialogue continues and evolves on Professional Learning Community. Faculty members participate in professional development opportunities.
May	Faculty members complete annual review.
Summer	Faculty members reflect on previous year and consider goals for the following year.

Table 2. Sample Strand Analyses

Faculty Goal	Conference	Conference Strand
Improved science-literacy connection	National Science Teachers Association—Regional Conference in Detroit, 2007	Science and Literacy
Effective strategies for introducing inquiry-based learning	Science Council of New York City, 2008	Science Content
Innovative programs for introducing STEM opportunities for young women	National Association of Independent Schools—Annual Conference in New York, 2008	The Classroom Experience

Program Details

At the beginning of the academic year, each department member undertakes a goal-setting exercise that requires identification of the following:

- Two or three teacher-centered professional goals to focus on during the academic year.
- The strategies that need to be undertaken to achieve those goals.
- The anticipated impact of these professional goals on student learning and instruction.

Use of this approach encourages teachers to "think about the relationship between teaching and learning in a cause-and-effect kind of way" and to "truly find new ways of teaching" as well as to be "exposed to alternatives" (Willis 2002, p. 8).

After completing the goal-setting exercise, each teacher meets individually with the department chair to review the goals, determine the goals' validity and appropriateness, and review the strategies being undertaken to achieve those goals. During the review process, unattainable goals, unmeasurable goals, and goals that cannot be linked to student learning are either discarded or improved upon. Clearly defined expectations, including a reasonable timeline, are developed for each faculty member. These expectations are written into a summary document that then becomes part of the teacher's professional development portfolio.

After each faculty member has finalized his or her goals for the year, this information is shared as part of the department's online Professional Learning Community. Each department member has, in effect, a digital portfolio. This allows faculty members to realize that "the focus on collaboration is a shift from making teaching completely private to realizing how much you can learn by letting your teaching be public and talking about it with your colleagues" (Willis 2002, p. 9). Members of the department are then able to review the goals of their colleagues, pose questions, seek advice, propose methods to work collaboratively to reach those goals, and discuss possible solutions to problems as they arise. Through this process, the department is able to create "a context in which everyone is really motivated to improve" (Willis 2002, p. 9).

This goal-setting exercise is then placed in the professional development framework. This framework is critical in supporting each faculty member's goals during the year. Without this framework, the concern is that teachers may see the entire program as yet another chore that is simply tacked onto their daily responsibilities. Unless teachers understand the ways in which these goals affect the learning outcomes of their students, when faced with the inevitably hectic schedule of daily responsibilities, efforts to follow through on professional goals and professional development are often the first to be jettisoned.

Faculty members are also provided with conference strands for a variety of local, regional, and national conferences. Table 2, page 267, shows the relationship between faculty goal, conference, and conference strand. Faculty members then match their specific goals with the provided conference strands. Faculty members are also encouraged to seek out additional professional development opportunities. Once this strand analysis is completed, faculty members meet with the department chair to review the following:

- Selected workshop or conference
- How this workshop or conference addresses one or more of their annual goals
- Possible methods of integrating workshop or conference material with the current curriculum

After attendance at the conference is approved, the faculty member posts their strand analysis on the Professional Learning Community.

Following the conference, the faculty member then completes a post-conference evaluation form that includes writing a brief review of each workshop attended and a description of ways that the material gained from each workshop may—or may not—be integrated into the curriculum. The faculty member also relates each workshop to their own goals and posts a summary of the workshop and related goals on the Professional Learning Community forum. Department members are then able to review these workshops and comment, which provides a context for each teacher's professional development opportunity to become less private and more public. Faculty members are expected to review the PLC on a continual basis. Moreover, an ongoing dialogue between science department faculty members is generated, and that dialogue often extends to other departments through inter-classroom discussion, or even informal chatting by the copy machine!

At the end of the year, each faculty member evaluates the progress made on his or her individual goals. Each considers the input, insights, and suggestions of colleagues; anecdotal evidence of the impact that each professional goal has on student learning and the curriculum; and the influence and impact of the professional development component on each goal. This information is then summarized and posted on the Professional Learning Community forum. The faculty member also meets with the department chair to review the annual summary. This annual summary then becomes material for the faculty member's summer reflection that is used to prepare for goal setting for the following academic year.

Educational Initiatives

As a result of each teacher's yearly goals and the professional development program, a number of new educational initiatives that seek to provide a 21st-century science curriculum for students of differing learning styles and abilities have been implemented. This section includes four examples of successful alignment of faculty professional goals, professional development opportunities, and curricular integration.

Case Study 1: Science and Literacy
Division: Lower School
Faculty Goal: I would like to more fully integrate literacy objectives into the lower school science curriculum.
Workshop: NSTA Detroit, 2007—Use High-Interest Science Content to Support Reading and Writing Skills
Curriculum Integration: Student-created book "What Is a Marymount Scientist?"

In this workshop, presented by representatives from the Battle Creek Area Mathematics and Science Center, participants learned how to integrate language arts and science through investigations and science journals. The faculty member used the knowledge gained from the workshop to develop a new project for students in first grade, the production of a short book entitled *What Is a Marymount Scientist?* Using digital photography and basic design skills, each student created a book that used the scientific method to review how a "Marymount scientist" (student) works in the laboratory.

This focus on scientific literacy has spurred additional science and literacy integrations at other levels. Students in Middle School now use *Science News* on a weekly basis to further their understanding of current issues in science, and students in the Upper School use Bill Bryson's *A Short History of Nearly Everything* in their Chemistry courses in order to more fully understand the development of atomic theory. Moreover, students in atmospheric science use Maude Barlow's *The Blue Covenant* as part of their debate on equal access to water resources (see Case Study 4).

Case Study 2: Authentic Learning Opportunities
Division: Middle School
Faculty Goal: I would like to integrate authentic learning opportunities into the classroom.
Workshop: NSTA Boston, 2008—FLEXE (From Local to Extreme Environments)
Curriculum Integration: FLEXE Integration in Class VII

FLEXE (From Local to Extreme Environments) is a GLOBE (Global Learning and Observations to Benefit the Environment) project involving the study of the deep ocean led by Pennsylvania State University, in partnership with Ridge 2000 and InterRIDGE Scientists. Through online interactions with project scientists, seventh-grade students were able to gain an understanding of local and deep-sea environments, specifically in the regions surrounding hot hydrothermal vents and cold hydrocarbon seeps. Students analyzed deep sea data and shared their results on the online FLEXE Forum. The students' experience is capped by scientific reporting, peer review, and communication with scientists at sea during a research cruise.

Additional authentic learning opportunities have been integrated into the curriculum in all divisions. The department's Women in Science Luncheon brings noted female researchers to the school to discuss current, cutting-edge science research, and the annual Light Up Your Mind event introduces Middle School parents and students to a variety of science topics, including genetic engineering and climate change.

Case Study 3: Inquiry-Based Learning
Division: Upper School
Faculty Goal: I am stymied by how to develop and implement inquiry-based learning objectives
Workshop: POGIL One-Day Introductory Workshop at MARM 2008—Queensborough Community College (Bayside, NY); The 40th Middle Atlantic Regional Meeting (MARM 2008) of the American Chemical Society
Curriculum Integration: Using POGIL in the high school chemistry classroom

According to their website, POGIL (Process-Oriented Guided-Inquiry Learning) is a classroom and laboratory technique that seeks to simultaneously teach content and key process skills such as the ability to think analytically and work effectively as part of a collaborative team. A POGIL classroom or lab consists of any number of students working in small groups on specially designed guided inquiry materials. These materials supply students with data or information followed by leading questions designed to guide them toward formulation of their own valid conclusions—essentially a recapitulation of the scientific method. The instructor serves as facilitator, observing and periodically addressing individual and classroom-wide needs" (*www.pogil.org*)

This technique was adopted in our 10th-grade Honors Chemistry course. The teacher redesigned her curriculum unit on the composition of matter. The same objectives were considered (i.e., differentiate between a compound and a mixture), but, in this case, students were provided with a model that reviewed chemical bonding. The students then explored the model by creating visual representations of chemical compounds. They extended their knowledge to distinguish between chemical and physical changes and developed their understanding of the concept of limiting reagents.

Case Study 4: Global Collaborations
NAIS 20/20
Faculty Workshop: NAIS Annual Conference in 2004
Faculty Goal: I would like to develop global collaborations for my students.
Curriculum Integration: Introduction of NAIS Challenge 20/20 into grade 12 Atmospheric Science curriculum

Challenge 20/20 is an internet-based program that pairs classes at any grade level (K–12) from schools in the United States with counterpart classes in schools in other countries; together the teams (of two or three schools) tackle real global problems to find solutions that can be implemented at the local level in their own communities.

We began our participation in this program in 2004 and have been partnered with schools in Italy and Canada. Our focus for the first three years was climate change and global warming. Students in the partner schools discussed these issues in their classrooms, posted the results of their research on a collaborative blog and continued the conversation about short- and long-term solutions on that blog. Currently, the focus of this project has been on equal access to water resources, and we plan to continue that partnership in the future with our sister school in Los Angeles, a school in Australia, and the United Nations. Video conferencing and online collaboration tools are used to support the projects.

Again, additional collaborations are currently in place. Many of these collaborations are possible through curriculum maps hosted on Rubicon Atlas, a web-based curriculum management tool. These maps cover all 21 schools in our international network. An online collaboration blog allows students in our school to discuss and debate key scientific and ethical issues with their peers at our sister school in Los Angeles.

Stories of Success

Occam's razor suggests that the innovative curricular enhancements are a direct result of the development and implementation of a sustainable, teacher-focused goal setting and professional development program. Members of the science department have a framework upon which this program easily sits, and the program has become part and parcel of each teacher's daily and yearly responsibilities. Faculty members have the opportunity to reflect on both instructional strategies and student learning in a supportive environment that allows teachers to become active participants in curriculum planning and implementation. Teachers now feel that they are leaders in the science classroom, leaders in educational innovation, and leaders in science education.

A survey of the science department faculty generated the following responses:

- I feel like I am now a leader in the classroom.
- I now have ownership over curriculum decisions.
- My goals are supported. It's been great to think about conferences in a whole new way.
- Everyone knows my goals for the year—and that's a good thing. I feel that this collaborative spirit has benefited me as a teacher.
- Now, I don't feel like I have to "do" professional development. It's really seamlessly integrated into the year.

A brief survey of the students shows similar insights.

- It's cool that our teachers are students too. They exemplify lifelong learning.
- Working with scientists is so interesting. I feel like I'm a scientist as well.

- I love it when our teacher comes back from a conference, because we get to try all sorts of new things. It shows that our teachers are willing to "think outside their comfort zone."
- We get to talk to students in other schools about scientific issues that affect us. We have learned so much from our peers!
- Our science education made me forget about all the stereotypes associated with STEM-related careers.

References

Danielson, C. 2007. *Enhancing professional practice: A framework for teaching*, 2nd ed. Alexandria, VA: Association for Supervision and Curriculum Development.

Flinn, L. 2002. Using video to reflect on curriculum. *Educational Leadership* 59 (6): 42–45.

From Local to Extreme Environments (FLEXE). Homepage. *www.globe.gov/fsl/html/templ.cgi?flexe*

Hoerr, T. R. 2004. New year, new goals. *Educational Leadership* 62 (1): 86–87.

NAIS Challenge 20/20. Homepage. *www.nais.org/resources/index.cfm?ItemNumber=147262*

Process Oriented Guided Inquiry Learning (POGIL). Homepage. *www.pogil.org*

Routman, R. 2002. Teacher talk. *Educational Leadership* 59 (6): 4.

Willis, S. 2002. Creating a knowledge base for teaching: A conversation with James Stigler. *Educational Leadership* 59 (6): 6–11.

Section Five

Leadership That Engages the Public in the Understanding of Science

Chapter 17

Leadership for Public Understanding of Science

George E. DeBoer

There is no question that American society places a high value on science and science teaching. Science is well established in the American school curriculum and has been since the 19th century. Each state requires students to take science courses to graduate from high school and, under the current No Child Left Behind Act of 2001 (NCLB), students must be tested in science at the elementary, middle, and high school levels. Some states also make passing a comprehensive science test a requirement for high school graduation. Science is part of the curriculum because the society believes it is a way to attract future scientists, to provide early experiences in science to those who will become scientists, and to provide nonscientists with a familiarity with science.

Society also invests significant amounts of its resources in science education at the college and university level, not only to prepare future scientists but also to increase nonscientists' understanding of science. In addition, the mass media, science centers, natural history museums, zoos, botanical gardens, and other informal science institutions play a significant role in educating the public about science.

The results of these efforts to engage the general public in science have been mixed. When compared to the youth of other countries, American students do not fare very well (PISA 2007; Gonzales et al. 2008). But when adult science literacy is compared internationally, American adults appear to be more knowledgeable about science than the adults of just about any other country (Trefil 2008, pp. 85–86). Jon Miller, who has conducted surveys of adult science literacy for decades, attributes the comparative success of American adults in science to the fact that college students in the United States are typically required to take at least some science in college regardless of their major field of study, which is not true in most other countries (Trefil 2008, p. 86). Some also have attributed the greater science literacy of American adults to the vast network of informal science institutions in the country.

The focus of this chapter will be on the formal system of schools and the role they have played in the public's understanding of science. Science is generally considered to be one of the most important subjects in the school curriculum, even if it does not receive as much attention as math and reading–language arts, which have always formed the central core of the elementary school curriculum and, to a slightly lesser extent, the secondary school curriculum as well. For example, citing a survey conducted by Achieve, Inc., the Center for Public Education reports that at present most states require students to complete either two or three years of science to graduate from high school, and two states require four courses. In comparison, 40 states require high school students to take four years of English to graduate, and 13 states require high school students to take four years of math to graduate (2008).

Also, although science must be tested once in elementary, middle, and high school under current federal legislation, reading and mathematics are tested annually from grades three through eight, and the test results are used to determine if schools are making adequate yearly progress (AYP). Schools have only recently (since the 2007–08 school year) been required to test students in science, and science is not included in the determination of AYP status. Furthermore, the National Assessment of Educational Progress (NAEP) is given every two years in reading and mathematics, but only every four years in science, social studies, and other subjects. As part of NCLB legislation, schools must participate in the national assessment of reading and mathematics, but science testing is voluntary, as is testing in social studies and other subjects. Also, the Common Core State Standards Initiative, which was recently introduced by the National Governors Association and the Council of Chief State School Officers (CCSSO), aims to create high-quality and internationally benchmarked national standards that could be voluntarily adopted by states; however, the new initiative is moving forward in math and reading but not in science (CCSSO 2009). Finally, school resources, including money spent on specialists and remedial services, are often allocated disproportionately to math and reading programs.

Yet there are many who believe that because of its central importance to our society, science should have the same status as mathematics and reading in the school curriculum. A number of proposals have been introduced in the past two years that would do that. For example, on October 30, 2007, the National Science Board (the governing body of the National Science Foundation) released the National Action Plan for Addressing the Needs of the U.S. Science, Technology, Engineering, and Mathematics (STEM) Education System. The plan recommends (1) the creation of a nonfederal National Council to facilitate STEM programs and initiatives throughout the nation, (2) the coordination of STEM education among the states including defining national content guidelines that would outline essential knowledge and skills needed at each grade level, and (3) the development of measures to assess student performance that are aligned with the national content guidelines. In addition, the Standards to Provide Educational Achievement for Kids (SPEAK) Act (S. 224 and H. R. 2790) that was introduced by Rep. Vernon Ehlers (R-MI) and Sen. Chris Dodd (D-CT) on January 9, 2008 was reintroduced on June 10, 2009. This legislation would create voluntary national standards in math and science that would be aligned with postsecondary and workforce needs and would be comparable to the best standards in the world. The legislation would provide incentives for states to adopt these standards through competitive grants, and it would add science to the biennial National Assessment of Educational Progress to place it on par with reading and math.

Progress in developing high-level policies that give science the status in the curriculum that many believe it deserves has been slow to materialize. Although scientists and science educators recognize the importance of science in the school curriculum and have argued vigorously to elevate the status of science in the curriculum, it is not clear how strong that support is among the general public or the legislators who represent them. For example, in a survey that was conducted for AAAS Project 2061 by Global Strategy Group in 2001, 800 interviews were conducted with a nationally representative sample of parents of school-age children (students in grades 4 through 10), that asked them about their attitudes regarding the importance of science in society and in the school curriculum, as well as their attitudes about the quality of the science instruction their children were receiving. When asked to reflect on the importance of mathematics, reading, and science in their own lives, 45% chose math, 41% chose reading, and 5% chose science as the subject that they used the most in their everyday life. When asked what subject their children needed to do well in to succeed in their chosen line of work, 18% chose science, but when the question was phrased to determine the subject parents considered most valuable to their children without regard to the job they would have as adults, 59% chose reading, 28% chose math, 3% chose history, and 1% chose science (2001). A similar result regarding student and parent attitudes about the relative importance of reading, math, and science was reported by the Carnegie-Institute for Advanced Study Commission on Mathematics and Science Education (2009, p. 12).

Clearly there is work to be done to convince the public of the importance of science—not only its importance for those who wish to pursue careers in science but also for all future citizens. Leadership is required at multiple levels of the system. This chapter will focus on the distributed leadership that exists in a decentralized system such as the U.S. education system. In a decentralized authority system, it is the power of well-crafted arguments and the ability to have those arguments heard that is most important. Because we operate in a free market of ideas, the ideas that can convince a critical mass of policy makers to act and that are consistent with the values and attitudes of the public are the ones that have the most influence on practice. Because many of the policy initiatives that would improve the public's understanding of science through improved science instruction require the allocation of resources, policy makers need to be convinced not only of the worth of the project but also of its value relative to the vast array of other policy initiatives that compete for attention. In this chapter we take a historical approach to the examination of three questions about leadership for public understanding of science.

- What arguments have been made for what the public should know about science and why they should know it?
- What have been the implications of these arguments for public understanding of science in K–16 education?
- What leadership has been successful in accomplishing the goals of public understanding of science?

This chapter examines the arguments for science at various points in time, the implications of those arguments for K–16 education, and the various contributors whose arguments were most compelling given the conditions in society at the time. In the space available, it is impossible to go into any significant detail regarding the ways in which various leadership influences intersected and ultimately led to the establishment of policies and practices, so for each time period we will only touch on the key individuals, professional organizations, published reports, and legislative decisions that have influenced society's perspective on science as well as the impact that this has had on education. This discussion is intended to provide a sense of the complexity of science education policy development in the United States, the fundamental consistency of the set of arguments over time, and the influence of broad social conditions on the presentation of and response to those arguments. The importance of the public's understanding of science is a common theme in all of these debates, and this idea will sound similar from one era to the next. However, there are also features that vary according to the prevailing social attitudes and the values of the individuals and groups making the arguments. In addition, the expectation is that a historical perspective will temper and refine the arguments we make today in support of the public's understanding of science.

Mid- to Late 19th Century

In the mid- to late 19th century, practicing scientists and supporters of science took the lead in arguing for the importance of public knowledge about science and the scientific way of thinking. Their arguments focused on two main points: Science as a way of thinking was more suitable for life in a democracy than the more authoritative methods offered by the classics and mathematics because the methods of science allowed individuals to be their own observers of the natural world and to draw conclusions independently based on those observations and the power of their own reasoning. Science was also thought to be important for the practical knowledge it provided to citizens, especially for maintaining personal health. In his classic essay "What Knowledge Is of Most Worth?" Herbert Spencer (1864) said that knowledge of the functions of the human body and how to maintain health were essential for self-preservation, and that knowledge of the apparatus, materials, and scientific principles involved in modern manufacture were important skills for employment. He also argued that an understanding of science was important for appreciating as well as constructing art. Proportion, balance, and physical form were all physical concepts that were important in the arts. Science also supported the development of the intellect. "The constant habit of drawing conclusions from data, and then of verifying those conclusions by observation and experiment, can alone give the power of judgment correctly. And that it necessitates this habit is one of the immense advantages of science," Spencer claimed (p. 88). Finally, science was important for developing independence of thought, perseverance, sincerity, and a willingness to abandon any preconceived notion that proved to be incorrect. Spencer called these qualities "moral discipline."

In 1867, Edward Livingston Youmans, science writer and public lecturer, argued that the study of science could provide useful knowledge about practical things such as sanitation, hygiene, health, and disease, as well as strengthen the intellect by offering an effective way of thinking that included observation, experimentation, and reasoning (DeBoer 1991, p. 8). In 1899, Thomas Huxley explained that a study of biology could be helpful in avoiding infection and would be valuable for farmers to improve crop yields and avoid plant disease. Each of these scientists argued that science deserved a place in the curriculum alongside the classics and mathematics because of its importance for life in a democratic society.

By the end of the 19th century, science was slowly becoming a legitimate study in the school curriculum, not just as preparation for technical careers but also as part of a liberal education for all students. In 1893, the science conferences of the National Education Association's (NEA) Committee of Ten worked to place science on an equal footing with Greek, Latin, and mathematics in the school curriculum. Again, it was the scientific community that took the lead in arguing for the value of science. As did the scientists a few decades earlier, these scientists argued for the value of science in two ways: First, the study of science would develop one's intellectual skills, especially the ability to reason clearly from empirical evidence; and because empirical observation was the starting point for scientific reasoning, science should be studied in the laboratory or out in the field. Second, the study of science offered practical knowledge related to personal health, agriculture, and manufacturing (NEA 1894). Alexander Smith, a noted chemist at the University of Chicago, said that if science could be shown to provide useful information and to have disciplinary value, the subject would be "practically indispensable" (Smith and Hall 1902, p. 14).

In support of these arguments, the Committee of Ten suggested four recommended courses of study that could lead to high school graduation and college admission, all of which included significant numbers of science courses. Even the classical course of study included three years of high school science. Overall, across all four proposed plans, approximately one-fifth of a student's total time would be devoted to the study of science. It was recommended that all of the courses of study be considered acceptable for college entrance because they were thought to provide equivalent intellectual preparation for college. Following the report of the Committee of Ten, the NEA met in 1895 to discuss the Committee's recommendations. At that meeting, the NEA created a joint committee from higher education and secondary education to make recommendations for implementation of the Committee of Ten Report. This committee, the Committee on College Entrance Requirements, took a less positive view of the value of science. They recommended that only one course (out of a total of 16) should be required in science for high school graduation and college admission, whereas a total of six courses should be required in linguistic studies—four in languages and two in English literature. However, six of the 16 courses would be electives, giving students additional opportunities for taking science (NEA 1899). The scientists had a significant impact on educators' thinking about the role of science in society and, therefore, the place it should have in the curriculum; but in the end, the powerful NEA took a more conservative approach in its recommendations and let the study of the classics continue to dominate high school graduation and college entrance requirements, at least into the near future.

The Early 20th Century

During the second half of the 19th century, arguments in support of the importance of science in society focused primarily on the value of science for the individual's personal intellectual development and acquisition of practical knowledge. In contrast, by the early 1900s most arguments in defense of science (and other subjects as well) were made in terms of its usefulness in a 20th-century industrial society. As society became more complex and the numbers of people immigrating to the United States increased, social stability and social utility became paramount. Schools were seen as one of society's major socializing forces, and all parts of the curriculum became justified in terms of their practical value. Practical studies were also seen as a way to attract more students into the educational system. In 1900, only 10.2% of children ages 14 to 17 were enrolled in public and private secondary schools, and most of the students did not graduate (National Center for Education Statistics 1981). For schools to have an impact on society, greater numbers of students would have to attend.

In order to emphasize the practical and applied benefits of education, the NEA, which had established standards for high school graduation and college admission in 1896 based on the recommendations of the Committee of Ten, significantly liberalized those recommendations in 1911 by moving away from a focus on classical and linguistic studies and toward more applied and vocational studies. The committee recommended that up to four electives could be chosen from vocational offerings, that the current graduation requirement in foreign language be reduced from four units to two, and that foreign language could be avoided altogether if substituted by a course in science or social studies (NEA 1911).

The commitment to social relevance in all parts of the curriculum was embodied in the report of the NEA's Commission on the Reorganization of Secondary Education in 1918. The commission argued that education should be aimed toward a democratic life for all, with neither the individual nor the society being subordinated to the other. The role of education was to prepare the individual for life in society, and educational goals should be developed based on the activities of individuals in society. The commission identified seven major categories of educational goals, which came to be known as "cardinal principles" of education: (1) health, (2) command of fundamental process, (3) worthy home-membership, (4) vocation, (5) citizenship, (6) worthy use of leisure, and (7) ethical character (NEA 1918). As part of the NEA's reorganization effort, its Committee on Science justified the presence of science in the curriculum on the basis of six of the cardinal principles. Only "command of fundamental processes"—that is, reading, writing, and calculating—was left out, because it was dealt with in other parts of the curriculum.

The committee said that science is valuable for maintaining "good health" because knowledge of pubic sanitation and personal hygiene can protect people from illness and help to control disease. Science contributed to "worthy home-membership" by teaching students about the functioning of electrical appliances, how to repair heating and ventilating systems, and the operation of other conveniences found in the home. With respect to "vocations," the committee said: "In the field of vocational preparation, courses in shop physics, applied electricity, physics of the home, industrial and household chemistry, applied biological sciences, physiology, and hygiene will be of value to many students if properly adapted to their needs" (NEA 1920, p. 13). Regarding the goal of "citizenship," science courses could give the citizen the ability to select experts wisely for specialized positions in society. Science could contribute to the enhancement of one's "leisure" through such avocations as photography by making the optical and chemical principles used in photography clear to students. And science study could contribute to the development of "ethical character" "by establishing a more adequate conception of truth and a confidence in the laws of cause and effect" (NEA 1920, p. 14).

The schools took these recommendations to heart and instituted programs to appeal to the practical interests of students. New programs provided students with knowledge that would be of use to them in their everyday lives, especially knowledge related to health, industrial manufacturing, and applications of technology in everyday settings, such as understanding how household appliances worked.

In addition to the very significant leadership of the NEA in these matters, the Association for the Advancement of Progressive Education, which was founded in 1919, and later renamed the Progressive Education Association (PEA), also provided leadership in the development of practical and applied studies aimed at the improvement of society. The association was inspired by the writings of John Dewey, an advocate for progressive principles in education and of the importance of science in society. In

Democracy and Education, Dewey, describing the importance of science for social progress, said:

> Man's life is bound up in the processes of nature; his career, for success or defeat, depends upon the way in which nature enters it. Man's power of deliberate control of his own affairs depends upon ability to direct natural energies to use: an ability which is in turn dependent upon insight into nature's processes (1916, p. 228).

But not everyone was enamored of applied science and a curriculum focused on the immediate practical needs of students. John M. Coulter, a science professor at the University of Chicago who had served as a member of the Conference on Natural History of the Committee of Ten, disagreed that science teaching should focus only on what was within the experience of the students: "That our science teaching should consist only in explaining to a student what he encounters in his own experience, is to limit his life, rather than to enrich it by extending his horizon" (1915, p. 99). Robert Bradbury, head of the Department of Science in the Southern High School in Philadelphia, speaking of the new practical approach to teaching chemistry, said, "We should firmly grasp the fact that in changing from chemistry to technology, we are deserting knowledge of proved permanent worth to deal in information whose chief characteristic is the evanescence of its value. The technology we teach now will merely mislead our students ten years hence" (1915, pp. 785–786).

One solution to the controversy over traditional versus applied science in discipline-based courses such as biology, chemistry, and physics was to place the more applied topics in the newly created general science course, a course primarily intended for junior high school students but sometimes taught at the high school level as well. This course would introduce them to the various areas of science, the experimental method, and the applications of science in society. The Thirty-First Yearbook Committee of the National Society for the Study of Education (NSSE) said that topics for that course should be chosen from "aspects of the environment which, from the point of view of science, are most significant in the everyday life of individuals and of society" (1932, p. 203). Topics would include "food, water, air, clothing materials, materials of construction, fuels, plant life, animal life, heat, light, electricity, sound, machines, the weather, the climate, the sky, the crust of the earth, and the soil" (p. 198). In addition, this course would teach students about the methods of science. According to the NSSE Yearbook Committee, "Science is essentially an experimental study of materials and phenomena and requires, therefore, learning activities that are designed to solve problems relating to concrete and objective instructional materials, whether in pure science or in its applied aspects" (p. 213).

Throughout the first half of the 20th century, progressive educators continued to argue for the value of applied science, but resistance to those ideas also continued, so that support for the approach was widespread but not universal. In 1940, for example, there were still many educators and scientists who believed that there was value in disciplinary science and in a traditional approach to science teaching. Thomas Smyth provided some insight into the nature of the debate as he reiterated the principles of applied, socially relevant science in a critique of a biology curriculum endorsed by the National Association for Research in Science Teaching. He asked:

> How important is it for high school students to go into details concerning the nature and properties of protoplasm, or how worthwhile is it to delve into cytology and know the morphology and physiology of the parts of a cell? Why burden the high school group with the intricacies of mitosis? Is there nothing more worth bringing to this group? If we are teaching for the enrichment of human life the time is here now when we must pack our high school science courses with life values and not fill them with a lot of stuff that few will ever use or even think of again the rest of their days (1940, pp. 258–259).

Leadership for teaching applied science and practical studies throughout the first half of the 20th century rested with the National Education Association, the Progressive Education Association, the National Society for the Study of Education (which was sympathetic to progressive ideals and whose Thirty-First and Forty-Sixth Yearbook Committees summarized the principles of progressive education and its applications to schooling) (NSSE 1932, 1947), and the many individuals associated with the progressive movement in education, especially John Dewey. The arguments focused on the practical value of science for the improvement of society and the individual as part of that society. Scientists were less of a presence in these arguments than they had been in the 19th century and in the years leading up to the turn of the century. The net effect of the efforts to increase the public's understanding of science through the applications of science was that, by the late 1940s, most students learned about science through the general science course and one other disciplinary course, usually biology (DeBoer 1991).

The 1950s and 1960s

By the late 1940s, arguments in favor of science knowledge began to head in a somewhat different direction. The social utility of science was still widely acknowledged, but it took on a new character following the experience of World War II. The loss of science students and faculty during the war produced several years when few scientists were being trained. Following the war, reducing this deficit in science personnel became a high-level national priority and led to efforts to quickly prepare scientists and technical personnel. This was of such concern for national security that all discussions about the importance of public understanding of science or science being included in the school curriculum must be viewed in the context of this immediate and pressing need. In 1944, President Roosevelt asked Vannevar Bush, Director of the Office of Scientific Research and Development, to report on a variety of issues, including the question, "Can an effective program be proposed for discovering and developing scientific talent in American youth so that the continuing future of scientific research in this country may be assured?" (Bush 1945, p. 4). In his report, *Science: The Endless Frontier*, Bush recommended that "the Government should accept new responsibilities for promoting the flow of new scientific knowledge and the development of scientific talent in our youth. These responsibilities are the proper concern of the Government, for they vitally affect our health, our jobs, and our national security" (1945, p. 8). This call for federal involvement and support for science and scientific training represented a turning point in the ways that society, through its governing bodies, would guide the development and dissemination of scientific knowledge. To a greater and greater extent, leadership in science education would come from the federal government.

Bush recommended the establishment of a national research foundation, which led to the creation in 1950 of the National Science Foundation, a unified agency for the funding and coordination of basic scientific research and the support of education through the dispersal of grants and scholarships to students. Bush had received a doctorate in engineering from MIT and held many influential science policy positions, especially during the war years, including Director of the National Defense Research Committee and Director of the Office of Scientific Research and Development, which controlled the Manhattan Project. He was also president of the Carnegie Institution of Washington, and in that position he was able to influence the direction of scientific research through the dispersal of research funds.

Then in 1946, to address the crisis of personnel shortages, President Truman created the President's Scientific Research Board. The Board began its report by saying:

> The security and prosperity of the United States depend today, as never before, upon the rapid extension of scientific knowledge. So important, in fact, has this extension become to our country that it may reasonably be said to be a major factor in national survival. (President's Scientific Research Board, vol. 1, 1947, p. 3)

The Research Board said that science was important for military and economic reasons, and because other countries were investing heavily in science, it was critical that the United States did so too. The Board asked AAAS to study the effectiveness of science education to meet these purposes at all levels of the educational system. In its findings, which were included in the report of the President's Scientific Research Board, the AAAS Cooperative Committee on the Teaching of Science and Mathematics emphasized the dual role of science education:

> While it is the primary object of this report to deal with the production of professional scientists, account must be taken of the degree of comprehension of science by the general population. For in a democracy it is upon the popular attitude toward science that the attractiveness of the profession, the resulting selectivity for those finally entering the profession, and the degree of support obtainable for their work will depend. (President's Scientific Research Board, vol. 4, 1947, p. 113)

This idea that the public should learn about science so that they would develop a positive attitude toward science went hand-in-hand with the argument that a robust scientific enterprise was needed for national security.

The importance of science as a part of general education was also taken seriously by a number of colleges. In 1945, the Harvard Committee on General Education published *General Education in a Free Society*, in which they argued the importance of science for the nonscientist as part of a general or liberal education.

At the same time that national leaders and the scientific community were becoming convinced of the national security importance of science and the importance of a public that was knowledgeable about and sympathetic to science, the practical education being offered in schools during the previous half century had become what was now being referred to as "life adjustment education." In 1947, the U.S. Commissioner of Education appointed a National Commission on Life Adjustment Education for Youth and a second national commission in 1950 to promote this concept (U.S. Office of Education 1951). The life adjustment programs that were being developed had a decidedly nonacademic focus, emphasizing instead the real-life needs of students such as their health and well-being, knowing how to drive and care for an automobile, and managing personal finances wisely (Sanford 1950). In the minds of many, the content of science had been almost completely removed from the curriculum. Although his comments were not aimed at science specifically, Mortimer Smith, a writer and advocate for academic excellence in elementary and secondary schools and later co-founder of the Council for Basic Education in Washington, said that social skills should not take the place of intellectual training. In his book *The Diminished Mind*, he said that although practical usefulness in the curriculum was legitimate, "a school program which teaches little beyond how to fix a fuse, drive a car, set the dinner table, and enhance your personal appearance, isn't useful enough if your aim is the development of maturity and intelligent citizenship" (1954, p. 3). To Smith, the primary mission of the school was the development of intelligence, a mission he believed the schools had abandoned.

National security–based arguments for the importance of science that were stimulated by personnel shortages following the war, and arguments for more rigorous intellectual training, brought on by the perceived excesses of progressive education, came to a head when the Soviet Union launched its Earth-orbiting satellite, *Sputnik*, in 1957. In response, a major effort to improve science education was launched by the federal government as a way to enhance the scientific capabilities of the nation. Based on recommendations of the scientific community, the United States embarked on an unprecedented program of science education reform. To accomplish these national security goals, the National Science Foundation, with significantly increased congressional funding, sponsored projects that brought an approach to science teaching that focused on the logical content structure of the discipline and the nature of scientific thinking. In addition, the National Defense Education Act of 1958 was designed to provide the country with specific defense-oriented personnel. It also provided financial assistance, through the National Defense Student Loan program, for thousands of students to enroll in colleges and universities in the 1960s.

In speaking of the importance of science in terms of national security, Joseph Schwab (1962), a key advocate for reformed science education in the United States, said:

> A hundred fifty years ago, science was an ornament of a leisurely society. It was still mainly pursued by amateurs and gentlemen. It was a gratuitous activity of the enquiring intellect, an end pursued for its own sake.... It is so no longer. Industrial democracy has made science the foundation of national power and productivity. Science now plays the part once played by exploration, by empire, and by colonial exploitation (p. 18).

Schwab described the need for science teaching to keep pace with scientific development as "urgent" and "compelling." The nation needed an increased supply of scientific and technical personnel, competent political leaders who could develop policy agendas based on the sometimes conflicting claims of scientists, and a public willing to support scientific research and discovery that was long-term and ongoing and to support science even when it did not yield obvious practical outcomes.

Some thought that the way to increase the supply of scientific and technical personnel was to improve the education of the most talented students. Proposals included the creation of separate schools for the gifted, honors classes, use of a two-track system so the most talented could advance more rapidly, and the use of gifted students as assistants in class (DeBoer 1991, p. 137). In 1955, Paul Brandwein published *The Gifted Student as Future Scientist*, in which he discussed the characteristics of gifted students, ways of identifying them, and proposals for increasing the number of gifted students taking science courses.

In the postwar and *Sputnik* years, the arguments for the importance of science in society had been transformed from ones that for half a century had emphasized its everyday personal and societal usefulness into arguments that emphasized the military and economic security of the country. Along with that change, the approach recommended for teaching science changed from one in which the technological applications of science were taught to one in which a rigorous and highly conceptual structure of the disciplines were to be taught. Leadership for the reform efforts came largely from the scientific community, supported by the federal government through the National Science Foundation. Scientists valued the disciplined thinking that science provided and the general applicability of the core concepts of the disciplines to a range of scientific and practical problems in society. The new curriculum materials offered scientific validity to course content, engaged students in independent scientific investigations that were characteristic of the way science was actually done, and attempted to present a realistic picture of the nature of the scientific enterprise.

But as effective as the arguments of scientists were in convincing high-level policy makers that students should be introduced to science that was intellectually rigorous, the new instructional approaches and curriculum materials generally ignored the technical applications of science, were unconnected to students' interests or to the concerns of everyday living (Hurd 1970), and often proved too difficult for many students. Because of the mismatch between curricular expectations and students' interests and capabilities, and because of a shift in the issues that the country as a whole saw as important, more changes would follow in the years ahead.

The New Social Relevance of the 1970s

By the late 1960s and early 1970s, the arguments for the value of science in society had again shifted, this time to a tone more reminiscent of the first half of the 20th century than of the previous 30 years. The term "scientific literacy" was used to describe what adults needed to know for effective citizenship and what they needed to know to create a more humane society (DeBoer 2000). Educators, concerned that the reforms of the 1960s had gone too far in moving science teaching away from practical interests of students and the technological applications they encountered in daily life, argued that social relevance justified and should guide the teaching of science. Science literacy included science content knowledge, knowledge of the methods of science, and awareness of the relationship between science and society. Some defined science literacy as the knowledge and skills that enabled one to engage in the scientific issues of the day (in other words, the ability to read and understand the science being discussed in the popular media; Koelsche 1965).

The theme of science literacy was identified by the National Science Teachers Association (NSTA) at its annual meeting in 1971 as the most important goal for science education for the 1970s. In its statement on scientific literacy, NSTA said: "The major goal of science education is to develop scientifically literate and personally concerned individuals with a high competence for rational thought and action" (1971, p. 47). The scientifically literate person is one who "uses science concepts, process skills, and values in making everyday decisions as he interacts with other people and with his environment" and "understands the interrelationships between science, technology and other facets of society, including social and economic development" (pp. 47–48).

In 1982, the NSTA board of directors adopted a similar position statement entitled Science-Technology-Society: Science Education for the 1980s. In that statement, they said:

> Many of the problems we face today can be solved only by persons educated in the ideas and processes of science and technology. A scientific literacy is basic for living, working, and decision making in the 1980s and beyond.... The goal of science education during the 1980s is to develop scientifically literate individuals who understand how science, technology, and society influence one another and who are able to use this knowledge in their everyday decision-making. (NSTA 1982)

Science was again seen as having utility for citizens—useful for helping people make decisions on issues having a scientific basis and for improving the quality of their own lives and the lives of their fellow citizens.

Leadership for this "new-progressivism" (Ravitch 1983) came mainly from professional educators—including classroom teachers, professors of science education, and professional organizations such as the NSTA, but less so from practicing scientists.

The 1980s: *A Nation at Risk* and the Beginning of the Standards Movement

During 1981 and 1982, the United States experienced its most severe recession since the Great Depression. The recession followed nearly a decade of high unemployment and high inflation rates. In this difficult economic environment, and at a time when American students' test scores in science and mathematics were low and declining, President Reagan established the National Commission on Excellence in Education (NCEE) on August 26, 1981. The report of the Commission, *A Nation at Risk*, was released on April 26, 1983, and called for the federal government, along with states and local school districts, to raise the level of competence of American students in all academic areas, with special emphasis on science and mathematics. Science and mathematics, rigorously taught, were seen as the route to new economic prosperity.

A Nation at Risk

The NCEE concluded that the nation had lost sight of its true educational mission and of the need for high expectations for students. It recommended a return to a more academic educational focus and more disciplined effort on the part of students. The NCEE also claimed that international competitors were well educated and highly motivated and that the United States needed to be as well if the nation was to compete successfully. The new raw materials of international commerce were knowledge, learning, information, and skilled intelligence. The NCEE pointed to the value of an education where comprehension, analysis, and problem solving were fostered, instead of rudimentary knowledge or technical and occupational skills. In high school, all students would learn the "New Basics," including English, mathematics, science, social studies, computer science, and, for the college-bound students, two years of foreign language.

A *Nation at Risk* recommended that schools, colleges, and universities raise expectations for academic performance and student conduct. Textbooks should be upgraded and updated to assure more rigorous content, and university scientists should be called on to help in this task. In science, students should be introduced to (a) the concepts, laws, and processes of the physical sciences; (b) the methods of scientific inquiry and reasoning; (c) the applications of scientific knowledge to everyday life; and (d) the social and environmental implications of scientific and technological development" (NCEE 1983, p. 25). The report also recommended more homework, longer school days and longer school years, better attendance policies, and placement and promotion of students on the basis of academic progress. Although these recommendations were broad, and included science content and the applications of science as well as the scientific way of thinking, what was most distinctive was the emphasis on academic rigor. The NCEE believed that higher standards and expectations were needed to raise the scientific competence of students and to give them a deep respect for intelligence, achievement, learning, and self-disciplined effort.

Educating Americans for the 21st Century

Just five months later, on September 12, 1983, the Commission on Precollege Education in Mathematics, Science, and Technology of the National Science Board, which acts as an advisory board to the National Science Foundation, issued its report, *Educating Americans for the 21st Century* (National Science Board 1983). The report echoed many of the ideas in *A Nation at Risk* and provided additional detail on how the vision of improved science education for all could be realized. They said that the educational system had undergone a period of neglect, resulting in unacceptably low performance levels in science and mathematics, that U.S. national security and economic health depended on its human resource development, and that a commitment to academic excellence would put the United States on a firm economic footing in its competition with other countries.

The recommended strategy to accomplish these priorities involved the development of national goals and curricular frameworks, local responsibility for meeting these goals, local variation in how the goals would be implemented, and strong national leadership for monitoring the quality of local efforts. The commission recommended increased student exposure to science, higher standards of participation and achievement (citing comparisons to Japan's system where students spent more time in school), and a system of objective measurement to monitor progress.

Educating Americans for the 21st Century provided more detail in its recommendations regarding the content of the science, mathematics, and technology curriculum than was in *A Nation at Risk*. The commission recommended drastically reducing the number of topics that students would study, in part by integrating topics within subject areas and by making connections between subject areas, especially between mathematics, science, and technology. Courses should focus on thinking, communication, and problem-solving skills. Students should have early hands-on experiences in school, and they should be given opportunities to formulate questions and seek answers from their observations of natural phenomena. The study of science should provide knowledge that would lead to civic responsibility and the ability to cope in a technological world. The commission recommended that the courses be oriented toward practical problems that "require the collection of data, the communication of results and ideas and the formulation and testing of solutions" (p. 45). Content recommendations were given for each subject area and organized into three grade bands within subject areas. For example, at the high school level it was recommended that biology should emphasize concepts and principles such as "genetics, nutrition, evolution, reproduction of various life forms, structure/function, disease, diversity, integration of life systems, life cycles, and energetics" (p. 98).

As had been true at previous times when the focus shifted away from the applications of science and toward the traditional content of science, there was concern that by emphasizing academic rigor, the commission's recommendations would be seen as advocating intellectual elitism intended only for those students who would pursue careers in science, mathematics, and technology. The commission addressed the excellence-equity distinction by saying: "these new basics are needed by *all* students— not only tomorrow's scientists—not only the talented and fortunate" (p. v). "While increasing our concern for the most talented, we must now also attend to the need for early and sustained stimulation and preparation for all students so that we do not unwittingly exclude potential talent..." (p. x).

The commission was also careful, as they recommended the development of standards written at the national level, to leave room for variation in the way states and local school districts would implement those standards. "This should not be construed as a suggestion for the establishment of a national curriculum; rather these are guides that state and local officials might use in developing curricula for local use" (p. 41). "No one course of study is appropriate for all students and all teachers in all schools in all parts of the country. Nor is there just one good curriculum. Various parts of the Nation must develop their total curriculum and revise it repeatedly to keep it suitable for students and teachers" (p. 92).

A *Nation at Risk* and *Educating Americans for the 21st Century* aptly summarized a vision and strategy for reform. The vision included an intellectually rigorous common core of science knowledge for all, which would lead to an understanding of science ideas that are personally fulfilling and can help build a knowledgeable and competent citizenry well-prepared for life in a free democratic society. The strategy involved national goals, local implementation, and accountability through student testing. Details of the vision and the strategy were to be worked out over time with the help of scientists and professional educators.

In response to the call for added rigor in the educational system, many of the state legislatures and state departments of education during this time implemented policy initiatives that were structural in nature but often did not pay attention to the broader goals of educational reform. As Paul Hurd said toward the end of the 1980s, "changes implemented... include lengthening the school day and year, requiring more science courses, intensifying course rigor, increasing student testing and school assessments, and raising graduation requirements; but, to what ends?" (1989, p. 16).

Science for All Americans

The first detailed and substantive response to the various calls for a comprehensive statement of what all students should know and be able to do in science came from the American Association for the Advancement of Science (AAAS) through the establishment of Project 2061, a long-term reform effort to define and promote science literacy. The work of Project 2061 began with the publication of *Science for All Americans* (AAAS 1990) and has continued to this day with the development of tools and resources to bring the vision of science for all into full realization. The creation of Project 2061 was led by F. James Rutherford, Executive Director of the Education Division at AAAS. Rutherford was a science educator who had worked with Gerald Holton and Fletcher Watson on the development of Harvard Project Physics (Holton 2003), and had served in the administration of President Carter as head of the National Science Foundation's Science, Mathematics, and Engineering education programs and as Assistant Secretary for Research and Improvement in the U.S. Department of Education.

Chapter 17

The 1990 publication of *Science for All Americans* (AAAS) was a bold statement of what Americans should know in science to participate fully in a democratic society. That core knowledge included concepts and skills in science, mathematics, technology, and the social sciences. It also included knowledge of the nature of science, the nature of mathematics, and the nature of the designed world. Furthermore, it included an understanding of historical perspectives; common themes dealing with systems, models, constancy and change; and issues of scale.

The language of *Science for All Americans* stressed both personal development and responsible citizenship:

> Education has no higher purpose than preparing people to lead personally fulfilling and responsible lives. For its part, science education—meaning education in science, mathematics, and technology—should help students to develop the understandings and habits of mind they need to become compassionate human beings able to think for themselves and to face life head on. It should equip them also to participate thoughtfully with fellow citizens in building and protecting a society that is open, decent, and vital. America's future—its ability to create a truly just society, to sustain its economic vitality, and to remain secure in a world torn by hostilities—depends more than ever on the character and quality of the education that the nation provides for all of its children. (AAAS 1990, p. xiii)

Science for All Americans suggested that schools should focus on the essentials of science literacy—a common core of ideas and skills that have the greatest scientific, educational, and personal significance. Consistent with statements made earlier in the decade, the recommendations for science content were meant for all students regardless of social circumstances or career ambitions. Criteria for content selection included (1) the utility of the content for employment, personal decision making, and intelligent participation in society; (2) the intrinsic historical or cultural significance of the knowledge; (3) the potential to inform one's thinking about the enduring questions of human meaning; and (4) the value of the content for the child's life at the present time and not just for the future (AAAS 1990, pp. xix, xx).

There were also recommendations regarding pedagogy. *Science for All Americans* suggested that: "Young people learn most readily about things that are tangible and directly accessible to their senses—visual, auditory, tactile, and kinesthetic" (p. 199). Other pedagogical approaches that would support conceptual understanding included applying ideas in novel situations and giving students practice in doing so themselves, having students express ideas publicly and obtaining feedback from their peers, allowing time to reflect on the feedback they receive, and having the chance to make adjustments and try again.

According to *Science for All Americans*, to appreciate the special modes of thought of science, mathematics, and technology, students should experience the kinds of thinking that characterize those fields: "To understand [science, mathematics, and technology] as ways of thinking and doing, as well as bodies of knowledge, requires that students have some experience with the kinds of thought and action that are typical of those fields" (p. 200).

Science for All Americans also pointed out the value of beginning instruction within the range of concrete experiences that students have already had:

> Sound teaching usually begins with questions and phenomena that are interesting and familiar to students, not with abstractions or phenomena outside their range of perception, understanding, or knowledge. Students need to get acquainted with the things around them—including devices, organisms, materials, shapes, and numbers—and to observe them, collect them, handle them, describe them, become puzzled by them, ask questions about them, argue about them, and then to try to find answers to their questions (p. 201).

It was also recommended that the content and methods of science be taught together:

> In science, conclusions and the methods that lead to them are tightly coupled. Science teaching that attempts solely to impart to students the accumulated knowledge of a field leads to very little understanding and certainly not to the development of intellectual independence and facility.... Science teachers should help students to acquire both scientific knowledge of the world and scientific habits of mind at the same time (pp. 201, 203).

Science for All Americans recognized that to be consistent with the nature of science, science teaching should encourage students to raise questions about the ideas being studied, help them frame their questions clearly enough to begin to look for answers to those questions, and support the creative use of imagination. It should promote the idea that one's evidence, logic, and claims will be questioned, and scientific investigations are subjected to replication. Students should be encouraged to ask: How do we know? What is the evidence? Are there alternative explanations? *Science for All Americans* makes clear that science is a way of extending understanding and not a body of unalterable truth. It also suggests that teachers and textbooks should not be viewed primarily as purveyors of truth. Because science ideas are often modified, an open mind is needed when considering scientific claims.

Benchmarks for Science Literacy

In 1993, the vision of science literacy laid out in *Science for All Americans* was translated into *Benchmarks for Science Literacy*, a statement of knowledge and skills that students should gain by the end of each of four grade bands (K–2, 3–5, 6–8, and 9–12) in order to achieve the goal of science literacy by the end of high school.

The call for higher standards in *A Nation at Risk*, the efforts of the Commission on Precollege Education in Mathematics, Science, and Engineering to begin to define the science content that all students should know, and the publication of *Science for All Americans*—the most comprehensive statement yet written describing what science literacy entails—were the first steps in a new approach to science education.

First, the vision for science education described in both *A Nation at Risk* and in *Science for All Americans* was broadly humanistic and inclusive. Although they recognized the importance of scientific knowledge for the nation's economic development and for individual occupation, those documents also acknowledged the personal intellectual value of science. For example, *A Nation at Risk* pointed to the importance of a high-level of common understanding in a free and diverse democratic society. The concern was not only for competitive success in industry and commerce; it was also for the intellectual, moral, and spiritual strength of the people who form the society. The educational system should contribute to the development of a common culture to help achieve a shared understanding of complex societal issues. Similarly, *Science for All Americans* asserted that science education "should help students to develop the understandings and habits of mind they need to become compassionate human beings able to think for themselves and to face life head on. It should equip them also to participate thoughtfully with fellow citizens in building and protecting a society that is open, decent, and vital" (p. xiii). Both documents also recognized the value of science for all, not just for an elite few, and that science education should include knowledge about how science is done as well as scientific knowledge.

Second, the idea of organizing curriculum, instruction, and assessment around clear and precise content standards (or learning goals), whether national in scope or defined by the state or school district, took hold in the subsequent years. Content standards were used to describe important goals of quality science instruction, and they were also used for accountability purposes through progressively more restrictive federal legislation that held states responsible for defining and measuring student performance with respect to specific science content standards.

Public Accountability

With respect to the specification of content standards called for in *A Nation at Risk*, following the publication of *Benchmarks for Science Literacy* in 1993, the National Research Council published the *National Science Education Standards* in 1996. Those two documents, which shared a high degree of content agreement between them (AAAS, 1997), were then used by virtually every state in the preparation of their own content standards.

The federal government was clearly on the path toward a system of standards and accountability when President George H. W. Bush met with state governors in September 1989 in Charlottesville, Virginia, to discuss a national agenda for education. Although the increasing role of the federal government in science education is traceable to the national security concerns of the post-war years, the launching of *Sputnik* in 1956, and the funding of science education through the National Science Foundation, the Charlottesville summit on education led to policies that vastly increased the federal government's role in science education. Whereas individual scientists, professional scientific societies such as AAAS, and teachers' organizations such as the NEA and NSTA had been the major influences on policy up to that point, this summit marked a significant shift in leadership for science education. At the summit, the president and the governors agreed to establish clear national performance goals and strategies to ensure U.S. international competitiveness. They also agreed that there should be annual reporting on progress toward meeting those goals. Then, on April 18, 1991, the president released *AMERICA 2000: An Education Strategy* (U.S. Department of Education 1991) which described a plan for moving the nation toward national goals. Six goals were identified that would be accomplished by the year 2000, one of which was to "make U.S. students first in the world in math and science achievement" (p. 4).

The strategy for accomplishing the national goals was to include an accountability package that would encourage schools and communities to measure and compare results and insist on improvement when the results weren't good enough. The package included national standards, national tests, reporting mechanisms, and various incentives. Content standards in each of five core subject areas and tests to measure achievement of that content would be developed in conjunction with the National Education Goals Panel. "These standards will incorporate both knowledge and skills, to ensure that, when they leave school, young Americans are prepared for further study and the work force" (p. 21). The tests would be national but voluntary and tied to the national standards. The president's proposals called for Congress to authorize the National Assessment of Educational Progress—which had been established by Congress in 1969 to provide national data on educational outcomes—"regularly to collect state-level data in grades four, eight and twelve in all five core subjects, beginning in 1994. Congress will also be asked to permit the use of National Assessment tests at district and school levels by states that wish to do so" (p. 22). This move toward state-level, and sometimes district-level, reporting represented a significant increase in accountability.

Although the specific proposals in President Bush's *America 2000* report were not enacted into law during his presidency, many of them became law when President Clinton signed the *Goals 2000: Educate America Act* on March 31, 1994. The act focused on educating workers for productive employment, with special reference to competition in international trade. Again, the government's primary interest in education was the development of human capital so the United States could remain economically competitive internationally (Spring 2001). In addition to stating national goals, the *Goals 2000* legislation also created the National Education

Standards Council, which had the authority to approve or reject the states' content standards. This body subsequently dissolved following the 1994 midterm elections when the Republicans took control of Congress and voiced objections to the increasing intrusion of the federal government in education (National Conference of State Legislatures, n.d.). Also in 1994, President Clinton signed the *Improving America's Schools Act* (IASA), which reauthorized the *Elementary and Secondary Education Act* of 1965 (ESEA), first enacted as part of President Johnson's War on Poverty and intended to improve education for disadvantaged children in poor areas. Under the education act, states had to

- develop challenging mathematics and language arts content standards that clearly define the knowledge and skills expected of students;
- develop performance standards representing three levels of proficiency for each of those content standards—partially proficient, proficient, and advanced;
- develop and implement assessments aligned with the content and performance standards in mathematics and language arts at three grade spans: 3–5, 6–9, and 10–12;
- use the same standards and assessment system to measure Title I students as the state uses to measure the performance of all other students; and
- use performance standards to establish a benchmark for improvement referred to as "adequate yearly progress" (AYP).

All schools were to show continuous progress or face possible consequences, such as having to offer supplemental services and school choice options to students or replacing the existing staff (National Conference of State Legislatures, n.d.).

The trend toward holding schools accountable for their students' performance through standards setting and assessment, begun in the early 1980s, was strengthened with the 1994 legislation. The legislation also provided the basis for the *No Child Left Behind Act* of 2001 (NCLB) as it moved the focus away from national standards combined with voluntary national testing to a state-by-state system of standard setting and accountability. In addition, as would be true under NCLB, the *Improving America's Schools Act* required states to test students in math and language arts but not in science. The pullback from national-level standards and toward state-level accountability was due to a continuing concern among many national policy makers about the nationalization of education, a concern that had been present from the earliest days of the country.

Leadership during the 1980s and '90s came from many places. Most notably, the federal government took a more and more active role through agency-sponsored reports such as the NCEE's *A Nation at Risk*, presidential goal statements such as *Goals 2000*, and enacted legislation such as the *Improving America's Schools Act*. In addition, professional scientific societies such as AAAS played a significant role in defining both the goals of a quality science education for all as well as the pedagogical approaches that could be used to accomplish those goals. But, although both AAAS and the National Research Council had written statements about the importance of science in the society, in the end, federal legislation focused on the teaching of reading and mathematics, but not on science.

Leadership for 21st-Century Science Education

This historical overview of arguments for the importance of scientific knowledge in our society and in our schools reveals how advocacy leadership came from many different places and in many different forms. Arguments by individual scientists such as James B. Conant and Vannevar Bush, influential books and essays such as Herbert Spencer's What Knowledge Is of Most Worth (1864) or Mortimer Smith's *The Diminished Mind* (1954), and national level reports such as the Report of the Committee of Ten in 1893 or the Report of the National Commission on Excellence in Education (*A Nation at Risk*) in 1983 all had a significant impact on the direction that science education took. But these arguments did not stand alone. They have to be viewed in light of the dominant social forces operating at the time. The events of the day often determined whether the justification for science was based on its importance for personal intellectual development, for building a civil society, ensuring national security, or improving economic competitiveness. We also see trend lines in the various influences affecting which arguments were made and which ones were listened to. For example, during the 19th century and early 20th century, the federal government played a relatively limited role in defining the knowledge considered to be of most importance to society or in establishing education policy. That role was greatly increased in the years following World War II as the federal government saw education in science much more strategically linked to national security and, following the economic troubles of the 1970s and early 1980s, much more linked to economic security. It should also be clear from this review that leadership is a complex phenomenon that involves the intersection of individuals, professional organizations, and government agencies among others.

Is it possible to describe where we are today in terms of the perceived value of science in our society and the nature of the leadership needed to affect K–12 science education to achieve our goals? Are opinions again coalescing around a particular idea or set of ideas? Are we headed in a new direction in science education? Who is providing leadership? Let us look briefly at what is being said about the importance of science today, the people making various arguments, and the implications of the proposals for K–16 education.

On June 10, 2009, Rep. Vernon Ehlers (R-MI) and Sen. Christopher Dodd (D-CT) introduced S. 224 and H.R. 2790, the Standards to Provide Educational Achievement for Kids (SPEAK) Act. Under the SPEAK Act, the National Assessment Governing Board would create or adopt rigorous content standards in math and science for grades K–12 that would be anchored to the math and science frameworks and achievement levels of the National Assessment of Educational Progress and voluntarily chosen by the states. The act also authorizes establishment of a fund to provide financial incentive to states willing to adopt the higher standards. In the legislation, it is argued that the reason common standards are needed is to ensure that all American students are given the same opportunity to learn no matter where they reside and how often they move from one state to another, instead of the current system of 50 individual states creating 50 different standards of varying quality and as many different variations in the sequencing of content. The key argument is that a lack of common standards has led to wide variation in the levels of knowledge, skills, and preparedness among America's student-aged population. The legislation also argues that science is important to prepare students for jobs in a global economy and to ensure the economic competitiveness of the country.

After a period of pulling back from national standards, this legislation, if adopted, would reestablish their role. The legislation is consistent with the Common Core State Standards Initiative recently introduced by the

National Governors Association (NGA) and the Council of Chief State School Officers (CCSSO) to create high-quality and internationally benchmarked national standards in math and reading that would be voluntarily chosen by the states (CCSSO 2009).

Another major effort to raise the profile of science education was undertaken by the Carnegie Corporation of New York and the Institute for Advanced Study of Princeton, NJ. Their joint Commission on Mathematics and Science Education issued its report, *The Opportunity Equation: Transforming Mathematics and Science Education for Citizenship and the Global Economy*, on June 10, 2009. In the executive summary of the report, the commission says:

> The nation's capacity to innovate for economic growth and the ability of American workers to thrive in the global economy depend on a broad foundation of math and science learning, as do our hopes for preserving a vibrant democracy and the promise of social mobility for young people that lie at the heart of the American dream. Our nation needs an educated young citizenry with the capacity to contribute to and gain from the country's future productivity, understand policy choices, and participate in building a sustainable future. Knowledge and skills from science, technology, engineering, and mathematics—the so-called STEM fields—are crucial to virtually every endeavor of individual and community life. All young Americans should be educated to be "STEM-capable," no matter where they live, what educational path they pursue, or in which field they choose to work. (Carnegie Corporation of New York 2009, p. vii)

A key observation made by Commission members is that many students and their parents do not think that it is important to do well in math or science unless the student intends to pursue a career directly related to them. According to Phillip A. Griffiths, cochair of the commission, "It is imperative that we impress upon all young people that knowledge of math and science is crucial to many more careers than they may realize. All young Americans should have a sufficient grounding in science, technology, engineering, and mathematics no matter where they live, what educational path they pursue, or in which field they choose to work" (Carnegie Corporation of New York 2009).

Clearly, there is a renewed emphasis within the scientific and science education community on common national standards in science. This is consistent with the push for common standards in math and reading within the National Governors Association. The arguments for science today primarily have to do with the role of science in keeping us competitive internationally in a global economy. The argument is that most jobs in the 21st-century workforce will require knowledge of science, mathematics, and technology.

The leadership for these initiatives has come from many different places. For one, there are members of Congress who are particularly aware of the role that science plays in society. For example, Rep. Vernon Ehlers (R-MI) and Sen. Mark Udall (D-CO) launched the bipartisan Science, Technology, Engineering and Mathematics (STEM) Education Caucus for members of Congress; dozens of members have joined the caucus. On their website (*www.stemedcaucus.org*) are listed three kinds of intellectual capital that STEM Education is responsible for providing our country:

- Scientists and engineers who will continue the research and development that is central to the economic growth of our country,
- Technologically proficient workers who are capable of dealing with the demands of a science-based, high-technology workforce, and
- Scientifically literate voters and citizens who make intelligent decisions about public policy and who understand the world around them.

As already noted, the Carnegie Corporation of New York and the Institute for Advanced Study has taken a leadership role in establishing the joint Commission on Mathematics and Science Education. In addition, the National Governors Association, in their alliance with the Council of Chief State School Officers, has shown significant leadership in bringing the idea of internationally benchmarked common standards in math and reading to the public attention, and may do so in science as well. The Secretary of Education, Arne Duncan, has supported the idea of common standards that is being proposed by the National Governors Association and has pledged the backing of the U.S. Department of Education, including support from the $4.35 billion Race to the Top Fund. With respect to common standards in science, professional societies such as AAAS have publicly argued the long-term economic and workforce advantages of providing all students across the country with access to a high-quality education in science, which begins with high-quality standards (Leshner

2007; Leshner and Roseman 2009). President Obama also has publicly supported the idea of improved standards in science education.

From this, it appears that support is coalescing around the idea of voluntary, common, internationally benchmarked standards in math and reading, and concerted efforts are being made to include science as well. There is also widespread support for the idea that science is important for economic competitiveness and for a scientifically literate public that can engage in discussions about science and make wise decisions regarding science issues. Time will tell whether the support that has been pledged by the current administration will be realized so that American students will be well-prepared for life in the twenty-first century.

But history should teach us that the debate will be ongoing, that education will forever be on the minds of American citizens and their leaders, and that leadership in science education needs to be continuously exercised by individual scientists, science educators, professional organizations, as well as by members of the administration and Congress. Leadership in our democratic society is truly a distributed activity.

References

American Association for the Advancement of Science (AAAS). 1990. *Science for all Americans*. New York: Oxford University Press.

——. 1993. *Benchmarks for science literacy*. New York: Oxford University Press.

——. 1997. *Resources for science literacy: Professional development*. New York: Oxford University Press.

Bradbury, R. 1915. Recent tendencies in high school chemistry. *School Science and Mathematics* 15: 782–793.

Brandwein, P. 1955. *The gifted student as future scientist*. New York: Harcourt, Brace.

Bush, V. 1945. *Science: The endless frontier. A Report to the President, July 1945* (1960 reprint). Washington, DC: National Science Foundation.

Carnegie Corporation of New York-Institute for Advanced Study Commission on Mathematics and Science Education. 2009. *The opportunity equation: Transforming mathematics and science education for citizenship. www.opportunityequation.org*

Center for Public Education. 2008. *Student graduation and beyond: What* courses do our students need to complete in order to graduate from high school? www.centerforpubliceducation.org/site/apps/nlnet/content3.aspx?c =lvIXIiNOJwE&b=5079529&content_id={C30C1763-A684-44B2-932C-AAC097ADD4DC}&notoc=1

Coulter, J. 1915. The mission of science in education. *School Science and Mathematics* 15: 93–100.

Council of Chief State School Officers (CCSSO). 2009. Forty-nine states and territories join common core state standards initiative. *www.ccsso. org/whats_new/press_releases/13359.cfm*

DeBoer, G. 1991. *A history of ideas in science education: Implications for practice.* New York: Columbia University Teachers College Press.

———. 2000. Scientific literacy: Another look at its historical and contemporary meanings and its relationship to science education reform. *Journal of Research in Science Teaching* 37 (6): 582–601.

Dewey, J. 1916. *Democracy and education.* New York: Macmillan.

Elementary and Secondary Education Act of 1965, 20 U.S.C. § 6301 *et. seq.* 1965.

Global Strategy Group, Inc. 2001. A public awareness initiative to build support for science literacy. *www.project2061.org/publications/articles/ psl/presentation.pdf*

Goals 2000: Educate America Act, 20 U.S.C. § 5801 *et. seq.* 1994.

Gonzales, P., T. Williams, L. Jocelyn, S. Roey, D. Kastberg, and S. Brenwald. 2008. *Highlights from TIMSS 2007: Mathematics and science achievement of U.S. fourth- and eighth-grade students in an international context.* Washington, DC: National Center for Education Statistics, U.S. Department of Education.

Harvard Committee on General Education. 1945. *General education in a free society.* Cambridge, MA: Harvard University Press.

Holton, G. 2003. The project physics course, then and now. *Science and Education* 12: 779–786.

Hurd, P. 1970. *New directions in teaching secondary school science.* Chicago: Rand McNally.

———. 1989. Science education and the nation's economy. In *Scientific literacy*, eds. A. Champagne, B. Lovitts, and B. Calinger, 15–40. Washington, DC: AAAS.

Huxley, T. 1899. *Science and education.* New York: Appleton.

Improving America's Schools Act of 1994, 20 U.S.C. § 8001 *et. seq.* 1994.

Koelsche, C. 1965. Scientific literacy as related to the media of mass communication. *School Science and Mathematics* 65: 719–724.

National Center for Education Statistics 1981. *Digest of education statistics.* Washington, DC: U.S. Government Printing Office.

National Commission on Excellence in Education (NCEE). 1983. *A nation at risk: The imperative for educational reform.* Washington, DC: U.S. Department of Education.

National Conference of State Legislatures. n.d. *No child left behind: History.* *www.ncsl.org/programs/educ/NCLBHistory.htm*

National Defense Education Act of 1958, 1 U.S.C. § 101, 72 Stat. 1581. 1958.

National Education Association. 1894. *Report of the committee on secondary school studies.* Washington, DC: U.S. Government Printing Office.

——. 1899. Report of the committee on college-entrance requirements. *Journal of Proceedings and Addresses of the Thirty-Eighth Annual Meeting.*

——. 1911. Report of the committee of nine on the articulation of high school and college. *Journal of Proceedings and Addresses of the Forty-Ninth Annual Meeting.*

——. 1918. *Cardinal principles of secondary education: A report of the commission on the reorganization of secondary education* (U.S. Bureau of Education, Bulletin No. 35). Washington, DC: U.S. Government Printing Office.

——. 1920. *Reorganization of science in secondary schools: A report of the commission on the reorganization of secondary education* (U.S. Bureau of Education, Bulletin No. 26). Washington, DC: U.S. Government Printing Office.

National Research Council (NRC). 1996. *National science education standards.* Washington, DC: National Academy Press.

National Science Board Commission on Precollege Education in Mathematics, Science and Technology. 1983. *Educating Americans for the 21st century: A report to the American people and the national science board.* Washington, DC: National Science Foundation.

National Science Teachers Association (NSTA). 1971. NSTA position statement on school science education for the 70s. *The Science Teacher* 38: 46–51.

——. 1982. *Science-technology-society: Science education for the 1980s.* Washington, DC: NSTA Press.

National Society for the Study of Education (NSSE). 1932. *A program for teaching science: Thirty-first yearbook of the NSSE.* Chicago: University of Chicago Press.

National Society for the Study of Education (NSSE). 1947. *Science education in American schools: Forty-sixth yearbook of the NSSE.* Chicago: University of Chicago Press.

No Child Left Behind Act of 2001, 20 U.S.C. § 6301 *et seq.* 2002.

President's Scientific Research Board. 1947. *Science and public policy*, vols. 1 and 4. Washington, DC: U.S. Government Printing Office.

Programme for International Student Assessment (PISA). 2007. *PISA 2006: Science competencies for tomorrow's world, vol.1–analysis.* Paris: Organisation for Economic Co-operation and Development.

Ravitch, D. 1983. *The troubled crusade.* New York: Basic Books.

Sanford, C. 1950. High school science and mathematics—For whom and for what? *School Science and Mathematics* 50: 307–319.

Schwab, J. 1962. The teaching of science as enquiry. In *The teaching of science*, eds. J. Schwab and P. Brandwein, 1–103. Cambridge, MA: Harvard University Press.

Smith, A., and E. Hall. 1902. *The teaching of chemistry and physics in the secondary school.* New York: Longmans, Green.

Smith, M. 1954. *The diminished mind.* Chicago: Regnery.

Smyth, T. 1940. Problems associated with the high school science sequence. *School Science and Mathematics* 40: 255–260.

Spencer, H. 1864. *Education: Intellectual, moral, and physical.* New York: Appleton.

Spring, J. 2001. *The American school: 1642–2000.* New York: McGraw-Hill.

Standards to Provide Educational Achievement for Kids (SPEAK) Act. H. R. 2790/S. 224, 111th Cong. 2009.

Trefil, J. 2008. *Why science?* New York: Teachers College Press.

U.S. Department of Education. 1991. *America 2000: An education strategy sourcebook.* Washington, DC: U.S. Department of Education.

U.S. Office of Education. 1951. *Life adjustment for every youth.* Washington, DC: U.S. Government Printing Office.

Chapter 18
Science Communication and Public Engagement With Science

Tiffany Lohwater

A scientist walks down a beach on the Outer Banks of North Carolina, catching a unique species of butterfly in her net and making observations about the butterfly's habitat and behavior. These little brown butterflies are threatened by waterfront development in this small coastal community, and the scientist's research is concerned with documenting their dwindling population numbers, their genetic makeup, and the changes to their habitat. When beachgoers and local residents see the scientist with her net and notebook, they often ask what she is doing and how they can help protect the butterflies. The combination of these kinds of questions and a request to speak with policy makers in Washington, D.C., led this young scientist to seek out opportunities for improving her ability to communicate about her research and its importance to society. This is the kind of story I hear time and time again.

At the American Association for the Advancement of Science (AAAS), I work with scientists and educators on ways to explain their work to a greater audience than the scientific and education communities, including the public, news media, and policy makers. Scientists are often in need of quality resources to help develop their public communication and outreach skills, since traditional scientific training does not typically prepare scientists to be effective communicators outside of academia. AAAS's Communicating Science program has trained hundreds of scientists and educators to discuss their work in ways that connect to people's everyday lives.

It is the responsibility of all who have a passion for science and science education to serve as ambassadors of science because we need as many great communicators of science as possible. Scientists and science educators are the individuals involved in the daily tasks of doing and explaining science, and they can be natural connectors between the world of science and the public. The first section of this chapter provides useful tips for educators and scientists who would like to improve their public communication skills.

Why is science communication important? In the United States, we find a public who has high regard for scientists and their work but also displays a lack of knowledge about scientific facts and process. The U.S. population continually recognizes science and technology as beneficial to society, but many continue to have reservations about scientific issues and technologies that touch upon personal or moral values (Pew Research Center 2009).

In response, the scientific and education communities have emphasized the need to improve science literacy among the public, in hopes that this would lead people to better know and appreciate science (Bubela et al. 2009). However, public surveys administered by the National Science Foundation and others over the last two decades have shown no marked increase in science literacy—in fact, numbers have remained largely flat (National Science Board 2008). How can we encourage people to learn more about science and understand its relevance to their everyday lives?

One approach that AAAS and other science, education, and civic organizations are increasingly using is known as *public engagement with science* (McCallie et al. 2009; Bucchi 2008; Center for Advances in Public Engagement 2008; Wilsdon, Wynne, and Stilgoe 2005; Leshner 2003). A later section of this chapter will summarize this approach.

Science Communication 101

In order to be a successful communicator—science or otherwise—there are a few basic principles to keep in mind.

Consider your audience. Since true communication is an exchange of information, it is really important to think about your audience: who they are, their interest in and experiences with your topic, and questions they may have. This will prepare you to exchange the information you have with the audience you'd like to reach. We've all attended public talks by scientists and educators who, unfortunately, had not spent time changing their academic talk into one that would be better received and responded to by a nonacademic audience. I cannot stress how important it is to really think about who those people will be in the seats, literally and figuratively. Regardless of the form of communication (writing, speaking, blogging), it is extremely useful to spend time planning based on your audience's likely experiences, knowledge of your subject, and—perhaps most importantly—their interests. Remember that communication is defined as the exchange of information. It does not take place in a vacuum. If you are giving a talk or communicating online, always leave ample time and space for questions and response. You will not only provide individuals with an opportunity to interact with you directly and have their questions answered, but you will also receive feedback from the audience on their interest in and knowledge of the topic. If you follow through with Q&A on multiple occasions, you may find that there are a few key questions that individuals ask repeatedly. This may help you improve your communication because you will have identified points of interest regarding the topic.

Identify the key points of your message. When first considering what you plan to say in your communication, it helps to determine the main points you would like to make. Think of it as a message outline that will keep you on topic and will help your audience follow you. Identify no more than three key points. Ideally, there should be a natural relationship or way to transition seamlessly between your points. Many scientists struggle to explain their research to the lay public. Thinking about your work in terms of three key things a public audience should know often helps define the most important and relevant pieces of your presentation, without use of unwieldy scientific jargon that could lose the audience. Creating an outline of three points to help communicate your message also allows you to provide multiple entry points into the conversation. An audience may pick up on point two, for example, and ask questions that will elicit additional information from you. This is success! It shows that point two is a topic of interest to your audience and provides you with useful information for further development of your message. Remember that your three points—and even your message—will likely change based on your audience, what you'd like them to know, and what kind of feedback you desire.

Use the form of communication best suited to your audience and your message. From speaking to writing to personal conversations to blogging, there are several ways to communicate a message. Take care to identify the best way for your intended audience to receive and respond to your message. If you would like to reach a local community and decision makers on a specific issue related to science or science education, writing an editorial for the local newspaper or its website may be one option for reaching that audience with your message. If you would like to encourage a more conversational approach among a specific group of individuals in order to explain an area of scientific research and learn more about the group's interests and concerns, a small, informal speaking engagement where individuals have the opportunity to ask questions and interact one-on-one may be a better fit. Whatever your message, make sure to consider your audience and the purpose of the communication when deciding how best to communicate.

Be conscious of tone. As previously discussed, Americans respect and value science but may not have a high level of knowledge about your particular topic. Keep in mind that your tone can set expectations for the kind of communication and the level of audience involvement. If you are prepared to provide an hour and a half lecture on a topic and leave no room for questions or audience involvement, you've conveyed an assumption that the audience cannot truly participate in the communication. Similarly, if you take on an expert tone that is laced with jargon and acronyms and inaccessible to your audience, you risk alienating those individuals with whom you'd like to encourage learning and response.

Practice, practice, practice. This point cannot be stressed enough! Practice is the key to success. Practice does not mean scripting a talk until it is memorized or needs to be read from paper. Practice means working on your message and your key points and thinking about audience questions in advance of communicating. I often encourage scientists who are preparing to give a public talk or make a public announcement about their research to practice by talking with nonscientists they know: family members, friends, or neighbors. Find someone who is far enough outside of your field to provide useful feedback. Try out your analogies and cultural references with them—not with a group of your peers who are intensely familiar with your work. In academia, we are encouraged to use technical terms, to speak to our peers, and to show our breadth of knowledge on a topic. These are not usually the best characteristics for communicating well with the public. The public will respond to an expert who is willing to explain a topic in a way that is of interest and relevant to them personally, not necessarily the same techniques that the expert would use to impress other experts.

The Changing Face of Journalism and Social Media

Changes in communication technology are having profound effects on journalism, including science journalism (Russell 2009). Emphasis has long been shifting from purely print stories to those that showcase multimedia—photography, video, blogs, and social media tools that enable user interaction.

The downside to these changes is the continuing disappearance of journalism mainstays that provide well-researched, well-edited content; the struggling newspaper industry is the most prominent example. The upside is that institutions and individuals, including scientists and educators, now have increased opportunities to provide information to and interact directly with the public through social media tools such as blogs, Twitter, YouTube, and Facebook. Perhaps the most interesting component of social media is the opportunity for multichannel communication. Information is not simply dispersed; it is shared and exchanged among users. There is a real need for science and education leaders to participate in and experiment with social media in order to discover new ways to provide science content to the public, and encourage interest, involvement, and participation.

Social media and tools for direct online engagement have proliferated in recent years. The state of social media is changing rapidly, and it may be impossible to know what new tools will develop in coming months. With that in mind, here are a few established social media tools with which you may want to experiment:

> *Blog:* A website that contains dated text entries in reverse chronological order. Blogs serve many purposes from online newsletters to personal journals. Written by one person or a group of contributors, entries contain commentary and links to other websites, images, and videos; additionally, a search facility may be included. Most blogs invite feedback and comments, which enables communication between readers and content posters. On controversial issues as well as mainstream subjects, blogs can quickly reach people around the world. The "blogosphere," which is the world of blogs, has become a forum for public expression and is routinely searched for reactions and opinions about ideas, politics, and issues of all kinds.

> *Twitter:* A website and service that allows users to send short text messages up to 140 characters in length from their computers or cell phones to a group of people. Launched in 2006, Twitter (*www.twitter.com*) was designed to keep friends and colleagues informed about daily activities. Twitter increasingly is used for commercial and political purposes to keep consumers or constituents informed, and it enables instantaneous response and feedback. Twitter messages ("tweets") are only distributed to recipients who have elected to become followers. An account option allows an individual's tweets to be accessed at a unique public web address, so you do not need necessarily to be a follower in order to read

someone's tweets. Messages can also be sent via instant messaging, the Twitter website, or a third-party Twitter application.

Social Networking Sites: Websites that provide a virtual community for people interested in a particular topic or for general socialization. Members create their own online profile with biographical data, photos, videos, links, and any other information they choose to post. They communicate with each other by voice, chat, instant message, videoconference, and blogs, and the service typically provides a way for members to contact friends of other members. Social networking has been described as the 21st-century "virtual community." Globally, hundreds of millions of people have joined one or more social networking sites. Popular sites include Facebook, LinkedIn, and MySpace.

YouTube: This is a popular video-sharing website that allows anyone to upload short videos for private or public viewing. Viewers are able to comment on posted videos. YouTube provides a venue for sharing videos among friends and family as well as a showcase for new and experienced videographers. In addition, YouTube has emerged as a major venue for excerpts from speeches, events, and topic-specific content. Videos are streamed to users on the YouTube site (*www.youtube.com*) and may also be embedded in blogs and other websites.

Public Engagement Can Help Communicate Science

Social media opens up a whole new world for educators and scientists to communicate directly to individuals and groups. A key characteristic of this shift to social media is the expectation on behalf of the "listeners," in this case, members of the public, to have the opportunity to participate in the conversation. Many institutions and governments are using various tools, including social media, to encourage the public to take on a more active role (Clark and Aufderheide 2009). One such approach taking place within the scientific community is known as *public engagement with science*.

The major issues of today, whether viewed locally, nationally, or globally, force us to consider what we know as well as how we want our world to be. To address such questions, we need science, but science alone does not provide all the answers to the issues affecting society. In order to make the best decisions, the contexts, goals, and vision in which to apply scientific knowledge should be better defined. These contexts and goals often come from other sources of knowledge and domains—ethics, vision for society, comfort level with uncertainty, and desire to explore the unknown.

Public engagement with science, in terms of science education, is characterized by mutual learning—not one-way transmission from "experts" to the public—among people of varied backgrounds, scientific expertise, and life experiences who articulate and discuss their perspectives, ideas, knowledge, and values. A public engagement with science activity may, but does not necessarily, directly inform the direction of scientific investigations, institutions, or public policy (McCallie et al. 2009).

Like other science and public models, public engagement with science includes a strong focus on increased overall interest, engagement in, and knowledge of science content and process. The goals of activities, whether of an individual or a community, often include one or more of the following:

- Mutual learning for the public and scientists, such that everyone who participates develops new or more nuanced understandings of issues and opportunities
- Empowerment and development of skills to participate in civic activities
- Increased awareness of the cultural relevance of science, science as a cultural practice, and analysis of science-society interactions
- Recognition of the importance of multiple perspectives and domains of knowledge, including science, values, and social and ethical concerns, to understanding and decision making around science-based societal issues

The key characteristic that distinguishes public engagement with science from other approaches in science education is that public engagement with science values and facilitates participation and learning on the part of both the public and the scientists with respect to the application of science and technology in modern society.

By incorporating perspectives and mechanisms of public engagement with science into an organization's offering, the possibility exists for the producers of science education experiences to operate not only as store-houses and disseminators of knowledge, but also as facilitators of the production of new knowledge and understanding through dialogue and interaction among the public, scientists, and policy makers. These processes seek to contribute to broader cultural change, including increased awareness, sense of shared responsibility, and civic participation in science and decision making (McCallie et al. 2009).

Get Involved

In conclusion, education and science leaders who can effectively communicate with the public, media, and decision makers are needed to facilitate better information exchange between science and society. We need to encourage educators and scientists at all levels to hone their public communication skills and become proactive in sharing their knowledge, and, perhaps more importantly, *listen* to what the public has to say and find significant ways to incorporate their knowledge.

References

Bubela, T., et al. 2009. Science communication reconsidered. *Nature Biotechnology* 27 (6): 514–518.

Bucchi, M. 2008. Of deficits, deviations and dialogues: Theories of public communication of science. In *Handbook of public communication of science and technology*, eds. M. Bucci and B. Trench, 57–76. Abingdon, UK: Routledge.

Center for Advances in Public Engagement. 2008. *Public engagement: A primer from Public Agenda*. Washington, DC: Public Agenda.

Clark, J., and P. Aufderheide. 2009. *Public media 2.0: Dynamic, engaged publics*. Washington, DC: American University Center for Social Media.

Leshner, A. 2003. Public engagement with science. *Science* 299 (5609): 977.

McCallie, E., L. Bell, T. Lohwater, J. H. Falk, J. L. Lehr, B. V. Lewenstein, C. Needham, and B. Wiehe. 2009. *Many experts, many audiences: Public engagement with science and informal science education. A CAISE inquiry group report*. Washington, DC: Center for Advancement of Informal Science Education.

National Science Board. 2008. *Science and engineering indicators*. Arlington,

VA: National Science Foundation.

Pew Research Center. 2009. Survey report: Public praises science; Scientists fault public, media. (July 9). *http://people-press.org/report/528/*

Russell, C. 2009. Science journalism goes global. *Science* 324 (5934): 1491.

Wilsdon, J., B. Wynne, and J. Stilgoe. 2005. *The public value of science: Or how to ensure that science really matters.* London: Demos.

About the Authors

Barbara A. Austin is an assistant professor of science education at Northern Arizona University. Her research interests include teacher growth and development and understanding the role that misconceptions play in teacher decision making.

Helen Bond is an assistant professor in the School of Education at Howard University in Washington, D.C. She teaches courses in technology, social foundations, and pedagogy. Prior to this appointment, Dr. Bond served as program director of the Master of Arts in Teaching program at the University of Maryland University College. She recently authored a chapter for *The Handbook of Research in Culturally-Aware Information Technology: Perspectives and Models*. Her research interests are human rights education and the use of science and technology to solve important social problems of the day.

Courtney Burns is an education analyst at RTI International in Research Triangle Park, North Carolina. As part of her honors studies in college, she conducted independent research on the effects of procrastination and extracurricular activities on academic performance. She presented this study at the NCPA conference at the University of North Carolina at Chapel Hill. Honors include membership in Psi Chi, Alpha Chi, and Phi Theta Kappa. She graduated from Peace College in May 2007 summa cum laude with a degree in psychology.

Rodger W. Bybee (retired) is the executive director of the Biological Sciences Curriculum Study (BSCS). Before this he was executive director of the Center for Science, Mathematics and Engineering Education at the National Research Council. Author of numerous journal articles, chapters, books, science curricular and textbooks, he also directed the writing of the content standards for the National Science Education Standards. Honors include the National Science Teachers Association's Distinguished Service Award and Robert Carleton Award.

Jeanne Century is director of science education and research at the Center for Elementary Mathematics and Science Education at the University of Chicago. Before this, she was at Education Development Center (EDC), where her work included curriculum, professional development, and research. She was responsible for STEM education and education research and development for the Obama-Biden transition team and most recently established *www.researcherswithoutborders.org*, an open-research environment to address complex problems that education and other fields share.

Karen Charles is a research education analyst at RTI International where she currently works on several projects related to the U.S. Department of Education's GEAR UP program and the Elementary and Secondary Education Act. Prior to joining RTI, she was the assistant director of the federally funded Southeast Eisenhower Regional Consortium at SERVE/UNCG where she directed the Technical Assistance Academy for Mathematics and Science Services. She is the past president of the North Carolina Science Leadership Association and the current treasurer of NSELA. Her doctorate is in curriculum and instruction with an emphasis on science and mathematics education.

George E. DeBoer is deputy director for Project 2061 of the American Association for the Advancement of Science where his work focuses on assessment in science and mathematics. Earlier he served as program director for the National Science Foundation and is professor of educational studies emeritus at Colgate University where he held several leadership positions. DeBoer also taught chemistry, biology, and Earth science at the high school and university levels and is the author of A *History of Ideas in Science Education: Implications for Practice* (Columbia University Teachers College Press 1991) and numerous articles, book chapters, and reviews.

Joel D. Donna began his career as a high school physics teacher and later received his PhD in science education from the University of Minnesota. His research interests include STEM teacher induction, online teacher professional development, and integrative STEM education. His dissertation work on online teacher induction programs for beginning STEM educators has earned him a Doctoral Dissertation Fellowship from the University of Minnesota. He currently serves as the STEM specialist for the Minnesota Department of Education.

Don Duggan-Haas is the education research associate at The Paleontological Research Institution and its Museum of the Earth in Ithaca, New York. Don has taught at Colgate, Cornell, and Michigan State Universities, Kalamazoo College, and Tapestry and Norwich (New York) High Schools. His work in science teacher education, teacher professional development and curriculum materials development marries deep understandings of how people learn with deep understandings of the Earth system.

Lois Brown Easton is a senior consultant for the National Staff Development Council and specializes in learning designs for adults and students. She has also served as Director of Re:Learning, a national high school reform initiative linking policy makers to schools with the Coalition of Essential Schools (Dr. Theodore Sizer) and Re:Learning, Dr. Ted Sizer) and Director of Curriculum, Instruction and Assessment for the state of Arizona. She has published four books, one of which was named outstanding education book of the year by Delta Kappa Gamma, an international organization for women educators. She has also published numerous articles, presented at national and international conferences, and served professional organizations in a variety of roles.

Izolda Fotiyeva is an assistant professor in the School of Education at Howard University in Washington, D.C. She teaches courses in mathematics, science, and pedagogy. Dr. Fotiyeva's experience includes mathematics and science curriculum development for public schools in Russia. In 2003, she authored a book titled *Math With Mom* that introduces early childhood mathematics topics through stories and activities. Her research interests are mathematics education, informal education, and the use of technology in mathematics and science education.

Julie Gess-Newsome is the J. Lawrence Walkup Distinguished Professor of Science Education at Northern Arizona University and the director of the Center for Science Teaching and Learning. With research interests in the development of teachers' knowledge and beliefs and their impacts on classroom instruction, she has authored numerous articles, chapters, and has acted as the editor of four books for researchers and teachers.

Ruth Heuer is a research education analyst at RTI International in Research Triangle Park, North Carolina. She has expertise in a broad range of educational survey and statistical methodologies and has led numerous tasks for national longitudinal studies of faculty and students, including the National Education Longitudinal Study, the Beginning Postsecondary Students Longitudinal Study, the National Study of Postsecondary Faculty, and the Baccalaureate and Beyond Longitudinal Study. She holds a doctorate in sociology from North Carolina State University.

Karen E. Irving is an associate professor in the School of Teaching and Learning at The Ohio State University. As a coprincipal investigator on the Institute of Education Sciences–funded Connected Classrooms in Promoting Achievement in Mathematics and Science project, Dr. Irving has investigated technology–facilitated formative assessment practices in secondary mathematics and science classrooms using wireless handheld devices. Dr. Irving received the 2004 National Technology Leadership Initiative Science Fellowship Award for her research in the use of educational technology in science teaching and learning.

Neelam Kher is a senior researcher at the Center for Research in Mathematics and Science Education. Before this she was professor in Educational Psychology and Coordinator of University Assessments at Northwestern State University of Louisiana and has made numerous contributions to the scholarly literature related to teacher preparation and student learning, teaching effectiveness and student outcomes in higher education, and other areas of institutional effectiveness.

Carolyn Landel joined the Science, Mathematics, and Technology Education program at Western Washington University (WWU), home to the state's largest teacher preparation program. Here, she serves as Project Director of a National Science Foundation–funded Mathematics and Science Partnership that unites scientists from Western Washington University and four community colleges with 28 small and rural school districts to improve science education K–16. Dr. Landel has authored numerous publications in scientific journals and, more recently, in the science education literature. She is the coauthor of *A Leader's Guide to Curriculum Topic Study* (Corwin Press).

Judith S. Lederman is the director of teacher education in the Department of Mathematics and Science Education at Illinois Institute of Technology. Dr. Lederman's experience with informal education includes her work as Curator of Education at the Museum of Natural History and Planetarium in Providence, Rhode Island. She presents and publishes nationally and internationally on the teaching and learning of nature of science and scientific inquiry in both formal and informal settings. She has served on the Board of Directors of the National Science Teachers Association and as president of the Council for Elementary Science International.

Norman G. Lederman is chair and professor of Mathematics and Science Education at the Illinois Institute of Technology. Dr. Lederman received his PhD in Science Education and he possesses MS degrees in both Biology and Secondary Education. Prior to his 20+ years in science teacher education, Dr. Lederman was a high school teacher of biology and chemistry for 10 years. Dr. Lederman is internationally known for his research and scholarship on the development of students' and teachers' conceptions of nature of science and scientific inquiry. Dr. Lederman is a former President of the National Association for Research in Science Teaching (NARST) and the Association for the Education of Teachers in Science (AETS). He has also served as Director of Teacher Education for the National Science Teachers Association (NSTA).

Tiffany Lohwater is public engagement manager at the American Association for the Advancement of Science (AAAS). Through its Center for Public Engagement with Science and Technology, AAAS provides a vehicle for boosting public awareness and understanding of the nature of science and the work of scientists, while at the same time increasing public input into scientific research and policy agendas by creating venues for dialogue among policymakers, the general public, and the scientific community. AAAS activities also encourage scientists to take a more personal and proactive interest in public engagement. Prior to joining AAAS, Lohwater worked with researchers, educators, and journalists at Johns Hopkins University and Rensselaer Polytechnic Institute.

James E. (Jim) McLean is currently a university professor and the dean of the college of education at University of Alabama. He has graduate training in statistics, measurement, evaluation, research, and educational psychology coupled with 35 years experience teaching and researching in these areas. He also has over 25 years of administrative experience as a program chair, area head, director, assistant dean, and dean. During the past 33 years he has directed, codirected, or administered over 100 research, assessment, and evaluation projects funded for more than $6,000,000. Dr. McLean holds BS, M.Stat., and PhD degrees from the University of Florida.

Barbara Miller is codirector of the Center for Leadership and Learning Communities at Education Development Center, Inc. Over the past 20 years, her work has included professional development and technical assistance for school district and program staff, research on professional development and teacher leadership in mathematics and science, evaluation of systemic reform efforts, and materials development for school leaders. She currently is the co-Principal Investigator for the National Science Foundation–funded Math and Science Partnership's (MSP) Knowledge Management and Dissemination project.

Natalie Nielsen is the director of research at the Business-Higher Education Forum (BEHF). Before joining BHEF, Dr. Nielsen was a senior education researcher at SRI International, where her work focused on high-school reform, out-of-school learning, and transitions to postsecondary education for underserved youth. She also has worked as a writer for Project 2061—the science education reform arm of the American Association for the Advancement of Science—and as a geology exhibit researcher at the Smithsonian Institution's National Museum of Natural History and the San Diego Natural History Museum.

Chris Roe is the deputy director of the Business-Higher Education Forum (BHEF). As part of his responsibilities, he works with BHEF's members to advance its science, technology, engineering and mathematics (STEM) initiative, which focuses on increasing the number of students graduating with degrees in these fields. Previously, he was managing director of the National Center for Postsecondary Improvement based at Stanford University. Roe also cofounded and serves as an advisor to Foundation for a College Education, a nonprofit dedicated to helping disadvantaged students prepare for and obtain a college degree.

Gillian Roehrig is the codirector of the University of Minnesota STEM Education Center and an associate professor in the department of Curriculum and Instruction. Her research focuses on the preparation and retention of secondary science teachers and STEM integration to provide more authentic and engaging contexts for student learning. Her work is supported by grants from the National Science Foundation, National Institutes of Health, National Institute on Drug Abuse, and the Administration of Children and Families.

Mistilina Sato is an assistant professor of Teacher Development and Science Education at the University of Minnesota, Twin Cities. She began her career as a middle school science teacher and received her PhD from Stanford University. Her research interests include practical reasoning in teachers' everyday work and leadership and standards-based assessment of teacher performance. Honors include the early career research award by the Teaching and Teacher Education Division of the American Educational Research Association and a Knowles Science Teaching Foundation Research Fellowship.

William H. Schmidt received his undergraduate degree in mathematics from Concordia College in River Forrest, Illinois and his PhD from the University of Chicago in psychometrics and applied statistics. He carries the title of *University Distinguished Professor* at Michigan State University and is currently codirector of the Education Policy Center, codirector of the U.S. China Center for Research and director of the NSF PROM/SE project and holds faculty appointments in the Departments of Educational Psychology and Statistics. Previously he served as National Research Coordinator and Executive Director of the U.S. National Center which oversaw participation of the United States in the IEA-sponsored Third International Mathematics and Science Study (TIMSS). He has published in numerous journals including the *Journal of the American Statistical Association, Journal of Educational Statistics,* and the *Journal of Educational Measurement.* He has coauthored seven books including *Why Schools Matter.* His current writing and research concerns issues of academic content in K–12 schooling, assessment theory and the effects of curriculum on academic achievement. He is also concerned with educational policy related to mathematics, science, and testing in general. He was awarded the Honorary Doctorate Degree at Concordia University in 1997 and received the 1998 Willard Jacobson Lectureship from The New York Academy of Sciences and is a member of the National Academy of Education.

Emily van Zee is an associate professor of science education in the Department of Science and Mathematics Education in the College of Science at Oregon State University. Her research has focused upon ways of speaking in which students express their own ideas and engage one another in discussing what they think. As co-organizer of Teacher Researcher Day at National Science Teachers Association conferences, she sponsors a Science Inquiry Group Network for teachers and teacher educators interested in sharing their inquiries and findings.

Eric A. Walters is the director of science and technology and a classroom teacher at the Marymount School of New York. Eric also serves as the Regiom B Director for the National Science Education Leadership Association and as the Chairperson for *The Science Teacher* Advisory Committee. Presenter at regional, national, and international science education conferences, Eric has worked with groups such as the National Association of Independent Schools in the areas of global education strategies and promoting K–12 STEM education for girls. Honors include the 2009 Vernier Technology Award.

Index